RULERS, RELIGION, AND RICHES

For centuries following the spread of Islam, the Middle East was far ahead of Europe. Yet, the modern economy was born in Europe. Why was it not born in the Middle East? In this book Jared Rubin examines the role that Islam played in this reversal of fortunes. It argues that the religion itself is not to blame; the importance of religious legitimacy in Middle Eastern politics was the primary culprit. Muslim religious authorities were given an important seat at the political bargaining table, which they used to block important advancements such as the printing press and lending at interest. In Europe, however, the Church played a weaker role in legitimizing rule, especially where Protestantism spread (indeed, the Reformation was successful due to the spread of printing, which was blocked in the Middle East). It was precisely in those Protestant nations, especially England and the Dutch Republic, where the modern economy was born.

Jared Rubin is an associate professor of economics at Chapman University in Orange, California. His research on the relationship between political and religious institutions and their role in economic development has appeared in numerous top economics journals.

D1282262

CAMBRIDGE STUDIES IN ECONOMICS, CHOICE, AND SOCIETY

Founding Editors
Timur Kuran, *Duke University*
Peter J. Boettke, *George Mason University*

This interdisciplinary series promotes original theoretical and empirical research as well as integrative syntheses involving links between individual choice, institutions, and social outcomes. Contributions are welcome from across the social sciences, particularly in the areas where economic analysis is joined with other disciplines such as comparative political economy, new institutional economics, and behavioral economics.

Books in the Series:

Rulers, Religion, and Riches

Why the West Got Rich and the Middle East Did Not

JARED RUBIN

Chapman University

CAMBRIDGE
UNIVERSITY PRESS

CAMBRIDGE
UNIVERSITY PRESS

One Liberty Plaza, New York, NY 10006, USA

Cambridge University Press is part of the University of Cambridge.

It furthers the University's mission by disseminating knowledge in the pursuit of
education, learning, and research at the highest international levels of excellence.

www.cambridge.org
Information on this title: www.cambridge.org/9781108400053
10.1017/9781139568272

First published 2017

A catalogue record for this publication is available from the British Library.

Library of Congress Cataloging-in-Publication Data
Names: Rubin, Jared, author.
Title: Rulers, religion, and riches: why the West got rich and the Middle
East did not / Jared Rubin, Chapman University.
Description: New York: Cambridge University Press, 2016. |
Series: Cambridge studies in economics, choice, and society |
Includes bibliographical references and index.
Identifiers: LCCN 2016045144 | ISBN 9781107036819 (hard back)
Subjects: LCSH: Europe, Western – Economic conditions. | Middle East – Economic
conditions. | Economics – Europe, Western – Religious aspects. | Economics – Middle
East – Religious aspects. | Rule of law – Europe, Western. | Rule of law – Middle East.
Classification: LCC HC240.R78 2016 | DDC 330.94–dc23
LC record available at https://lccn.loc.gov/2016045144

ISBN 978-1-107-03681-9 Hardback
ISBN 978-1-108-40005-3 Paperback

To the loves of my life: Tina, Nadia, and Sasha

Contents

Figures

Tables

Preface

I began research for this book in 2004, my third year of graduate school at Stanford University. Conflict between the "West" and the "Islamic world" was one of the enduring stories of the time: 9/11 was still fresh on everyone's minds, and wars in Iraq and Afghanistan dominated headlines. Not much has changed on this front in the intervening twelve years. If anything, the conflict has heightened. Terrorist attacks around the globe, the spread of al-Qaeda and ISIS, and the devastating Syrian refugee crisis all suggest that many of the West's political and economic struggles of the foreseeable future will take place in the Middle East.

Understanding the roots of conflict between the Middle East and the West is therefore of first-order importance, and it is the primary reason I wrote this book. It is my opinion that the most important driver of the conflict is the vast disparity in economic fortunes of the two regions. The economic disparity is real; while it is true that a few of the Gulf States gained significant oil wealth in the latter half of the twentieth century, only a small fraction of the population has seen any of its benefits. In any case, this wealth is fleeting; there is little evidence to my knowledge that any of the wealthy oil nations have built anything close to an economy that will stay strong as the world shifts away from petroleum as a primary energy source.

The economic disparity between the "West and the Rest" permitted Western occupation and colonization of the Middle East in the nineteenth and twentieth centuries. This disparity also permitted authoritarian rulers, generally supported by the West, to dominate Middle Eastern politics throughout most of the twentieth century. These outcomes have deep historical roots, and it is the goal of this book to discover and analyze these roots. The arguments laid out are inherently comparative; the causes of what went wrong, if anything did indeed go wrong, in the Middle East are easier to ascertain by analyzing what went right in parts of Western Europe. The goal of the book is therefore twofold. On the one hand, it provides insight into some of the necessary determinants for long-run economic success. On the other hand, it spells out how and why an economy might stagnate if those determinants are absent.

Upon deeper reflection, the reasons for the vast disparity of economic fortunes between the Middle East and the West are not so obvious. Any account of this disparity must also account for the fact that it has not always been this way. For centuries after the founding of Islam, the Middle East was ahead of Western Europe by practically any metric: economics, politics, culture, and science. The Fertile Crescent was the Western Eurasian economic and cultural hub for most of the high medieval period. At some point, this obviously changed. Almost no scholar I know of would argue that the Middle East was close to the leading European economies on the eve of industrialization in the mid-eighteenth century. After industrialization, what were already readily apparent economic differences were exacerbated many times over. The real questions, then, are: Why did a region that was so far ahead for so long ultimately fall behind? Why did the Industrial Revolution begin in Great Britain instead of, say, the Ottoman Empire?

This book attempts to shed light on the answers to these questions. In doing so it addresses head on the elephant in the room that is all too frequently invoked by Western media outlets and "intellectuals" as an explanation for Middle Eastern problems: Islam. I believe that such claims are ridiculous, but they cannot be simply dismissed offhand without providing a compelling alternative explanation. I provide such an explanation, although it is up to the reader to decide whether it is compelling. My explanation is deeply grounded in economic theory, and it considers the incentives of all the players who may have played some role in the divergence. It is my hope that the reader will come away from this book with a more nuanced view of the role that Islam played in Middle Eastern economic stagnation and, ultimately, conflict with the West.

The argument is hopefully clear about one key point: Islam itself is not the problem. However, economic success *is* less likely to occur where religion plays an important role in politics. But this is not to lay blame on religion in general, either; *any* interest group that has a powerful seat at the political bargaining table but does not have interests consistent with economic growth will play a retarding role in a society's economy. Historically – for reasons emphasized in this book – religious authorities had an outsized seat at the political bargaining table in both the Middle East and Western Europe. Understanding the process through which this was undermined in the latter but not in the former is therefore of utmost importance for understanding the long-run economic divergence between the two regions.

This book does not offer a solution for closing the economic disparity between the Middle East and the West. It merely diagnoses the problem and its causes. But just like a doctor must make a correct diagnosis before prescribing treatment, a proper diagnosis of the divergence is essential if we are to understand what political and economic actions could be taken to help close the gap. The diagnosis provided by this book is not based on some simplistic notion of Islam, and this book does not blame Islam more than any other religion for substandard economic performance. It does suggest that getting religion out of politics will be a crucial and necessary step for the Middle East, but even this is not a complete solution.

There is no reason to expect a quick fix in the Middle East; the process of getting religion (mostly) out of politics took centuries in the West. It is also true that context matters, and the economic and political contexts of the two regions are very different. An important difference noted in this book is that Islam is more conducive to legitimizing political rule than Christianity is, a fact that certainly influences the set of changes that are possible in the Middle East. But even if religion is removed from politics, this is only a first step. It matters dearly who replaces the religious elite at the bargaining table. For instance, replacing religious elites with autocrats is almost certainly worse for economic and personal well-being.

The rise and spread of Islamic fundamentalism is likely to be one of the enduring stories of the twenty-first century. The best way to contain it – indeed, the best way to contain radicalism of any kind – is through economic development. Radical ideas, be they religious or secular, are much more appealing when there is little hope for a better future. Such ideas, and the violent extremist tactics employed to carry them out, are a by-product of a world that has been left behind economically. It is my sincere hope that this book takes us one step closer to understanding the sources of such economic stagnation while shedding some light on what a path toward long-run, sustained economic growth might look like in the Middle East.

Acknowledgments

This is my first book, and as such it brings together most of the research I have conducted over the past decade. So many people have influenced my thoughts, publications, and career. There is a temptation to thank them all, beginning with graduate school. I will gladly succumb to this temptation; I see no reason to leave out anyone who has influenced me. A caveat, of course, is that so many people had a hand in shaping my thinking that I am sure to miss a few. If this is you, I apologize.

Some of this book comes from work I started in my dissertation, completed in the economics department at Stanford University. A number of my classmates at Stanford – in economics, political science, and the Graduate School of Business – contributed to my thought process at seminars, in class, and late at night over cheap beer. They include Will Tadros, Josh Lustig, Max Gulker, Jon Meer, Ed Van Wesep, Andres Santos, Steve Nuñez, Sri Nagavarapu, Bryan Keating, Gopi Shah Goda, Saumitra Jha, Luz Marina Arias, David Patel, Peter Lorentzen, Ben Ho, Kıvanç Karaman, Ta-Chen Wang, Erik Snowberg, and Lars Boerner. Equally important were the many faculty who helped at some stage in the process with insight and encouragement, including Petra Moser, Gavin Wright, Paul David, and Brent Sockness.

I feel blessed to have had fantastic collaborators, some of whom have worked with me on projects highlighted in this book. I have collaborated with Latika Chaudhary on multiple projects on the role religion plays in Indian political economy. She is one of the nicest people I know and is always full of insight. Mike Makowsky is a good friend and a heck of an agent-based modeler. He is always willing to give spot-on comments. Erik Kimbrough, Roman Sheremeta, and Tim Shields have been a blast to work with and have given me great insight into how experimental methods can further our understanding of economic phenomena. Murat Iyigun has been a huge advocate of mine since we first met in 2008. It is an honor to have someone as accomplished as him in my corner. The same can be said for Sascha Becker, Steve Pfaff, and Debin Ma. I have enjoyed every minute of working with all of you and I cannot wait to see what the final product of our efforts will look like. One collaborator who deserves special mention is Metin Coşgel. Along with Tom Miceli, Metin and I wrote two papers that form much of the argument for Chapter 5. He and Tom graciously allowed me to use the material we worked on together in this book. This is one of the key chapters in the book, as it links the theory in the first part to the consequences laid out in the final part. Metin has been a great friend over the years; I am in his debt as a scholar.

So many other people have influenced my work through events I regularly attend, especially the Association for the Study of Religion, Economics, and Culture (ASREC) annual conference, Association for Analytic Learning about Islam and Muslim Societies (AALIMS), and Chapman's Institute for the Study of Religion, Economics, and Culture (IRES) graduate student workshop. Since 2010 I have been a board member of ASREC, serving as both Executive Director and Program Chair along the way. I have made a great many friends in the process, but some really stand out, including Robbie Mochrie, Sriya Iyer, Sascha Becker, Dan Hungerman, Chris Bader, Jean-Paul Carvalho, and Mike McBride. I regularly see a great number of people at AALIMS who have helped shape my view on the role the social sciences can play in shedding light on various aspects of the Islamic world, including Cihan Artunç, Lisa Blaydes, Jean-Paul Carvalho, Eric Chaney, Murat Iyigun, Saumitra Jha, Timur Kuran, Avital Livny, Erik Meyersson, David Patel, Tom Pepinsky, and Mohamed Saleh. Regular graduate student workshops at IRES have also introduced me to a number of fantastic scholars. I am indebted to the "regulars" who show up to Chapman every year for our event: Jean-Paul Carvalho, Tony Gill, Mike McBride, Steve Pfaff, and Carolyn Warner. The John Templeton Foundation sponsored these workshops, numerous ASREC events, and various research projects through two grants I was awarded with Larry Iannaccone. Indeed, these grants funded course reductions that allowed me to focus on writing this book. For all of this I am very grateful to the John Templeton Foundation and especially to Kimon Sargeant, who has always been supportive of our work.

I have met so many others at workshops, conferences, or over coffee, drinks, and e-mail who deserve mention for influencing my thoughts. Many of these people have given me detailed comments on a book chapter or one of the papers that forms the backbone of this book. I know I will miss mentioning some of you, but it is not for a lack of appreciation. I consider many on the following list good friends; it is a pleasure to work in a field with so many genuinely nice people. These include Jason Aimone, Dan Bogart, Feler Bose (who brought me out for a great trip to Alma College to talk about the book), Davide Cantoni, Jeremiah Dittmar, Price Fishback, Andy Gill, Yadira González de Lara, Josh Hall (who sponsored a fantastic trip to Beloit College to talk about the book), Gordon Hanson, Phil Hoffman, Noel Johnson, Shawn Kantor, Elira Karaja, Mark Koyama, Deirdre McCloskey, Joel Mokyr, Julius Morche, Steve Nafziger, Gary Richardson, Jean-Laurent Rosenthal, John Tang, John Wallis, and Ludger Woessmann. There are many more I am sure. Sorry if I left you out!

Claire Morgan organized an invaluable book conference at the Mercatus Center, which helped sharpen my arguments significantly. I am deeply indebted to all the attendees, all of whom took the time to read an entire early draft of the manuscript and give excellent feedback: John Wallis, Pete Boettke (also a coeditor of this book series), Carmel Chiswick, Metin Coşgel, Stephen Davies, Noel Johnson, Timur Kuran, Karen Maloney, Peter Mentzel, John Nye, Scott Scheall, and Mario Villarreal-Diaz. I owe a special thanks to Karen Maloney, my primary editor at Cambridge, who has been supportive of this project throughout. Scott Parris, my original editor at Cambridge, was also supportive from the beginning and helped get this project off the ground.

I owe a great deal of debt to a number of people at Chapman University. Few people have helped me advance in my career as much as Larry Iannaccone, who was the primary force in bringing me to Chapman in 2011. I treasure Larry's friendship and insights. The institute we have built at Chapman, IRES, is a testament to the field he has revolutionized. Larry and I are not alone in building the institute; my IRES colleagues, Chris Bader, Beth Hofeldt, Andrea Molle, Celia Perez, and Linda Williams, have also been great friends. It is a fantastic environment to work in. Outside of IRES, I have greatly benefited from interactions with a number of my other Chapman colleagues. They include, but are not limited to: Gabriele Camera, Brice Corgnet, Lynne Doti, Dan Kovenock, Dave Porter, Steve Rassenti, Roman Sheremeta, Tim Shields, Vernon Smith, Nat Wilcox, and Bart Wilson.

Three people deserve extended thanks. The first is Ran Abramitzky, one of my dissertation advisors at Stanford. Ran has been one of the most positive forces imaginable on my career. When I embarked in graduate school on research in the economics of religion, I knew this was not likely to yield me a top job like many Stanford graduates expect to get. But I was never in it for the name brand of the university I worked at, the salary, or any other perks. I was in it because I loved the topic and I felt I had something significant to contribute. Ran never wavered in supporting my research. From the beginning, he advised me to do what I find interesting. Even if it were not the most mainstream of topics, he consistently told me that if done well, others will come around to my view that my research is interesting and important. It has been vital to hear such words of encouragement from a scholar as excellent as Ran. I do not think I have let him down, and I hope he views this book as a testament to that.

I do not know where my career would be without the friendship, mentorship, advice, comments, and encouragement of Timur Kuran. Timur was also on my dissertation committee. Timur's work is one of my primary sources of inspiration, and I think it really shows in this book. From the first time I met him when he was visiting Stanford in 2004, Timur has been a top advocate of mine. I am not sure what I did to deserve this honor, though I will gladly accept it. At every step in my career path Timur has been there with advice and support. It is difficult to put into words how important this has been for me, both for my confidence as a scholar and for providing me with opportunities I otherwise might not have had. Indeed, he is the primary reason this book is being published with Cambridge. He went through numerous drafts of the manuscript in his role as editor. Each draft improved substantially from his comments. Simply put, this book is leagues better than it would have been without Timur's supervision. I am deeply honored to call Timur a collaborator, mentor, and (most importantly) friend.

I would also be nowhere near where I am today without the mentorship, advice, and encouragement of Avner Greif. Avner had no idea at the time I first introduced myself to him, while taking his class in my second year, that I was on the precipice of leaving Stanford's Ph.D. program. The first year of the program was disillusioning; graduate economics was not what I was expecting or hoping it would be. This all changed when I took Avner's class. I always had an interest in religion – not out of personal conviction, but simply from its power to affect decision-making. Indeed, I minored in religion at the University of Virginia simply out of interest in the topic, not because I planned on doing anything with it in my career. Avner introduced me to the possibility that the very thing I was interested in was something that economists actually studied and provided insights deeper than I thought possible. Overnight I changed my mind from almost certainly leaving Stanford to almost certainly pursuing this line of research for the rest of my life. I vividly remember going to Avner with my first half-baked ideas about the role that religion and politics play in economic outcomes.

He told me flat out something that is not so easy to hear as a second-year graduate student: it will be hard to get an academic job pursuing this topic. However, he also encouraged me to tackle the topic head on if it were something I was passionate about. This is precisely what I needed to hear. I did not need to have illusions about what the market might hold for me, but I did need to know that I would have support if I decided to pursue it. And Avner's support has not wavered to the present day. Along with Timur Kuran, Avner's work has been the primary inspiration for my own work. And, as with Timur, I am deeply honored to call Avner a collaborator, mentor, and friend.

The greatest supporters I have had throughout my life are my parents, Thom and Linda Rubin. I have the incredible luck to have the greatest father one could imagine – he is supportive, caring, loving, and kind. I aim to emulate him every day now that I am a father. He was dealt an incredibly difficult hand when my mother passed away, but he somehow managed to raise me, my sister Samantha, and my brother Tyler into well-adjusted, interesting, and caring adults. I am constantly amazed at the father he is to me and my siblings and the grandfather he is to my children; and so is Debbie, my loving and caring stepmother. I miss my mother, Linda, dearly; not a day goes by that I do not think of her. Although her time on Earth was way, way too short, she managed to instill in myself, Samantha, and Tyler so much about what it means to be a good human being. I cannot imagine being anything close to who I am today had she not been a part of my life. Samantha and Tyler also deserve much credit for me being the person I am today; I certainly do not take it for granted how lucky I was to grow up in such a loving family.

Finally, this book – and everything else I do on a day-to-day basis – would be unthinkable without the support of the three loves of my life: my wife Tina, my daughter Nadia, and my son Sasha. Tina has always been there for me since we met in 2004. We have been through so much together: job changes, location changes, and the births of our two beautiful children. I do not have the words to convey how much Tina means to me. The same is true of Nadia and Sasha. The best part of my day is the time I spend with the three of them and our dog, the ever-loyal Watson. I cannot imagine what my world would be like without them. Tina, Nadia, and Sasha: this book, and everything else I do, is for you.

Introduction

By almost any available metric, there is a wide gap between the economic and political fortunes of the Middle East and the West.[1] Even after accounting for oil wealth, which benefits only a small portion of Middle Easterners, Westerners are on average about six times wealthier. They can also expect to live, on average, eight additional years and have nearly twice the education (see Table 1.1). One cause – and consequence – of Middle Eastern economic retardation is poor governance and violence. The average Middle Easterner lives in a much more fragile and autocratic state and is subject to much more civil and ethnic violence than the average Westerner. This is undoubtedly the primary reason for the political tensions between the Middle East and much of the rest of the world, and it is at the root of the political and economic grievances espoused by Islamists.

This gap between the West and the Middle East – indeed, the West and the rest of the world – is a relatively recent phenomenon. In the preindustrial period, Western Europe was not obviously ahead of the rest of the world, and it was not so far ahead of the Middle East that the Ottoman Empire (the leading Middle Eastern state) felt economically or politically inferior. Over time, a vast economic, political, military, and technology gap emerged between the two. This divergence allowed Europeans to dominate the rest of the world economically and politically, a fact most clearly manifested in their colonization of a large portion of the world's inhabitable land. Meanwhile, by the nineteenth century, the Ottoman Empire was considered the "sick man of Europe" – a once mighty empire on its final legs. The leading Western European powers ultimately carved up the Middle East into states with artificial boundaries that suited European geopolitical needs.

It is undeniable that the fortunes of the Middle East diverged wildly from those of the West. But what caused this divergence? The difference in fortunes is more puzzling than it might seem from a twenty-first-century

Table 1.1 *Economic and Political Health, the "West" and Middle East/North Africa (MENA), 2012–2014 (weighted by population)*

	The "West"	MENA	Interpretation/Notes
Per Capita GDP	$48,269	$8,009	In 2013 US Dollars
Life Expectancy	80.4	72.6	2013 Life Expectancy at birth
Mean Years of Schooling	12.1	6.8	2012 data
State Fragility	1.42	11.11	0–25 (25 is most fragile)
Civil and Ethnic Violence/War	0.00	1.03	0–10 (10 is most violent)
Autocracy	0.00	3.58	0–10 (10 is most autocratic)

Sources: GDP – World Bank (2014); Schooling – UN Development Program (2014); State Fragility, Violence, Autocracy – Marshall and Cole (2014); Population – CIA World Factbook (2014); all data weighted by 2014 population; GDP and Fragility are in 2013; Violence and Autocracy are in 2014.
Western Europe includes Australia, Austria, Belgium, Canada, Denmark, Finland, France, Germany, Ireland, Luxembourg, Netherlands, New Zealand, Portugal, Spain, Sweden, Switzerland, the United Kingdom, and the United States.
MENA includes Algeria, Bahrain, Egypt, Iran, Iraq, Jordan, Kuwait, Lebanon, Libya, Morocco, Oman, Qatar, Saudi Arabia, Syria, Tunisia, Turkey, UAE, West Bank & Gaza, and Yemen.

perspective. For most of the last millennium or two, Westerners had more contact with Middle Easterners than they did with the rest of the world. Cross-cultural learning between Western Europe and the Middle East occurred more frequently than it did between Western Europe and the rest of the world. The similarities between the two regions and their relative integration make the relative success of the West even more mysterious: What allowed Western economies to succeed where Middle Eastern ones stagnated?

This is the question addressed in this book. At its core, this book is about why some economies succeed and others stagnate. It is tempting to ask whether Islam is to blame for the relative poverty and poor governance of the Middle East. It is impossible to avoid this question, even if it may be offensive to some; it is simply bad science to reject a hypothesis because it is offensive. And there is reason not to dismiss this possibility offhand. The famed scholar of Islamic history Bernard Lewis seemed to suggest just this late in his career,[2] and there is a long Orientalist tradition ascribing bad consequences to Islamic doctrine and practice. This is also a common trope of the Western media, where simplistic associations between Islam and "bad" socio-political-economic events are all too common. Even if most stories in the media are easy to dismiss upon only slightly deeper inspection, it is not so easy to dismiss the more intelligently construed arguments of the Orientalists. Lewis and others knew a *lot* about the Middle East and Islamic history. And indeed, Islam harbors numerous rules relevant for trade and governance.

So, why isn't Islam to blame? The answer is simple: even if one accepts the idea that religious doctrine matters for economic performance, the facts simply do not line up. The histories of these regions in the millennium prior to industrialization do not align with the idea that Islam is antithetical to economic growth. The most important fact to account for in *any* theory of why the modern economy was born in Western Europe and not the Middle East is that the Middle East was ahead of Europe economically, technologically, and culturally for *centuries* following the spread of Islam. From the seventh through twelfth centuries, Islamic empires dominated Western Eurasia. For its first four or five centuries, Islam was associated with *positive* economic growth.

The worldwide distribution of wealth was much different eight to ten centuries ago than it is in the twenty-first century, both within and across economies. Western Europe was a relatively poor area – the rule of law existed only in small, settled regions, little interregional commerce existed, populations were small and scattered, and science and technology were far behind other regions. By almost any available economic measure, the Middle East was ahead of Europe. It had access to far more advanced science and technology, its trade flowed in higher volumes and over longer distances, and it employed more complicated financial instruments. There is plenty of evidence to support this assertion. Major advances in mathematics, medicine, philosophy, art, and architecture were hallmarks of the Islamic world through the thirteenth century. The data are of course sparser the earlier back in time one travels, but one indication of wealth in the premodern setting for which we do have data is urban population size. Urban population works as a metric of premodern economic performance because large urban populations meant there was enough food to feed people who were not producing for their own sustenance, and urbanites generally produced and consumed the luxuries of life. In short, greater urban populations generally meant greater wealth.[3]

Urban population data confirms the suspected trend, showing a slow but clear reversal of economic fortunes between Western Europe and the

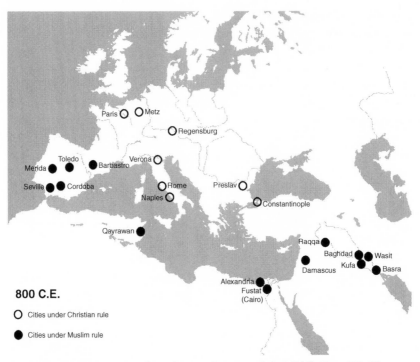

Figure 1.1 Twenty Most Populous Cities in Europe and the Middle East, 800 CE
Source: Bosker et al. (2013).

Middle East over the last 1,200 years. Figure 1.1 indicates that in 800, the urban share of the population of the Islamic world was much greater than in Christian Europe.[4] Fourteen of the twenty-two largest cities in Europe and the Middle East, including by far the largest city – the Abbasid capital Baghdad – were under Islamic rule. The Umayyad (Cordoba) Caliphate in modern-day Spain and the Abbasid Caliphate, centered in modern-day Iraq, ruled the most populous and wealthiest areas. Seven of the eight most populous cities were Muslim-ruled, with only the Byzantine capital Constantinople containing a large urban population of Christians. In fact, the *combined* population of the top thirteen cities of Christian Western and Central Europe (Naples, Rome, Verona, Regensburg, Metz, Paris, Speyer, Mainz, Reims, Tours, Cologne, Trier, and Lyon) was less than the population of Baghdad in 800.

Fast forward 500 years. The scene described in the preceding paragraphs certainly changed by 1300, but even so the Middle East was far from a laggard, in spite of the decimation of some urban populations by the Mongols.

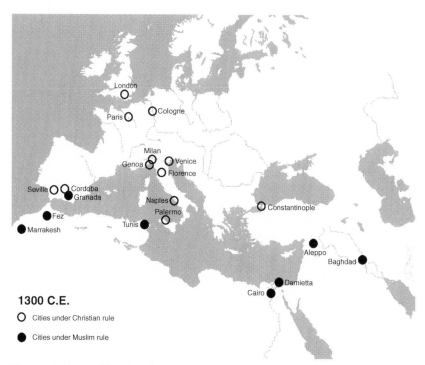

Figure 1.2 Twenty Most Populous Cities in Europe and the Middle East, 1300 CE
Source: Bosker et al. (2013).

By 1300, the economies of Western Europe were again thriving following the long post-Roman downturn, especially in Northern Italy, and many parts of Western Europe were well on their way to recovery. Figure 1.2 suggests that the balance of power between the Christian and Islamic worlds was more equal, with twelve of the top twenty cities ruled by Christians (including the most populous city, Paris). The center of European growth was located in Italy – six of the twelve Christian cities were Italian, with four of those located in the wealthy northern region. The city-states of Northern Italy, especially Venice, Genoa, and Florence, were among the wealthiest places in the world, birthing many aspects of modern banking, finance, accounting, and trade. Northwestern Europe was only slightly wealthier in per capita terms in the early fourteenth century than the wealthiest Muslim region (Egypt), while Italy was about twice as wealthy as any other part of Western Europe, let alone the Middle East.[5]

By 1800, the reversal of fortunes was complete. Seventeen of the twenty most populous cities in the region were not only Christian but located in

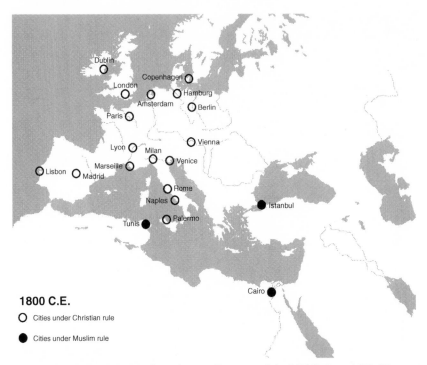

Figure 1.3 Twenty Most Populous Cities in Europe and the Middle East, 1800 CE
Source: Bosker et al. (2013).

either Western or Central Europe. The Industrial Revolution had commenced in Great Britain, and the European powers had colonized much of the rest of the world. Real wages were much higher in northwestern Europe than they were in the wealthiest parts of the Muslim world.[6] The divergence was not solely between northwestern Europe and the Middle East. By this time, real wages diverged dramatically between northwestern Europe and China, Japan, and India as well.[7]

Figure 1.4 summarizes this trend in economic fortunes. This figure presents the "urban center of gravity" of Western Eurasia for each century from 800 to 1800. This is a simple metric of the average longitude and latitude of the region weighted by where urbanites lived. More populous areas "pulled" the center of gravity closer to themselves. The path in this figure is clear. In 800, the urban center of Western Eurasia was just west of the Anatolian Peninsula. It was pulled strongly to the southeast by the Abbasid Caliphate, which was centered in Iraq, while it was pulled south by the bustling urban areas of Egypt. The primary reason

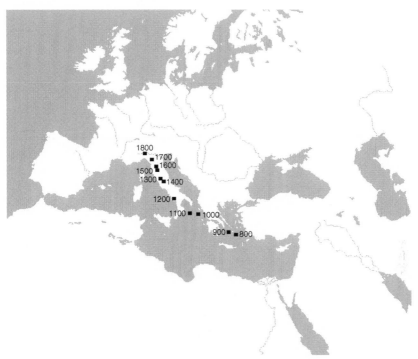

Figure 1.4 Urban Center of Gravity in Europe and the Middle East, 800–1800
Note: Maps in Figures 1.1–1.4 are for representational purposes only. Europe is on a slight tilt in this map relative to its conventional representation in order to accommodate the entire region.
Source: Bosker et al. (2013).

the center was so far west of the Abbasid capital was the presence of large Muslim urban populations in the Iberian Peninsula. Over time, the urban center shifted to the northwest; first toward Italy as the northern Italian city states expanded beginning in the late tenth century, and ultimately toward northwest Europe in the sixteenth–eighteenth centuries as urban populations in England and the Dutch Republic grew relative to the rest of the region. By 1800, the urban center of Western Eurasia was located in northwestern Italy, near Milan – about 2,000 miles away from the old Abbasid capital Baghdad, but only about 500–600 miles from the two great commercial cities of northwestern Europe: London and Amsterdam.

Ultimately, any satisfactory explanation of the reversal of fortunes must account for two historical features. First, it must account for both the rise of the great Muslim empires as well as their relative stagnation. Second, although it is not clear from Figures 1.1–1.4, the modern economy was very much a product of *northwestern* Europe – England and, before that, the Netherlands. An understanding of where modern wealth comes from must therefore account for long-run differences both between Western Europe and the Middle East *and* within Western Europe.

It is the purpose of this book to address these two issues within one consistent framework. The framework eschews simplistic notions that Islam is at the root of the divergence or, on the contrary, that Catholicism or Protestantism are causes of European success. It does argue, however, that how political authorities used religion to legitimize their rule did matter, and the exact mapping from religion to legitimacy to economic outcomes is dependent on historical processes.

Implications and Limitations of the Argument

The consequences of this "long divergence," as Timur Kuran has called it, are still with us in the twenty-first century. If it were not for the temporary shock of oil wealth, the Middle East would be one of the poorest places on earth, rivaled only by sub-Saharan Africa and parts of Southeast Asia. Historical curiosity should be enough to warrant an investigation into how this region – once the wealthiest and most cultured region in the world – fell so far behind.

But historical curiosity is not always enough. Historians and other intellectually minded individuals may appreciate the uncovering of historical connections as ends in themselves, but others consider historical research of this type worthwhile only if it sheds light on contemporary problems. This book should satisfy such a reader. It is first and foremost a book of *economics*. It uses economic theory to search for the general features of an economy that yield success under some conditions and stagnation under others. It uses Middle Eastern and Western European history as a testing ground for the theory. History provides one of the best testing grounds for economic hypotheses: what happened is behind us, and the long-run consequences are clear. This is certainly true of the long-run divergence between Western Europe and the Middle East. One set of economies was clearly much more successful than the other in the long run despite falling well behind early on.

This book addresses this issue with a general economic argument. When economists say that an insight is "general," they tend to mean that it applies to many situations, and the insight may predict different outcomes depending on the parameters involved. This book aims to provide such a general insight into how and why economic success and stagnation occur over very long periods. It should be obvious that this is not just an issue of concern for the Middle East and Western Europe: the arguments made in this book have implications for the difficult process of alleviating human suffering associated with economic underdevelopment around the world. After all, Western Europe was at one point an economic backwater, and the average wealth of medieval Europeans was lower than most of the poorest parts of the world today. Understanding the mechanisms through which Western Europe escaped such poverty – and the Middle East, for the most part, did not – clearly has implications for the possibilities and limits of economic growth in the twenty-first-century developing world.

The history of the long-run divergence between Western Europe and the rest of the world is therefore important to understand not just for the sake of historical interest, but because it has real implications for how we view the world and how we can change it. Using the economic framework outlined in Chapter 2, this book delves into the historical past to find out what worked in Western Europe and what did not work in the Middle East. Yet, it never implies that merely transplanting what worked in Western Europe into the Middle East will solve all its economic problems. Quite the opposite is true; the solutions that worked in Western Europe arose and evolved in a *specific context*. Understanding this context is essential for establishing the limits of how previous experience can inform the present.

Nor does this book imply that the Middle East is helpless to change its fortunes. In fact, one of the primary insights gathered from the book's framework is that there are many forks along the path of a society's economic, political, and institutional progression. Once a society takes one path along the fork, it becomes more difficult over time to revert to the other side. Yet, new forks arise all the time, often for unanticipated or unforeseeable reasons such as new technologies or natural disasters. How societies respond to these opportunities can have enduring consequences. But nothing predetermines how a society will respond or when an opportunity will arise. History is *not* deterministic; we are not slaves to our historical and institutional past.

This book also does not suggest that the type of economic success that Western Europe experienced could have only happened there. The twentieth-century successes of South Korea and Taiwan are prima facie evidence against such a claim. Instead, this book urges a more nuanced view of why long-run economic success occurs, while searching for general features linked time and again to economic success.

Thinking in Terms of Incentives

Economists like to think in terms of incentives. This book is no different. At every historical turn, it asks the question: Why did the relevant parties act in the manner they did? The answer given in this book always boils down to: "They were *incentivized* to act in that manner." Incentives come from a host of societal attributes: politics, religion, social norms, laws, and culture are just a few. The inquiry cannot stop there: simply noting the incentives that individuals face is the last step. It is critical to take a step back and ask: Why were those incentives there in the first place? Why do the incentives people face differ in different places and at different times, and why do they change over time? Why do they sometimes not change over time?

Thinking in terms of incentives means tossing simplistic ideas of long-run economic divergence out of the window. Take, for instance, the idea that the root of economic divergence between the Middle East and Western Europe lies in the "conservative nature" of Islam. This is no straw man argument. A long tradition of Eurocentric explanations for the divergence suggests that the "conservative" or "mystical" nature of Islam discouraged curiosity and prevented risk-taking, innovation, and mechanization.[8] In this view, Islam is inherently hostile to commerce and finance. Indeed, in varying times and places, Muslim religious authorities advocated laws that inhibited economic development, such as regulations on taking interest and printing, suppression of women, laws discouraging mass education, and adherence to antiquated inheritance and partnership laws. So, at a minimum, there is a *correlation* between the presence of Islam and laws antithetical to economic development.

But correlation is not causation. A simple economic example illustrates the problem with arguments relying on "inherent conservatism." Consider the fact that elderly individuals are less likely to use computing technologies than teenagers are. On the surface, it may seem like older people are inherently more conservative – they prefer sticking with writing letters over sending e-mails. This, however, is a too simplistic argument. Older people are less likely to use advanced computing, not because they prefer the old ways more than teenagers do, but because the costs and benefits of learning a new technology are different. It may in fact be less costly in terms of time for a seventy-year-old to become Internet proficient. Yet, a shorter life horizon for the elderly not only means that they will enjoy the fruits of learning to use the Internet for a shorter period of time, but the opportunity costs associated with the time taken to learn new technologies are much greater as well. Moreover, since their friends are much less likely to be on the Internet, the benefits associated with larger networks are also lower. Hence, older people often take actions that lead to more conservative *outcomes*, but this is not necessarily a result of an inherent resistance to change. Instead, the incentive structure is such that the elderly have less incentive to learn new technologies.

This book applies a similar logic to economic history. Chapter 2 provides a framework based on the incentives the relevant players face in the bargain over laws and policies. It shows the conditions that incentivize these players to choose laws and policies that respond to changing economic environments. "Conservative" outcomes result when these conditions are not present, in that laws and policies do not change in spite of a changing world. But these are *outcomes*, not *preferences*. This book does not rely on some ad hoc theory of a "conservative nature" of certain groups of people; instead, it shows why certain people *act* conservatively.[9]

In the context of the Middle East–Western Europe divergence, an implication of this way of thinking is that conservatism is an outcome to be explained – it is not itself a cause of stagnation. While there is indeed evidence suggesting that Islamic political and religious thought became more conservative starting sometime around the turn of the first millennium, this does not mean that we should take the false path connecting a conservative outlook to economic stagnation. Instead, the correct questions to ask are why some cultures are more conservative than others and were there incentives in the Middle East which eventually led to conservative outcomes. A deeper answer requires that we look beyond cultural differences and analyze the key drivers of incentives, be they economic, religious, social, or political. Where do incentives come from? If not from culture, from where?

The Argument Summarized

Chapter 2 lays out the central framework of the book. It focuses on the players in an economy who affect the enacted set of laws and policies: rulers and their agents. One of its central ideas is that there are people or organizations in society that, due to their identity or access to resources, can help rulers stay in power. I call these people *propagating agents*. The framework focuses on two types of propagating agents: coercive agents and legitimizing agents. Coercive agents propagate through force – people follow the ruler because they face punishment otherwise – while legitimizing agents propagate through legitimacy – people follow the ruler because they believe he (or, much more rarely, she) has the legitimate right to rule. Propagating agents can provide immense benefits to the ruler, but they also come at a cost: the ruler gives them a seat at the bargaining table in return for their support. The laws and policies resulting from this bargain are reflective of the bargaining power of each player and their preferences.

Religious legitimation is especially attractive to rulers because it is inexpensive. Thus, rulers rely on religious authorities when those authorities have the capacity to legitimize their rule. In such a world, rulers are loathe to update laws in response to changing economic circumstances if doing so would undermine the religious establishment. As a result, those with the most to gain from modernizing a society's laws and policies – producers, merchants, and commercial farmers – have little incentive to push for change. Not only are rulers unlikely to side against the religious establishment, but such a request is also a sin. Consequently, laws and policies do not change in response to changes in the outside world, and the result is economic stagnation. This logic indicates that conservatism is a *result* of the incentives faced by the relevant players, not an ultimate *cause* of bad economic outcomes.

The upshot is that differences in laws and policies across societies and over time within societies are a result of differences in the identities of propagating agents. These differences are themselves a result of differences in costs and benefits to rulers of using propagating agents. At any one given point in time, a society's *institutions* impose these costs and benefits on rulers. Institutions are those aspects of society that help form the "rules of the game" by which all players abide. All societies have numerous types of institutions – religious, political, social, and economic – all of which help shape the "game" played between rulers and their propagating agents.

Chapter 3 brings the framework to the economic histories of Western Europe and the Middle East, exploring the historical reasons that rule-propagating institutions were different in the two regions. It argues that the circumstances surrounding the births of Islam and Christianity had important consequences for the manner in which rule was propagated. Islam was born in the seventh-century Arabian Peninsula, and it formed as the early Islamic empires were rapidly expanding. Many aspects of Islamic doctrine were a response to this environment, including doctrine supporting a ruler's right to rule as long as he acted "Islamic." Christianity, on the other hand, was born in the Roman Empire, with its previously established, well-functioning legal and political institutions. Early Christianity never formulated a corpus of legal or political theory that came close to rivaling that of early Islam for the simple reason that early Christian thinkers did not need to do so. This is not to say that religious legitimacy was unimportant in

European history – it merely entails that Islam was *more* conducive to legitimizing rule than Christianity was, meaning that the benefits of religious propagation were greater in the Middle East than in Western Europe. The framework therefore predicts that, all else being equal, religious authorities should have had a greater seat at the bargaining table in the Middle East than in Western Europe.

It matters who sat at the bargaining table for two reasons: (1) doctrine exists in both Islam and Christianity that affects economic practices; (2) the interests of religious elites do not always align with the types of laws and policies that favor economic success. Chapter 4 brings to light one consequence of this insight, overviewing the history of an economic doctrine common to Islam and Christianity: laws against taking interest on loans (usury). This chapter employs the framework to shed light on why usury doctrine diverged in the two religions. It highlights the different ways that political and religious authorities interacted in the two regions and how this in turn affected the willingness of rulers to permit interest. This chapter hardly claims that differences in interest laws were the reason Western European economies surpassed the Middle East. Yet, it does show that these restrictions were not completely innocuous. The type of financial instruments employed in the two regions reflected doctrinal differences and, more importantly, the lack of banking institutions in the Middle East prior to the nineteenth century.

Chapter 5 analyzes the spread of the printing press. The framework sheds light on a historical puzzle: while the printing press spread rapidly in Western Europe after its invention by Johannes Gutenberg in 1450, the Ottomans prohibited its use for *almost 250 years*. The argument for the different reactions to the press is straightforward. The printing press threatened the Ottoman religious establishment's monopoly on the transmission of knowledge – a key source of their influence in society – and they therefore had incentive to encourage the sultan to prohibit it. The sultan obliged because religious authorities were important legitimizing agents, and permitting the press would have undermined them. Meanwhile, Christian religious leaders were in no position to ask rulers to block the press, and it consequently spread rapidly throughout Europe.

The analyses of interest and printing restrictions suggest there is nothing inherent in Islam that fosters an environment supporting anti-commerce laws. In fact, early Islamic religious and political doctrines were quite flexible and possibly even growth promoting. Reinterpretation of religious law was frequent as demanded by economic and social conditions, and as a result the Middle East was an economic, technological, and cultural leader for centuries after the founding of Islam. Many of the Islamic laws that eventually inhibited economic development were well suited to the needs of the early Islamic economy. Yet, as economic conditions advanced, the legitimizing relationship between political and religious authorities had an increasingly dampening effect on further economic development. Religious doctrines such as those banning interest or reproducing words and images, which were not a problem in the premodern economy, came to the fore as an impediment to overcome.

The printing press was arguably the most important information technology of the last millennium, and Western European economies grew rapidly where it spread. But the indirect consequences of the spread of the press were even more important. Chapter 6 highlights one of these consequences: the press facilitated the spread of the Protestant Reformation. The printing press permitted widespread, rapid dissent, allowing the Reformation to succeed where previous anti-Church movements failed. This chapter reports the results of empirical analyses that show that the Reformation was much more likely to take hold in towns with access to printed works. This is a classic case of a "fork" in a society's long-run institutional trajectory. Such an anticlerical movement, which was so dependent on the rapid flow of information, was much less likely to happen in the Ottoman Empire, where access to printed works was minimal. The lack of information technology in the Ottoman Empire capable of quickly transmitting ideas allowed established interests to maintain their grip on power, permitting the institutional status quo to hold for centuries. As a result, religious authorities remained powerful political forces in the Middle East for centuries after their influence waned in Western Europe.

The remainder of the book argues why the Reformation was such an important event for the economic trajectory of Western Europe – and why a lack of a similar undermining of religious authority was important for the trajectory of Catholic Europe and the Muslim Middle East. The primary insight is that the Reformation fundamentally transformed the manner in which rule was propagated. The already weak legitimizing capacity of religion eroded further in Protestant states following the Reformation, forcing Protestant rulers to change the agents that propagated their rule. The most common response was to seek propagation by the economic elites who served in parliaments. By economic elite I simply mean those people primarily engaged in commerce: merchants, craftsmen, money changers, commercial farmers, and anyone else engaged in either producing for market or facilitating market transactions. The transition to propagation by the economic elite was an important development, because their preferences tended to align more with those types of policies that also portend economic success, such as secure property rights and public good provision. Consequently, Protestant rulers more frequently enacted laws and policies favoring long-run economic success than did Catholic or Muslim rulers.

This is not to say that the economic elite were more "public spirited" than other types of propagating agents and therefore desired policies in the public interest due to altruistic motives. Quite the opposite, it suggests that the economic elite pursued their own interests, which just so happened to coincide with policies that benefited the broader economy. Nor is it to say that everything the economic elite desired was good for the economy; history is replete with examples of rent seeking by the economic elite. This is also not to say that a political system run solely by the economic elite would be a good thing for an economy. It does imply, however, that a political system where the economic elite have a nontrivial seat at the bargaining table enables better economic outcomes than one where they have no voice at all.

Chapters 7 and 8 dig into the relevant histories to support these assertions. Chapter 7 overviews the post-Reformation economic and political changes made in the two leading Protestant economies: England and the Dutch Republic. Chapter 8 overviews the histories of one Catholic economy that fell behind, Spain, as well as the primary Middle Eastern economy of the time, the Ottoman Empire. These are not trivial comparisons cherry-picked to support the argument. These were the most important economies of the time, save possibly France, adhering to Catholicism, Islam, and some form of Protestantism.

The framework therefore accounts for the "little divergence" that happened between northwestern Europe and the rest of Europe as well as the larger divergence between Western Europe and the Middle East. It is not sufficient to say there was "something about Western Europe" that eventually led to economic success. The emergence of the modern economy was *not* a pan-Western Europe phenomenon – it was very much an English and Dutch phenomenon. While I do not claim that the framework explains everything – the argument stops before industrialization, which requires its own explanation – I *do* claim that the places where the modern economy was eventually born had a very different political economy equilibrium by the end of the sixteenth century – one that was more conducive to long-run economic growth.

This framework thus turns simplistic Weberian notions connecting a "Protestant ethic" to economic success on their head.[10] Max Weber (1905 [2002]) argued that Calvinist predestination doctrine encouraged believers to show that they were one of the "elect" by working hard and having worldly success. The "spirit of capitalism" thus pervaded the Protestant countries and placed them on a different economic path. The observation that inspired this hypothesis is valid: many of the Protestant nations had a head start on modern economic growth. But, while recognizing that there is a *correlation* between Protestantism and economic success, this book argues for a very different *causal* channel than one based on culture or religious tenets. It suggests that the changes in political economy brought on by the Reformation – specifically the replacement of the religious elite with the economic elite at the bargaining table – was the key feature connecting Protestantism to economic success. This of course does not mean that the modern economy had to emerge in Protestant northwestern Europe. It simply entails that if one living in 1600 had to choose which part of the world industrialization and the associated explosion of economic growth would commence 150 years hence, Protestant northwestern Europe would have been a good choice.[11]

Other Explanations

The explanation proposed in this book for the "rise of the West" is far from the only one out there. The rise of the West is one of the big issues that economic historians tackle, and consequently there have been many words dedicated to furthering our understanding of its causes. Many of the existing hypotheses nicely complement the one proposed in this book. Such explanations focus on other aspects of the rise of the West or relative stagnation elsewhere, providing explanations that reinforce the mechanisms highlighted in this book. There are also explanations that are clearly contradictory to the ones proposed in this book. I also address these below and indicate why I believe my explanation succeeds where those fail.

Complementary Hypotheses

The explanations for the "rise of the West" most closely related to the one presented in this book are those proposed by Avner Greif, Douglass North, and Timur Kuran. Greif and North both provide useful frameworks for understanding the economic implications of institutions. Greif shows in a series of articles and his book, *Institutions and the Path to the Modern Economy*, how decentralized institutions worked to facilitate trade in the medieval period in the absence of centralized political and legal institutions. Greif focuses primarily on economic institutions that emerged outside of the state and how these institutions facilitated economic exchange. The focus of the present book is on a different slice of economic life: the incentives faced by the key Middle Eastern and Western European political players. The institutional changes analyzed by Greif were necessary precursors of the historical factors explored in this book. Greif's work therefore provides a necessary complement to my argument.

One set of institutional differences studied by Greif that deserve explicit attention are those related to family structure. The European family structure resulted from the policies of the medieval Church that discouraged certain practices in order to weaken kinship ties (adoption, polygamy, remarriage, consanguineous marriage). According to Jack Goody (1983), the Church imposed these policies in the hope that people would donate their property to the Church at their death rather than to their kin.[12] In contrast, kinship ties were much more important in the Middle East, where consanguineous marriage was commonplace. Greif (1994a, 2006a, 2006b) argues that, as a result, European culture was more "individualistic" than Middle Eastern culture, which was more "collectivist." Europeans therefore created institutions that created trust outside of the group, as the nuclear family was too small of a unit to engender gains from exchange.[13] This advantaged the Middle East when the scope of trade was limited, as trade within the kin group could occur without further institutional development. However, impersonal exchange emerged on a wide scale once late medieval European communities established institutions that facilitated trust beyond the kin group. These arguments are entirely consistent with the ones presented in this book. For one, they employ the same argument for why Islam may have been beneficial to economic growth in the premodern context: it connected Muslims through the concept of *umma*, which views the entire Islamic community as one. And Greif's argument for the ultimate success of the European economy nicely complements my explanation. Strong kin ties may have ultimately discouraged impersonal exchange in the Middle East, but this alone does not explain why the economic elite were never able to get a seat at the bargaining table. The argument presented in this book fills in this gap, arguing that the economic elite never had a place at the bargaining table because Middle Eastern rulers were strong enough, due to the legitimizing capacity of Islam, to exclude them.

Another set of works from which the present book draws inspiration and insight are Douglass North's works on institutions, especially his books *Structure and Change in Economic History* and *Institutions, Institutional Change, and Economic Performance*. A primary focus of North's works is connecting political institutions to the expansion of property rights. The emergence of such institutions in northwestern Europe were undoubtedly important, and they play a key role in the theory laid out in this book.

North extended his contributions to this literature in a seminal article with Barry Weingast (1989), which suggests that the imposition of institutionalized constraints on executive authority in England following the Glorious Revolution of 1688 was the key turning point, since it gave an increased political voice to wealth-holders. North, John Wallis, and Weingast extend this argument even further in their book *Violence and Social Orders*, claiming that opening access to impersonal and impartial legal and economic institutions is the key to economic growth. In their view, open access is important because it encourages a wider swath of the population to use resources efficiently. Daron Acemoglu and James Robinson (2012) make a similar argument in their book *Why Nations Fail*, arguing that governments that permit extraction are the primary historical hindrances to economic growth. These arguments are all consistent with the one presented in this book. By and large, this book takes the year 1600 as its stopping point. One implication of my argument is that by 1600, there were certain parts of Western Europe that were primed for an economic takeoff in the spirit of what North and others describe. Hence, this book merely pushes their arguments back a few centuries, noting why such events were *more likely* to happen in England than, say, the Ottoman Empire.

The comparative approach employed in this book is similar to the important works of Timur Kuran. Kuran, in a series of papers and his book, *The Long Divergence*, argues that there were numerous aspects of Islamic law that helped stimulate commerce in the premodern economic environment but stifled economic progress as the environment changed. He employs a similar tactic to the one used in this book, searching for an explanation that can explain both why early Middle Eastern economies succeeded and why Western Europe eventually pulled ahead. Kuran primarily focuses on the demand – or lack thereof – for legal change in Middle Eastern history, while my argument primarily focuses on its supply.[14] Our works are thus necessary complements to each other; it is impossible to fully understand the demand side without a complete comprehension of the supply side, and vice versa. As with Greif's and North's works, Kuran and I ask the same big questions but tackle different parts of them.

Jan Luiten van Zanden employs the insights of Greif, Kuran, North, and many others in his book, *The Long Road to the Industrial Revolution*. van Zanden argues that one specific phenomenon – the "European Marriage Pattern" – contributed to the institutional formation that took place in early modern Western Europe and helped set it off from the rest of the world. Specifically, van Zanden suggests that the propensity of northwestern European men and women to get married later in life encouraged them to acquire more human capital, which was an important determinant of how institutions evolved.[15] Like Greif, van Zanden argues for the importance of decentralized institutional developments in the economic rise of Europe in the late medieval period (950–1350). Without such developments, many of the processes discussed in this book could not have occurred. Like the present book, van Zanden also stresses the importance of the printing press and the Reformation, although he is more concerned with their human capital consequences and I am more concerned with their effects on politics.

Another set of hypotheses focusing on political and legal institutions argues that fiscal and legal capacity – the power to tax and provide law – played an important role in the rise of the West. This argument in its recent form can be traced to Charles Tilly (1975, 1990), who argues that the need for mutual defense and war created incentives for governments to invest in revenue generation; Tilly's (1975, p. 42) oft-cited statement is "War made the state, and the state made war."[16] It is undoubtedly true that the growth of fiscal, legal, and state capacity in Europe played a large role in the growth of states and economic fortunes.[17] Yet, one shortcoming of this literature is that it assumes the existence of a ruler who can choose to expand tax collection efforts or legal jurisdiction without delving too deeply into why the ruler has the capacity to do so in the first place. This shortcoming is justified; any analysis must start somewhere, and assuming the existence of ruler is a reasonable place to start in most historical settings. But the argument laid out in this book suggests that the manner in which rulers are propagated matters for the types of policies they pursue – and, ultimately, their ability to reap the benefits of fiscal and legal capacity. Although I only indirectly discuss investments in fiscal capacity in relation to rule propagation (in Chapters 7 and 8), it clearly follows that the two are intimately linked.[18]

A related set of explanations based on the unique political history of Europe focuses on the fact that Europe was relatively fractured into small states that were frequently at war, whereas much of the rest of the world was dominated by large empires that faced less political competition. The main idea in this literature, formulated by Paul M. Kennedy (1987) in *The Rise and Fall of the Great Powers*, is that the constant demand for warfare in Europe created incentives to improve military technology at a different rate than the rest of the world, which in turn gave Europe the upper hand in colonizing starting in the sixteenth century. A more nuanced version of this hypothesis, put forward by Philip Hoffman (2015) in his book *Why Did Europe Conquer the World?*, argues that competition between European rulers only led to massive improvements in military technology when combined with gunpowder, which came to Europe in the late medieval period.[19] Yet, one of the key insights in the present book is that the Middle East ultimately suffered precisely *because* their rulers were strong: the strength of their rule, due in part to religious legitimation, permitted them to grow empires without having to negotiate with the economic elite. The opposite was the case in Europe, where rulers were relatively weak due in part to low levels of religious legitimation. This argument complements the fractionalization literature because it provides an explanation for Europe's fractionalization.[20] Indeed, it goes beyond this literature by providing an account for *intra*-European differences in long-run economic outcomes. The modern economy was born in northwestern Europe, not just Europe. This fact is difficult to account for in an argument based solely on European fractionalization.

A different set of hypotheses focus on the economic effects of rhetoric, intellectualism, and the Enlightenment. A compelling example from this literature is Deirdre McCloskey's *Bourgeois Dignity*, which suggests that the way people talked mattered. In particular, a shift in language, particularly in England and the Netherlands, more favorable to commerce and trade was instrumental in changing mindsets and encouraging talented and wealthy individuals to pursue commercial activities previously considered base. Joel Mokyr (2002, 2009) presents a complementary argument, suggesting that new ways of thinking and acquiring knowledge, particularly in association with the seventeenth–eighteenth century Enlightenment, augmented the economic behavior of producers and entrepreneurs in favor of experimenting toward more efficient techniques. Both McCloskey and Mokyr clearly point out important aspects of the growth of the modern economy; it is difficult to imagine a modern economy in which an inquisitive and experimental impulse was lacking in business or those engaging in commerce were pariahs. Yet, it is unclear what the prime mover is in these arguments. Could it possibly be true that a change in attitudes toward merchants occurred without a concurrent rise in the power or wealth of these classes? Is it not possible that the Enlightenment and other intellectual movements were responses to economic or political conditions? The arguments made in the present book help shed light on these problems by providing insight into the conditions that made such movements possible in the first place.

Contradictory Hypotheses

The most important set of contradictory hypotheses to the one proposed in this book centers around differences in culture. I already stated the primary problems with explanations based on culture – they often confuse correlation with causation, suggesting that a "conservative" culture is the cause of the problem when it is actually a result of deeper forces also affecting economic and political differences. Of course, culture matters to economic outcomes. Yet, hypotheses of this ilk tend to treat culture as unchanging. An important example of such an argument yet again comes from Max Weber (1922), who famously ascribed the relative economic retardation of the Middle East to the "conservative nature" of Islam. Such a claim was seconded in more recent expansive histories by David Landes (1998, ch. 24), Eric Jones (1981, pp. 179–84), and even Joel Mokyr (1990, pp. 205–6), who in a fantastic book on technology and economic development suggests that a shift to a more conservative outlook contributed to the long-run technological backwardness of the Middle East.[21] The present book suggests an alternative explanation: conservatism is not an inherent feature of a society, but an outcome based on a lack of incentive to change.[22]

Gregory Clark's meticulously researched *A Farewell to Alms* presents a different strand of cultural argument. Clark offers the theory that noble and middle-class values slowly spread throughout English society during the late medieval and early modern periods because the rich had higher reproduction rates than did the poor, and this did not occur elsewhere in the world. As people with a more bourgeois background spread throughout all layers of the economy, virtues generally associated with capitalism spread with them, allowing England to escape the Malthusian trap of persistent subsistence income. In Clark's view, institutions play no role in the rise of modern wealth. It is a fascinating hypothesis that has sparked an important debate about the "big question" of why some are wealthy and others are poor.[23] Yet, it does not adequately address one important aspect of the argument: the onset of modern economic growth was a northwestern European phenomenon. Clark's argument applies to England but not to the rest of Western Europe, and it cannot explain the clear differences that arose by 1750 between the Ottoman Empire and northwestern Europe, not just England.[24]

Another explanation, more prevalent in the popular press than in academia, is that Western colonialism is the cause of Middle Eastern economic stagnation and political violence. In this view, the nineteenth- and twentieth-century plundering of North Africa and the Middle East by European powers inhibited the region's economic development. The most popular variant of this argument is that the carving up of the Middle East under the Sykes-Picot Agreement of 1916 without regard to tribal, ethnic, or religious identities set the stage for internal conflicts from which the region has yet to escape.[25] This is an attractive idea to those who want to absolve Middle Eastern political, religious, and economic leaders from contributing to economic stagnation. While it is certainly true that the European powers did not have the best interests of Middle Easterners at heart – and that many aspects of twentieth-century Middle Eastern political economy have colonial roots – it is hard to see how colonialism is the root source of Middle Eastern problems. Such explanations raise a more important question than they answer (also noted by Timur Kuran): Why were Western European powers able to colonize the Middle East in the first place? Colonization cannot be the root cause of economic differences, but instead must be an outcome of other, more historically distant economic or political causes.

Another hypothesis that cannot explain many of the phenomena discussed in this book is Jared Diamond's "geography hypothesis" put forward in *Guns, Germs, and Steel*. Diamond claims that the shape of land masses, the ability to domesticate certain animals, and crop endowment had numerous consequences for how societies formed over time. Likewise, Jeffrey Sachs (2001) argues that disease environment, ability to produce food, and energy endowments help explain why tropical climates have performed worse than temperate ones. A related set of hypotheses are those of Stanley Engerman and Kenneth Sokoloff (1997, 2000), who argue that resource endowments helped shape the economic paths of different regions in the New World. If geography is the ultimate determinant of long-run economic success, it is difficult to see why some regions of the world could be so far ahead at one point in time and then fall so far behind later. After all, geography is practically constant. The geography thesis therefore has difficulty answering the primary question posed in this book: Why was the Middle East so far ahead of Western Europe for so long only to ultimately fall so far behind?[26]

A final argument meriting discussion is the one proposed by Bernard Lewis late in his career in *What Went Wrong?* Lewis argues that the lack of separation of church and state in the Islamic world had a long-run detrimental effect on Islamic economies. This fact is also at the heart of the argument in the present book, although the conclusions drawn from it are very different than in Lewis. Lewis argues that there was never a separation of church and state in Islam due to the fact that Muhammad conquered his holy land in his lifetime and became the head of the first Muslim state. Consequently, the concept of "secularism" remained foreign and unthinkable in the Islamic lands. Lewis goes on to argue that this meant that societal features associated with secularism in the West – civil society and representative government – never evolved in the Islamic world. Lewis's argument is a bit too simplistic. Why should a concept be unthinkable for more than *one thousand years* merely because it was not a part of early Islamic doctrine? Both the religion of Islam and the political structure of Middle Eastern states changed on numerous fronts in the last 1,400 years, especially in the first four Islamic centuries. There is apparently nothing inherent to Islam that would forbid change in the manner that Lewis implies. The present book provides an answer where Lewis is lacking one. Instead of simply assuming that differences in how rulers used Christianity and Islam were "built into" the system, it provides an explanation for why the legitimizing relationship between rulers and religious authorities diverged over time. Unlike Lewis, my explanation does not rely on a Eurocentric assumption of the "Orient" merely being stuck in its ways. Instead, I argue that where we do not see change it is not because of some inherent conservatism or alternatives being "unthinkable," but because it was in the interests of enough of the relevant players to maintain the status quo.

The Audience of this Book ... and a Caveat

This book provides insight into the statement made in its subtitle: Why the West got rich and the Middle East did not. It tackles the question of where modern wealth came from, and why its origins were found in the West and not elsewhere. This is one of the most important inquiries economists and economic historians make, which is why so many have addressed it in the past and many more will continue to address it in the future. A satisfactory answer has implications that clearly go well beyond historical curiosity. First and foremost, gaining a better understanding of the origins of modern wealth is a topic of central interest to economists, especially development economists and economic historians. Political scientists are interested in the role that rulers and political institutions played in the process that yielded the modern economy. I also attempt to repudiate simple but false claims about the direct connections between religious doctrine and economic outcomes. To the extent that they are willing to listen to such an economic argument, this is a topic of interest to scholars of religion. Finally, and most importantly, this book has implications for what promises to be one of the most enduring stories of the twenty-first century: the role of Islam in politics and economics. This topic should interest anyone concerned with the future of Middle Eastern political economy or the important role the Middle East will play in twenty-first-century Western political economy. Interest in this topic obviously extends well beyond the academy, and I have written this book in a manner that reflects this. To the extent possible, I avoid using economics jargon, and I have replaced all equations with words.

Whenever an economist writes for a general audience, it is difficult to avoid writing in a manner that prevents misinterpretation. This is even truer when writing on religion, a topic in which many people have preconceived notions on what they want the answer to be. I attempt to preempt any such misinterpretation throughout the book, wherever it is appropriate, and I re-address the major misconceptions of the argument in the concluding chapter. But there is one misconception worthy of addressing at the end of this introductory chapter. This is, namely, that this book is very much *not* a diatribe against religion. Nor is it a diatribe against Islam. It is true that this book seeks an explanation for why the Middle East fell behind Western Europe, and that it finds "getting religion out of politics" to have played a major role in this process. But there is almost nothing about Islam or Christianity per se that is at the root of these differences, save their capacity to legitimize rule. Nor is there anything specific to religion that is "bad" for economic outcomes: propagation by *any* entity with interests not aligned with broader economic success will likely lead to laws and policies detrimental to long-run economic fortunes. More importantly, while this book tackles a controversial topic, it does so with no underlying agenda besides being a quality work of economics. It is not pro- or anti-Islam or pro- or anti-religion. It is simply an argument that uses economic logic to improve our understanding of the origins of the modern economy and why it emerged – and did not emerge – when and where it did.

PART I

PROPAGATION OF RULE: A THEORY OF ECONOMIC SUCCESS AND STAGNATION

2

The Propagation of Rule

The introductory chapter posed an important puzzle: Why did the economies of the Middle East fall behind those of Western Europe after leading them for centuries following the spread of Islam? This chapter provides a framework for answering this question. The starting point follows from the most basic of economic dictums: people respond to incentives. Digging one step deeper, the questions arise: What type of incentives lead to economic success when present and to stagnation when absent? Why are incentives different in different societies? What determines the incentives that people face?

There are a variety of societal features shaping the incentives individuals face. For instance, religion can incentivize people to do certain things and not do other things. Islam disincentivizes Muslims to eat pork and consume alcohol, and it does so by imposing a *cost* on these actions. The costs are both intrinsic (fear of displeasing Allah) and social (what will other Muslims think?). The point is not that Muslims never eat pork or drink alcohol; it is simply that it is more costly for them to do so than it is for non-Muslims. And people perform actions less the more costly they are.

This book focuses on the types of incentives that shape a society's economic outcomes. The central focus is on the incentives that shape the *laws* and *policies* that a society enacts. The contents of laws and policies, as well as how they are enforced, are among the most important determinants of whether a society is economically successful or not. When laws and policies favoring commerce are impartially enforced – for example, those favoring property rights, innovation, investment in public goods, reasonable taxation, freedoms of speech, press, and information – people are more likely to invest in highly productive enterprises.[1]

Laws and policies favoring commerce sow the seeds of economic growth. Production rises when investors direct capital toward its most highly productive use, allowing for more consumption in the future. This process compounds itself over time as investment in increasingly productive activities occurs. Conversely, when lawmakers enact and enforce laws and policies dissuading commerce – handouts to privileged citizens, burdensome taxation, abuse of property rights, harsh restrictions on free markets, or overinvestment in war – people are likely to either invest in low-productivity ventures or not invest at all. For instance, as property rights became weaker in the Islamic core around the tenth century, water mills and building cranes practically disappeared.[2] These are precisely the type of capital investments that pay off handsomely only if rights to their rents are secure over long periods. Their absence prevented the realization of potential productivity gains. The resulting economic losses grew even greater in the long run, as these economies never realized the benefits of compounding.

Why do laws and policies favoring commerce emerge in some regions but not others? As subsequent chapters show, pro-commerce laws and policies became much more commonplace in certain parts of Western Europe prior to the Industrial Revolution, but Middle Eastern rulers rarely enacted similar laws and policies. To understand why this was the case, it is first necessary to understand where laws and policies come from and why they might be different in different regions. This is not an easy task. There are many groups with the ability to create and influence the content of laws and policies, and understanding how these groups interact is essential to understanding what types of laws and policies emerge. This chapter focuses on these interactions, exploring how and why groups get their voice heard, and why this results in the creation of certain types of laws and policies.

Any inquiry into the forces underlying the content of laws and policies must focus on the incentives of political actors and the constraints they face. Even dictators cannot enact any law or policy that they please; they have constituents to whom they must account, and citizens may revolt against certain laws.[3] The simplest way of analyzing the decisions made by political actors is in terms of costs and benefits. What are the benefits to political authorities from promoting a certain law or policy? What are the costs? Only when the benefits outweigh the costs will the political actor fight to enact a law or policy.

But who are the relevant players? How and why can they constrain rulers? Historically, European monarchs had to negotiate laws and policies with religious authorities, military and landed elites in parliaments, and, occasionally, commercial leaders from urban areas. Meanwhile, Middle Eastern rulers negotiated with a mixture of religious authorities, military figures, and tribal power brokers. Why were the players different in the two regions? Why and how did rulers' interactions with these players differ? More importantly, what did this mean for the economic fortunes of these regions? These questions are necessary to answer in order to address the puzzling "reversal of fortunes" between the Middle East and Western Europe.

Who Makes Laws and Policies and Why Are They Followed?

A number of questions require addressing in order to understand where laws and policies come from and why they differ in different regions. Which parties create laws and policies? What are their interests? What is the bargaining power of each of the parties in the fight over laws and policies? Why do people follow laws and policies?

This chapter answers these questions by focusing on the role that *elites* play in creating laws and policies and encouraging others to follow them. I define elites as anyone who can influence how people whom they do not know act.[4] In much of European and Middle Eastern history, religious authorities were among the most important elites. Their dictates encouraged people to do minor things such as fast during Ramadan or give alms to the poor, as well as major things like go on a Crusade or fight a holy war. Other types of elites abound in the historical and contemporary record. Tribal elders use wisdom and moral authority to resolve disputes and give advice, military elites use force to influence others to do things they would rather not do, and economic elites wield their purse strings to garner influence. Because elites influence others, they can help shape laws and policies that people follow. It is therefore the interactions between different types of elites that dictate laws and policies.

People will not follow any law or policy enacted by an elite. For example, when King Charles I of England (r. 1625–1649) attempted to collect ship money – a tax levied without the consent of Parliament that was widely viewed as illegitimate – the tax largely went evaded, with nobles openly refusing to pay it. Why? Why did Charles I's subjects follow laws and policies in some instances but not others? What constrains rulers? How do they convince people to follow their laws and policies?

The answers to these questions are central to the framework proposed in this chapter. Research that I conducted with Avner Greif (Greif and Rubin 2015) provides some insight into these answers. We argue that there are two reasons why people follow laws and policies (which I henceforth call *rules*): because they believe that the person who enacts the rules has the right to do so, and because they believe that punishment will result if they do not follow the rules. In other words, people follow a rule either because the ruler is *legitimate* or because he has access to some form of *coercion*, or both. Two features of rules therefore explain why people follow them: who *establishes* them and who *enforces* them.

For some rules, simply knowing who establishes them is sufficient to understand why people follow them. If the person enacting the rule is one who is widely believed to have the legitimate right to do so, then people will follow the rule because they believe that it is the right thing to do.[5] For instance, European kings historically made proclamations or decrees that their subjects generally followed as long as the proclamations were within the realm of what a legitimate king had the right to enact. Likewise, Ottoman sultans often issued decrees to supplement Islamic law. These decrees formed a corpus of law known as the *kanun*, which had authority largely due to the legitimacy of the sultan. In most modern democracies, citizens believe that elected officials are legitimate because they are in office due to the "will of the people," and they thus have the right to legislate. People follow all sorts of religious rules because a legitimate religious authority favors it. Christians abstain from certain practices during Lent and Muslims fast during Ramadan due to beliefs that it is the "right" thing to do. In such cases, there may be explicit sanctions for disobeying the authority figure, but such sanctions do not always need to be in place to encourage rule following. Instead, individuals follow rules because someone whom they believe has the right to set certain rules of behavior establishes them.

In other cases, the enforcement of rules is a much more important determinant of why people follow them, regardless of who sets them. It is costly to break rules when doing so may lead to imprisonment, physical brutality, or confiscation of wealth. This is why rulers often invest in police and military force, especially if their legitimacy is weak. One needs to look no further than the autocratic states of the pre–Arab Spring Middle East to find examples of weakly legitimized rulers supporting their rule via force. When people follow rules due to coercion, the identity of the person or organization who establishes the rules is irrelevant as long as the punishment associated with breaking the rules is credible.

It is often the case that legitimacy and coercion work in tandem to encourage rule following. Many people follow laws imposed by rulers because they believe the rulers have the right to impose laws *and* they know what the punishments are if they break them. But knowing why people follow rules and what type of rules they will follow is only a small part of the overall story. If the only types of laws and policies that are enacted are ones that are followed to some degree, this still leaves a wide range of possible rules that can be successfully implemented, and this range increases as the ruler gains legitimacy or coercive power. The next question, then, is: Which laws and policies do rulers choose out of their many available options?

A more "economics" way of asking this question is: What gives rulers utility? Historically, rulers sought to achieve many goals: raising tax revenue, conquering territory, basking in their own glory, providing protection to their subjects, and giving favors to constituents. For the sake of simplification, assume the aim of all of these actions is achieving one goal: *propagating rule*. Simply put, any factor that keeps a ruler in power propagates his or her rule.[6]

The implication is that rulers choose rules – within the set of those that people follow – that best propagate their rule. A particularly gruesome example is the practice employed by numerous Ottoman sultans of having their half-brothers murdered upon ascending to the throne. The incentive for new sultans to have their kin murdered was to prevent rival factions with claims to the throne from forming during the sultan's reign – in other words, to increase the probability that the new sultan stayed in power. Less dramatic and more ubiquitous examples of laws and policies enacted in order to propagate rule include building up military force; spending on public goods such as roads, bridges, parks, and education; giving privileged government positions to the economic, religious, and political elite; and imprisoning those who publicly dissent against the regime.

To summarize, rulers primarily desire to propagate their rule, although they may have other motivations. A primary means of propagating rule is through rules that increase the likelihood they will stay in power. People follow these rules because the ruler is legitimate, has access to some coercive power, or both.[7] Figure 2.1 summarizes this logic.

The foregoing discussion has left out an important feature of this process: how rulers *attain* legitimacy and coercion. It is useful to think of legitimacy and coercion as intermediate goods, meaning that they are the products of some production process, while there is another process in which they are an input into the production of the propagation of rule. Legitimacy can come from numerous sources. One source is what Max Weber (1922) called the "traditional grounds of authority," which are based on a widespread belief held in society's traditions. For example, being an heir to the throne has historically been an important source of "traditional" legitimacy in societies all around the world: subjects perceive an heir as having a right to rule that non-heirs do not have. Another source of legitimacy is what Weber called "charismatic grounds of authority," which are based

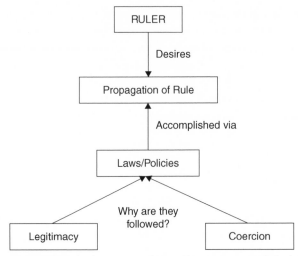

Figure 2.1 Rulers' Desires and How They Are Accomplished

on personality traits and achievements. A strong personality or record of achievement can give a ruler legitimacy when it strengthens the devotion of his or her people. Genghis Khan, Napoleon, Alexander the Great, Elizabeth I, and Saladin are all examples of individuals who legitimized their rule in part by the strength of their personality and achievements.

It is also possible for outside individuals or groups to confer legitimacy onto the ruler. Any individual or group who can bolster subjects' beliefs in the ruler's right to rule are called *legitimizing agents*.[8] Legitimizing agents are individuals or groups that people turn to for guidance due to some characteristic that makes people believe that their guidance is worthwhile to take. Legitimizing agents are by definition elites, since they can influence how people act.

Historically, one of the most important types of legitimizing agents were religious authorities.[9] The medieval Catholic Church could turn a king into an emperor; for instance, the Pope generally crowned the Holy Roman Emperor in Rome. The Pope dubbed Isabella and Ferdinand of Spain the "Catholic Monarchs" after they expelled the Muslim Moors from Spain and used the Inquisition to expel the Jews and Jewish converts. Medieval and early modern Middle Eastern rulers were also renowned for using religious authorities to bolster their legitimacy. They often acquired fatwas from important muftis before doing anything controversial, since fatwas were powerful proclamations that Muslims should abide by the ruler's policies. For example, the famous Ottoman mufti Ebu's-su'ud (1490–1574) was asked by the sultan for fatwas on controversial actions ranging from licensing an attack on the Venetians to approving the consumption of coffee, and the Abbasid caliph al-Muntasir (r. 861–62) secured a fatwa from top Iraqi religious scholars before hatching a plan to assassinate his father, the reigning caliph.[10]

Any elite with the power to influence people's opinions about their obligation to follow the ruler can serve as a legitimizing agent. Local elites, such as tribal elders or the landed elite, often act as legitimizing agents. They can confer legitimacy to the ruler because they have influence over the local population. For instance, the Ottoman sultan used local notables to propagate his rule in the provinces after the seventeenth century. The notables had local power due to tribal or military ties and were thus able to collect taxes and provide law and order that the sultan may have otherwise been unable to provide. These types of legitimizing agents have the capacity to legitimize rule based on what Weber (1922) called "rational grounds," which relies on "a belief in the legality of enacted rules and the right of those elevated to authority under such rules to issue commands."

Rulers can also use *coercive agents* to propagate their rule. These are individuals or groups with the power to enforce laws and policies through coercion. Examples of coercive agents include military elite, police officials, and warlords. Such individuals impose the ruler's will by force, often after the ruler enacts unpopular policies. For instance, Ottoman sultans gave their cavalry elite large tracts of land under the *timar* system, and in return the latter collected taxes and dispensed justice. Feudal lords in medieval Europe had a local monopoly on force, which they used to provide protection and local order in return for rights to collect the fruits of the land. Rulers use militaries throughout the modern Middle East to quash dissent and keep themselves in power. Together, legitimizing agents and coercive agents make up a broader class of actors called *propagating agents*.

Why do propagating agents propagate rule? What is in it for them? Propagating agents do not support the ruler without expecting something in return; they are "paid" in laws and policies that benefit their interests. When enacting rules, a ruler must cater to the interests of his propagating agents if he wants the same agents to propagate his rule in the future. If a ruler is powerful because the military terrorizes the citizenry, the ruler would be unwise to promote rules that upset the military. Indeed, members of the Janissary corps murdered more than one Ottoman sultan who attempted to reform the corps. Likewise, a ruler who is ordained by the religious establishment as ruling by divine right would find enacting laws contrary to religious doctrine quite costly, since it might undermine beliefs

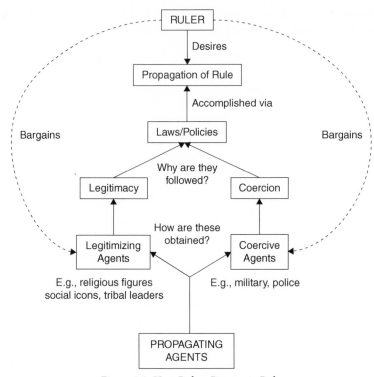

Figure 2.2 How Rulers Propagate Rule

in his divineness. Eric Chaney (2013) provides a fascinating example of such a bargain. In a study of Islamic Egypt from the twelfth through the fourteenth century, he finds that religious authorities were less likely to be replaced when the Nile River was either much lower than normal (meaning drought-like conditions unsuitable for agriculture) or much higher than normal (meaning flooding). The intuition is straightforward – it was precisely in those times when food was scarce that the ruler was most vulnerable to revolt. The benefit of religious legitimation was greatest at such a time, because religious authorities could dissuade the populace from revolting. As a result, religious authorities had a greater say in the bargain over laws and policies during Nile failures: "[During a failure] the sultan would bow to … pressure [from the head judge] and enforce decrees against … prostitution, hashish eating, beer drinking, the wearing of immodest or over-luxurious dress [or] Christian and Jewish functionaries lording it over Muslims."[11] Figure 2.2 extends upon Figure 2.1 to summarize the interactions between all of the relevant players in such a setting.

There is, therefore, an intimate relation between the types of rules that a ruler enacts and the *identity* of his propagating agents. When religious authorities propagate rulers, laws aligned with religious precepts and policies that keep religious authorities in power are likely to result. Religious authorities desire policies favoring religious precepts because such policies make it easier for them to maintain moral authority over the population. When Muslim rulers impose Islamic law, religious authorities benefit because the rules they tell individuals to follow are also the laws of the land. The policies that religious authorities want rulers to enact are occasionally growth-enhancing, such as support for the poor and education or prohibitions on violent acts. Their desired policies are also sometimes growth-retarding, such as restrictions on taking interest, rent-seeking, and prohibitions on certain actions taken by women.

The relationship between military propagation and economic outcomes is also mixed. On the one hand, merchants are much more likely to send expensive goods long distances if they are reasonably secure that naval power will protect them from piracy and overland travel is free from banditry. For instance, the Mongol invasions of the thirteenth century were largely destructive, but the "Pax Mongolia" they ushered in by placing much of Eurasia under the rule of one empire expanded the flow of ideas, techniques, goods, and people.[12] On the other hand, propagation by military elites can be bad for economic growth, as the Mongol destruction of many parts of Eurasia attest. The military can also suppress citizens – and economic activity – since they have an advantage in employing violence.

Propagation by the economic elite is more likely to lead to economic success because their motivations align to a greater degree with economically beneficial laws and policies. It is not because the economic elite are smarter or have the interests of the nation at heart more than other types of propagating agents. Quite to the contrary, it is *precisely* because they look out for their own self-interest that they contribute to overall economic success. While it is certainly true that the economic elite desires damaging policies such as handouts, monopolies, and other privileges, it is also true that public good provision, secure property rights, and impartial law and order benefit the economic elite more than they do other segments of society.

How the propagating process results in specific laws and policies is by no means simple. An analysis of this process must consider the ruler's various alternatives in propagating agents, how their policy desires affect these choices, and the nature of the quid pro quo between the various actors. These interactions quickly become complicated, and they depend on a host of variables that are different in different circumstances. Fortunately, economists have a tool – game theory – to help analyze situations in which individuals or groups interact strategically.

Game Theory and the Role of Institutions

The situation described in the preceding section is comprised of numerous actors, each with their own, often conflicting motivations. Each of these actors must take into account how the others will act and react when making their own decisions. In other words, when these actors get together to formulate laws and policies, they act strategically. Their interactions are therefore well suited for a game theoretic analysis.

Game theory is the study of how people and organizations act in strategic settings. Economists have used it to gain insight into all sorts of settings where economic actors have to account for the actions of others when making decisions. It is used to show how firms set prices, where firms locate, how markets for kidney donations work, why people marry their partner, how soccer players decide in which direction to kick a penalty, how countries negotiate over peace, and even why countries choose whether or not to detonate nuclear bombs. In the setting described earlier, game theory can shed light on how rulers interact with their propagating agents under varying conditions.

Thinking in game theoretic terms is valuable because it focuses attention on the salient aspects of the relationship between rulers and their propagating agents. The point is not to capture all of the factors that go into a decision, but to focus on the driving forces. This entails addressing numerous questions. First, who are the relevant players? Second, what are their motivations? Third, what is the relationship between the players? Fourth, how do these interactions help them achieve their goals?

A game theoretic framework answers each of these questions. Once the framework is established, it is possible to analyze how the players act under different settings. In the present situation, it is possible to craft a general game where the relevant players are a ruler and propagating agents. Generality has its limits, though. When studying the situation in medieval Europe or the Middle East, the identity of the propagating agents matters. In medieval Europe, the Church, economic elite, and the military propagated kings. In the Middle East, religious authorities and the military were the primary propagating agents. Knowing the identity of the relevant players is important because it informs us about their motivations as well as their relationship with the ruler.

When solving game theoretic models, economists usually focus on states of the world in which all of the players' actions are consistent with their motivations and the actions of others. In other words, they focus on *equilibrium* actions. An equilibrium is a state of the world where nobody has incentive to do anything different than what they are currently doing. In the context of the present framework, an equilibrium occurs when the ruler gets the best bargain he can, given his desires and how his agents act in the bargaining process, while the agents get the best bargain they can, given their desires and the actions of the ruler.

A key component of the game theoretic framework proposed in this chapter is the outside, or exogenous, factors that affect the incentives of the players. One of the most important of these factors is the society's *institutions*. A simple and powerful definition of institutions, proposed by Douglass North (1990), is that they are the rules of the game, means of enforcement, and players of the game.[13] Institutions come in many forms. They may be political, economic, religious, social, legal, or penal. Medieval manorial courts provide a straightforward example of a legal/economic institution: they resolved disputes between those living on the manor, each court had its own laws based on the custom of the manor, and the lord generally presided over cases. Hence, these courts provided the rules of the game (they helped specify which laws would be enforced), the means of enforcement (the losing party could be punished by the lord), and the relevant players.

In other words, institutions place *constraints* on human behavior. These constraints influence behavior because they affect the costs and benefits of different actions. For instance, rulers are much more likely to propagate their rule via religious legitimation if the "rules of the game" are such that religious doctrine is consistent with permitting religious legitimation. In such a case, the benefit of religious legitimation is greater than if there were no doctrine whereby religion could ordain rulers.

How institutions affect interactions between rulers and their propagating agents is only half of the story. Institutions also *evolve* over time along with the rules of the game they impose. Over long periods, institutions change when people stop following the old rules of the game and start following new rules created by new institutions.[14] Such change is often good for an economy: institutions that change to reflect economic conditions incentivize behavior that puts economic inputs to their most highly productive use. Conversely, if institutions do not adjust to their surroundings, the rules of the game do not change to account for economic realities, and economic opportunities are likely to be lost. Why does this happen? Why do institutions sometimes fail to change when economic conditions change?

The "Game" Played between Rulers and Their Propagating Agents

The first task of any game theoretic framework is to identify the relevant players.[15] In the present case, those players are a ruler and the set of potential propagating agents. This includes propagating agents that the ruler does not actually end up choosing; they may still play an important role in the game because they represent the outside option available for the ruler. A final set of players that have received little attention so far are the "citizenry," or the "nonelite." For the most part, they are in the background of the framework, since most policies result from the bargain between the elite. However, the citizenry place an important constraint on the actions of all parties; a ruler cannot stay in power if he does not have the support of the citizens, and a propagating agent loses its ability to support political power if it holds no influence over the citizens.

The next step is to consider the motivations of the players. Building on the previous analysis, the framework assumes that the ruler's primary goal is to stay in power, which he can achieve through some combination of legitimacy and coercion. The motivations of propagating agents depend on their identity. The military elite generally desires policies such as greater military spending, campaigns of conquest, or increased capacity to collect taxes. Economic elites generally support policies that increase their own wealth. Religious authorities often desire tax exemption, policies consistent with religious precepts, and suppression of rival religions.[16]

The next task is to determine the nature of the relationship between the players. All players must get something out of interacting with each other, otherwise they would not do so. The benefit to the ruler of playing the game is clear: propagating agents bolster his claim to rule, which in turn helps keep him in power. The benefit to the agents of playing the game is whatever they receive in return for their support. For example, a ruler may enforce a religious law or subjugate a rival religious movement in order to maintain good standing with the religious establishment. Numerous pre-Reformation European kings did just this, assisting the Church in suppressing heretical movements. Or a ruler may provide public goods to satisfy the economic elite. Early Islamic leaders commonly endowed *waqf*s (pious trusts) that provided schools, hospitals, mosques, and other public goods.

The enacted policies ultimately result from the ruler's choice of propagating agents and the bargaining strength of those agents. In other words, the keys to understanding which policies result from the bargain are found in the answers to the following questions: How much do rulers need the agents to propagate their rule? Are the agents effective at propagating rule at relatively low cost? Are there good alternative sources of propagation for the ruler? What determines the magnitude of the costs and benefits of different laws and policies? This is where the society's institutions enter the game. By providing the "rules of the game" institutions dictate the costs and benefits that a ruler faces of having rule propagated in different manners and thus the relative costs and benefits of enacting different policies.

Propagating agents are effective when they are able to strengthen the ruler's likelihood of staying in power. They are able to do so only when the rules of the game permit it. In some societies, religious authorities are highly effective at legitimizing rule. They are only effective, however, when they are influential with the population and when there is historical or theological content that permits them to effectively legitimize rule.[17] When such doctrine exists, one of the rules of the game is that religious leaders have the capacity to propagate rule. And indeed, such doctrine exists in both Christianity and Islam. Equally important, the costs associated with religious legitimation are generally trivial relative to the costs of other types of propagation. As Anthony Gill (1998, p. 51) notes, "Ideology … is a relatively cost-effective form of control since people obey out of the belief that what the government does is right. By creating a system of values and norms, a strong ideology regulates citizens' behavior by providing an internal guide to acceptable and unacceptable activity."

The costs and benefits of using specific propagating agents therefore depend on the society's institutions. For instance, Eliana Balla and Noel Johnson (2009) show that both Ottoman and French rulers provided elites with tax farms to collect revenue. But due to differences in incorporation laws, French tax farmers were able to pool their capital and thus coordinate to constrain the king if he chose fiscal policies undesirable to them. There was no mechanism for Ottoman tax farmers to do this, and they were never able to credibly constrain the sultan. In other words, as French tax farmers became more coordinated, it became more costly for kings to use them to collect taxes, since they had more bargaining power and could thus extract more from him. For the Ottomans, using tax farmers was a rather inexpensive manner of collecting taxes, as the sultan had to give relatively little to tax farmers in return for the right to collect taxes.[18]

In sum, the cost to the ruler of receiving propagation from an agent is how much the ruler has to give up in the bargain over propagation. These costs can take many forms, depending on whether the propagating agent(s) are members of the economic, military, or religious elite, or some combination of the three. The magnitude of these costs is dependent on the society's institutions.

Taking these institutionalized rules as given for the moment, let's turn to the equilibrium actions of all the players. To solve for the equilibrium, consider what each player is thinking when they come to the bargaining table. First off, the ruler wants to stay in power. He knows that to do so he needs propagation from his agents. He also knows there are a host of policies that otherwise weaken his hold on power but are consistent with the interests of the agents. Meanwhile, the agents have some objective they wish to obtain in the bargain. The agents can withhold or provide less propagation as a bargaining tactic. If these tactics are credible, the agent can force the ruler's hand.

The parties' relative bargaining power determines the equilibrium outcome of the bargain. The ruler considers how much propagation he needs to stay in power and rule effectively, how much propagation each agent can provide him, and the cost of receiving propagation from each of the agents. He then weighs these costs and benefits and chooses some combination of agents to propagate his rule in the most effective way possible.

There are two possible outcomes of this bargain. First, if the chosen propagating agent(s) is highly effective or inexpensive, it is in a good bargaining position. In this case, the agent can threaten to withhold legitimacy, leaving the ruler without an important source of propagation. If this threat is credible, the ruler will make significant policy concessions to the agent even if those policies otherwise reduce his likelihood of staying in power.

The game becomes more complex if the agents' desires do not align with those of the citizens. In this case, the ruler must choose between supporting his propagating agents and enacting policies that benefit the citizenry. If the ruler ends up supporting a policy favored by the agents, any citizen who violates the policy faces a "double penalty," since they are subject to sanctions from both the ruler and the agent. For instance, anyone attempting to break Saudi laws that subjugate women may face both spiritual sanctions from the religious establishment as well as jail time or fines. This creates an extra disincentive for citizens to push for changes to such a rule in the future. A vicious cycle is thereby created where, over time, citizens have little incentive to push for change, and the ruler and propagating agents do not need to bargain over these laws and policies because they are not of concern of the public.[19] It is even possible that society forgets arguments in favor of change once they fall out of the mainstream, meaning that over time a push for change in these rules is not even a preference of the citizens.[20]

The contrary logic holds when the agent(s) chosen in equilibrium is costly or ineffective. In this case, if the agent's demands are too great, the ruler can credibly threaten to choose another form of propagation. Hence, the laws and policies emanating from the bargain are more reflective of the ruler's desires. This outcome also has dynamic consequences when the actions of the citizenry are considered. If economic conditions incentivize some citizens to push to change rules that are contrary to the agents' desires, the ruler is more likely to enact these changes, since he does not fear losing the propagation the agent provides. Hence, the citizens are encouraged to push for even more rule changes in the future. Although they face costs imposed by the agent from doing so, they do not face penalties from the ruler. This can lead to a cycle moving in the other direction, where the ruler permits more and more as the citizens ask for more, to the point where the rules of the society are radically different than before the initial push.

Institutional Change (and Stagnation) in the Long Run

When laws or policies change dramatically over time, institutions may change to accommodate the new reality. In the long run, it is possible that the ruler's cost-benefit calculation changes over time *precisely* because people act in their own interest. When this occurs, institutions change *endogenously*. Figure 2.3 represents this process in simplified form.

This book focuses on why institutions change – or do not change – when political rule is legitimized by religion. Religious propagation is effective when religious authorities exert influence over the population and when religious doctrine is conducive to legitimizing rule. This is even truer of the monotheistic faiths such as Islam and Christianity. Murat Iyigun (2015, ch. 2) argues, with support from an extensive data analysis, that monotheisms are good for propagating rule because they imbue both political and religious authorities with monopoly powers. But religious authorities cannot simply claim that rulers are legitimate if this is inconsistent with doctrine.

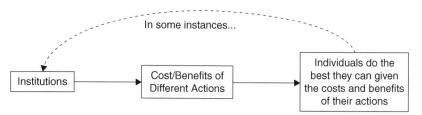

Figure 2.3 Endogenous Institutional Change

Religions are somewhat unique in this way – *consistency matters*, and a primary reason that religious authorities are able to propagate rule in the first place is that they hold the keys to the "eternal" word of God. These "keys" are highly valued in most civilizations, historic and present, perhaps for evolutionary reasons: humans desire answers to the unknown and the unknowable, and religion offers these answers. This gives religious authorities power over the citizens – it is what makes them "elite" – but only to the extent that their answers are consistent. Inconsistent proclamations indicate that religious authorities do not have access to "eternal" laws, and such proclamations therefore undermine the ability of the authority to legitimize political rule.[21] Religious authorities may attempt to rationalize big changes as being consistent with doctrine, but they are still constrained to choose from the set of rationalizations that are believable. In other words, the "rules of the game" are such that the efficacy of religious statements that legitimize rule are constrained by being consistent with doctrine. This does not mean that religious doctrine remains stagnant under all conditions; it simply indicates that the cost to religious authorities of changing their proclamations is greater than it is for other types of propagating agents.

One upshot is that religious authorities are in a no-win situation when people flagrantly violate their dictates. Religious authorities have a full menu of policy objectives, with their views on the issue at hand being one of them. They stand to lose credibility – and hence the ability to propagate rule – if large swaths of the population openly transgress their position on one issue. For instance, the contemporary Catholic Church stands to lose members as it continues to cling to its positions on contraception, divorce, and homosexuality, although these issues represent a miniscule fraction of the Church's overall doctrinal concerns. Hence, on this one issue, religious authorities have a short-term incentive to update their views. Yet, religious reinterpretation carries an important long-run cost: it undermines the very nature of the religious authority's power. This is the main feature that distinguishes religious authorities from other types of propagating agents: intertemporal consistency matters.

This religion-specific institutional feature means that the legitimizing relationship between the religious and political elite can change over time. If religious authorities reinterpret doctrine to maintain their relevance with the citizenry, they undermine their ability to legitimize rule in the long run, thus reducing the benefits of religious propagation. On the other hand, if they permit individuals to flagrantly violate their dictates without a response, they stand to lose their ability to influence actions in both the short run and the long run, as transgressing religious doctrine will become a norm. The upshot is that religious authorities with weak ability to propagate rule become even weaker over time. This process may continue to the point where rulers remove religious authorities from the set of agents who propagate their rule.

Such long-run change does not occur, however, when religious authorities are highly effective at legitimizing political rule. In this case, it is unlikely that citizens transgress religious dictates in the first place, since the ruler will not support their transgressions. The religious authority therefore never has to make the "no-win" decision because it never faces any pressure to reinterpret doctrine. This means that the legitimizing relationship between religious authorities and the ruler reinforces itself over time.

One consequence of this logic is that what are initially small institutional differences between societies can blossom into very large differences over time. Once a society begins moving toward an equilibrium where open violation of religious dictates is the norm, a cycle begins where these actions feed into institutional change, exacerbating the degree to which religious dictates are transgressed, which itself feeds into even more institutional change. Such a cycle is unlikely to occur when religious authorities are highly effective in legitimizing rule, since there is no impetus to initiate the cycle. An institutional divergence can occur even if the economic benefits from institutional change are the same in both societies: the mechanism described above rests on the narrow self-interest of the ruler and his agents, not the efficiency of their bargaining outcome.

These insights are related to the second mechanism through which institutions change in the long run: *path dependence*. A path-dependent series of events is one in which the initial impetus that triggers a series of events is far, far removed from the eventual outcome, and the initial raison d'être that sparked movement down a certain pathway has no direct influence on long-run behavior. This occurs when each step along the path depends on what happened at the last step. The first chapter described these steps as "forks" along a society's economic or institutional path. Once the society chooses one side of the fork, a new path emerges, far removed from the reasons the society chose the original path in the first place.[22]

In the context of economic history, path dependence entails that institutions can originate in situations in which humans found a solution to a problem, but they can also persist long after that problem is relevant. In such a situation, institutions still provide the rules of the game, even though important parts of the game were unforeseen at the time of the institution's creation. The historical setting on which this book focuses is case in point: rulers in the medieval Middle East and Western Europe legitimized

their rule in part via religion because the rules of the game indicated that
this was the most efficient solution to their problem of propagating rule
given the conditions that they faced. Once these rules of the game were
established, the desires of religious agents affected the laws and policies that
arose in response to *unanticipated and unforeseen* events. An important
historical example of such a process is the subject of Chapter 5, which analyzes why the Ottoman Empire failed to adopt Gutenberg's movable type
printing press. In short, the printing press threatened the sultan's ability to
propagate his rule, since it threatened the status of the religious establishment. The invention of the printing press was unforeseeable at the time that
Ottoman propagating arrangements emerged. The suppression of printing
in the Ottoman Empire was therefore a result of a path-dependent series of
events and is thus only explainable by digging into history and searching for
the events that caused these events to arise in the first place.

Testable Predictions

Any good economic framework should provide *falsifiable, testable predictions*. Otherwise, there is no way to know whether it is correct or if it tells
us anything about the real world. To this end, this chapter concludes by
summarizing the framework's major implications as they relate to the main
question posed in this book: Why did Western European economies catch
up with and eventually far surpass those of the Middle East?

The first, and most straightforward, testable prediction relates to the
outcome of the short-run bargain between rulers and their agents. If the
religious establishment legitimizes the ruler, we should expect to see laws
favoring religious authorities. The same is true if the economic or military elite propagate the ruler. In other words, the following prediction
should hold:

> Testable Prediction #1: The laws and policies of a society should in part
> reflect the desires of the ruler's propagating agents.

Testable Prediction #1 implies that the motivations of propagating agents
matter. If they primarily desire laws and policies that benefit themselves at
the expense of the rest of the population, economic success is unlikely to
result: even though their desires are harmful, they *still get their voice heard*
because they play a valuable role in propagating rule. In an ideal world,
the motivations of the propagating agent are consistent with economic success, meaning that agents benefit from the provision of public goods, secure
property rights, impartial law and order, investment in public education,

protection for long-distance traders, and so on. This ideal world has never come to fruition, but some societies have come closer than others to realizing it. These societies are ones where the economic elite have a nontrivial seat at the bargaining table. Unlike religious or military elites, economic elites have interests that align with the types of laws and policies listed above. Testable Prediction #2 summarizes this insight.

> Testable Prediction #2: Societies in which the economic elite play some role in propagating rule will be more successful in the long run than societies in which the economic elite play no role in propagating rule.

The framework also suggests that when religious legitimation is important, it tends to remain important even as the world changes. And barriers to long-run success arise when laws or policies that would change in the natural course of a growing economy's progression instead persist. Such a sequence of events does not transpire when religious legitimacy is less effective or more costly. In such a case, the religious establishment has less capacity to impose restrictions that are harmful to long-run economic growth, and other forms of propagation become more appealing over time. It follows that institutional change proceeds in a manner shaped by the economic – and not the religious – incentives of the relevant actors. In turn, the society's institutions are likely to be more conducive to economic growth, and this outcome grows stronger over time. Testable Prediction #3 summarizes these insights.

> Testable Prediction #3: When religious legitimacy is highly effective or inexpensive, rulers propagate their rule with religion in the short run and the long run, even if economic circumstances change. If religious legitimacy is less effective or more expensive, its use will diminish in the long run once circumstances arise that decrease its effectiveness or decrease the cost of other forms of propagation.

One upshot of Testable Prediction #3, summarized in Testable Prediction #4, is that what were at one point in time small differences in propagating arrangements between societies can blossom into large differences over time as one economy stagnates and the other adjusts to changing economic realities.

> Testable Prediction #4: A society in which religious authorities are an important source of political legitimation will eventually stagnate as institutions do not change in response to changing economic conditions. As a result, a society in which religious authorities are a less

important source of political legitimation may pull ahead economically, even if it were once behind.

Testable Predictions #3 and #4 therefore suggest a possible answer to one of the historical puzzles posed in the first chapter: Why did the successful economies of the Middle East eventually fall behind Western Europe, which was once an economic laggard? If religious authorities more heavily legitimized Middle Eastern rulers than their Western European counterparts, then the "reversal of fortunes" is explainable in the context of the framework.

Testable predictions are one thing. Whether the historical record bears them out is quite another. The next chapter addresses this issue, exploring why religious propagation was important in Islam and Christianity and why its benefits to rulers differed in the two religions.

3

Historical Origins of Rule Propagation

In 1521, the Italian War of 1521–1526 broke out between Spain and France. The Holy Roman Empire sided with Spain – Charles V was both the king of Spain and the Holy Roman Emperor – as did England. The wealthy Republic of Venice sided with France. Pope Leo X (r. 1513–1521) needed an ally to stop the spread of the Reformation in the Holy Roman Empire, and he therefore involved the Papal States on the side of Charles V. The war culminated in January 1526 with the French King Francis I ceding significant territory to Charles V. But the new pope Clement VII (r. 1523–1534) did not welcome this outcome, as he felt that the Spanish were growing too powerful. Within weeks of the signing of the treaty, the pope gave his blessing to Francis I of France to attempt to reclaim what was lost in the Italian War. The Pope helped establish the League of Cognac – consisting of France, the Papal States, England, and the Republics of Venice and Florence – to drive the Spanish from Italy. This precipitated the War of the League of Cognac (1526–1530) and ultimately another Spanish–Holy Roman Empire victory. Although there were many factors determining the various alliances and causes of the wars, it is notable that within the span of one decade, almost all of the major Western European powers – France, Spain, the Holy Roman Empire, and Venice – were involved in wars *against the papacy*. Ironically, England was the only nation that sided with the pope in both conflicts, which occurred just before Henry VIII kicked the Church out of England.

To the southeast of these conflicts, the Ottoman Empire just concluded some important conflicts of its own. Prior to the reign of Selim I (r. 1512–1520), the Ottoman territories were confined to the western half of the Anatolian Peninsula (Turkey) and southeastern Europe. The Ottomans had long desired the territories controlled by the Egyptian Mamluk Empire, who ruled over the eastern half of the North African coast, much of the Levant including Syria, and the Arabian Peninsula including the holy cities Mecca and Medina. These territories were wealthy – they covered the fertile Nile Delta and the avenue to the Indian Ocean–Red Sea transit trade – and included the most important religious sites in Islam. But despite having superior force, the Ottomans could not simply attack the Mamluks, who, like the Ottomans, were Sunni Muslims. Prior to attacking the Mamluks, Selim I sought a fatwa from the Grand Mufti (*şeyhülislam*, the head of the Ottoman religious establishment) Ali al-Jamali to authorize an attack. Ali al-Jamali gave Selim permission for the attack, which was ultimately successful and brought extensive land and wealth under Ottoman purview.

Although these historical episodes take place near the end of the period covered in this book, I mention them here because they reflect differences in the importance of religious legitimation in the Middle East and Western Europe. In Western Europe, the major political players did not hesitate to enter into wars against the papacy. Meanwhile, the most important Middle Eastern power sought legitimation for military actions that would have been successful even in the absence of religious blessing. These differences are important, for reasons highlighted in the last chapter. Specifically, reconsider Testable Prediction #4: *A society in which religious authorities are an important source of political legitimation will eventually stagnate ... [and] a society in which religious authorities are a less important source of political legitimation may pull ahead economically, even if it were once behind.*

How was it determined who propagated rule in the Middle East and Western Europe? Why did the identity of propagating agents differ across the two societies? This chapter addresses these questions, exploring the historical determinants of religious legitimation in Middle Eastern and Western European history. Religious legitimation was important in both regions for one simple reason: it was relatively inexpensive. But this only explains why rulers frequently used religious legitimation in European and Middle Eastern history; it does not explain why rulers used it differently in the two regions. More to the point, it does not explain why religious legitimacy was historically more important in the Middle East than in Western Europe. This chapter makes the case that historical differences in the two regions arose from the unique circumstances under which Islam and Christianity were born. These circumstances shaped how political and religious institutions interacted with each other at the births of the religions and persisted long after the original circumstances were relevant.

The Doctrine of Religious Legitimation in Islam and Christianity

Islam arose in the seventh century in the western half of the Arabian Peninsula between the powerful Byzantine and Sasanid empires. The Bedouin tribes who dominated the area engaged in trade with each other and with neighboring empires. Their trade networks reached at least as far away as Syria and Iraq. Mecca was at the center of this trade. The tribal confederation of Mecca constructed a regional trade network that reached throughout the Peninsula. Mecca was also a center of worship due to its housing the Ka'ba, and by the sixth century it was an important pilgrimage destination.[1]

Muhammad was born into the Meccan tribal confederation. The trade network familiarized Muhammad with the religions and cultures of the Peninsula, including Christianity and Judaism, as well as the economic realities of trade and the power of religious symbolism. Muhammad's initial message, which he carried to Medina, focused on faith and morality. The community he established in Medina accepted God as the ultimate source of authority, with this precept providing a basis for all aspects of life. As Muhammad's influence spread beyond Medina, he oversaw the formation of a new religion, a new polity, and a new legal system – all of which were intimately connected. The proto-institutions created in Muhammad's lifetime had the ability to establish laws, dispense justice, collect taxes, and conduct diplomacy. These institutions drew from the existing, pre-Islamic framework of the Arabian Peninsula, which included Judeo-Christian monotheism but also included unique Islamic elements covering both morals (e.g., prohibition of alcohol) and laws (e.g., inheritance).

The new Islamic polity spread rapidly after Muhammad's death, reaching as far west as the Iberian Peninsula and as far east as the Indian subcontinent. The three empires following Muhammad (the First Caliphate, the Umayyad Empire, and the Abbasid Empire) were among the largest in terms of land mass in world history up to that point – much larger than the Roman Empire or Alexander's Macedonian Empire (see Table 3.1). The economic benefits of Islam were an important reason the new religion spread. It initially spread along old trade routes, and many of the initial converts were those who benefited from trade.[2] Indeed, a pre-Islamic merchant might reasonably suspect that foreigners would rip him off, meaning that he would be wary of conducting trade in the first place. The Arab conquests of the seventh and eighth centuries helped mitigate this problem.

Table 3.1 *Largest Empires in World History, through 1750*

Empire	Birth Year	Death Year	Peak Land Mass (million km²)	Muslim
Mongol Empire	1206 CE	1502 CE	33.2	No
Russian Empire (Muscovy)	1462 CE	1795 CE	16.5	No
Umayyad Empire	661 CE	750 CE	13.2	Yes
Qing Empire (China)	1644 CE	1911 CE	12	No
Qin Dynasty (China)	247 BCE	209 BCE	12	No
Abbasid Empire	750 CE	861 CE	11	Yes
First Four Caliphs (Rashidun)	632 CE	661 CE	9	Yes

Source: Iyigun (2010).

The spread of a relatively consistent Islamic legal framework helped foster a unifying ideology that accommodated divergent tribal interests while providing greater security for traders carrying expensive and easily stolen goods. This ideology respected trade – Muhammad himself engaged in commerce – unlike early and medieval Christianity, which largely disdained trade.[3] Islam therefore served as a unifying force for groups with very different natural resource and geographic endowments, and early Islamic ideals associated with wealth redistribution were in part reflective of this fact.[4] The creation of a network of coreligionists who spoke a common language, employed a consistent monetary system, and used similar Islamic financial instruments reduced other transaction costs associated with trade. This setting contrasted with both post–Roman Europe and the pre-Islamic Middle East, where the most significant impediments to trade were high transaction costs and a lack of trust between rival groups. New crops and agricultural techniques were also introduced to the newly Islamized lands, and the ensuing agricultural surplus and local agricultural trade that followed permitted the rapid growth of cities throughout the Islamic world.[5]

The new Muslim polity founded by Muhammad evolved conterminously with Islam. This meant that when new questions of governance arose, rulers answered them in an Islamic context. Muhammad himself claimed that, "Islam and government are twin brothers. One cannot thrive without the other. Islam is the foundation, and government the guardian. What has no foundation, collapses; what has no guardian, perishes."[6] Bernard Lewis

(1974, p. xviii) argues that as a result of the coevolution of Muslim political and religious institutions, the concept of a separation of church and states is absent in Islamic thought: "[S]uch pairs as spiritual and temporal, lay and ecclesiastical, and religious and secular have no equivalents in the classical languages of the Muslim peoples."

Importantly, since the growth of the first Muslim state occurred in the early stages of Islamic doctrinal development, early thinkers codified Islamic ideas of the state in the Qur'an. The Qur'an lists at least three ways that rulers can gain legitimacy: appointment from God, inheriting authority from a legitimate ruler, and having an "oath of allegiance" from the populace.[7] The following three Qur'anic verses detail these means of legitimacy:

2:247 And their prophet said to them, "Indeed, Allah has sent to you Saul as a king." They said, "How can he have kingship over us while we are more worthy of kingship than him and he has not been given any measure of wealth?" He said, "Indeed, Allah has chosen him over you and has increased him abundantly in knowledge and stature. And Allah gives His sovereignty to whom He wills. And Allah is all-Encompassing [in favor] and Knowing."

27:16 And Solomon inherited David. He said, "O people, we have been taught the language of birds, and we have been given from all things. Indeed, this is evident bounty."

48:10 Indeed, those who pledge allegiance to you, [O Muhammad] – they are actually pledging allegiance to Allah. The hand of Allah is over their hands. So he who breaks his word only breaks it to the detriment of himself. And he who fulfills that which he has promised Allah – He will give him a great reward.

Regardless of how a ruler obtained legitimacy, the Qur'an and subsequent Islamic doctrine are explicit on one point: good Muslims should follow a ruler who acts according to Islamic dictates, and Muslims have a duty to rebel against a ruler who acts contrary to Islam. Islamic doctrine therefore tells Muslims exactly what type of rules a ruler can legitimately enact, as indicated in the following Qur'anic verses (italics added):

4:59 O you who have believed, obey Allah and obey the Messenger and *those in authority* among you. And *if you disagree over anything, refer it to Allah* and the Messenger, if you should believe in Allah and the Last Day. That is the best [way] and best in result.

2:190–191 Fight in the way of Allah those who fight you but do not transgress. Indeed. Allah does not like transgressors. And kill them wherever you overtake them and expel them from wherever they have expelled you, and fitnah [i.e., persecution] is worse than killing.

The first verse cited above suggests that Muslims should follow worldly authorities, but only if their statements are consistent with those of Allah and Muhammad (the Messenger). The second verse suggests that it is better to kill one who persecutes – one who transgresses Allah – than live under persecution. The hadith of al-Bukhari makes much clearer statements on which rulers Muslims should or should not follow. Hadiths are the reports of the teachings of Muhammad that scholars handed down orally over generations. They are among the most important sources of authority in Islam. Al-Bukhari's hadiths were compiled two centuries after Muhammad and are considered among the most reliable of all the hadith literature. Of importance are the following two hadiths:[8]

The Prophet said, "It is obligatory for one to listen to and obey (the ruler's orders) unless these orders involve one disobedience (to Allah); but if an act of disobedience (to Allah) is imposed, he should not listen to or obey it." (Vol. 4, Book 52, No. 203)

The Prophet said, "A Muslim has to listen to and obey (the order of his ruler) whether he likes it or not, as long as his orders involve not one in disobedience (to Allah), but if an act of disobedience (to Allah) is imposed one should not listen to it or obey it. (Vol. 9, Book 89, No. 258)

From its inception, Islamic doctrine provided a mechanism to legitimize rulers: it commanded Muslims to follow the laws and policies of rulers who acted in accordance with Islamic dictates and to not follow those who did not.

The circumstances under which Christianity was born were quite different than those found in the seventh-century Middle East. Unlike Islam, which coevolved with a growing empire, Christianity was born in the Roman Empire, where well-functioning legal and political institutions already existed. Hence, there was not an opportunity for Christianity to spread in the manner that Islam did in its first century. There were already established institutional means for propagating Roman rule, such as the military, Senate, and Roman ideology.

For these reasons, Christianity did not legitimize political rule in its first three centuries. Early Church leaders were not concerned with legitimizing political rule because, quite simply, the Church was not in a position to legitimize. In order for an agent to have the capacity to legitimize, it must be able to augment subjects' beliefs regarding the ruler's right to rule. Religious authorities can do this when they are able to claim moral authority, but this is only useful if the religion is widespread, its institutions are entrenched deeply enough in society, or if the political or economic elite ascribe to them. The early Christian Church was neither widespread nor had it infiltrated the elite. Prior to the fourth century, Christianity consisted primarily of individuals willing to take on great risk of persecution and social ostracism, and it consequently was a religion of the "middling" classes. Although some of the elite were attracted to the fledgling religion, most churches owned little to no land and the clergy largely came from lower social classes.[9]

In the first three Christian centuries, the Church sought to survive and expand within an empire that was sometimes hostile to it, as large polities often are toward groups of non-privileged citizens who meet regularly and in private. Indeed, the Romans occasionally charged early Christians with cannibalism, as word spread of their eating the "body of Christ" during the sacrament. The Church could not confront the empire and hope to survive, and so early Church leaders advocated a separation between political and religious institutions.[10] The most famous support for this position came from Jesus: "Render unto Caesar the things which are Caesar's, and unto God the things that are God's" (Matthew 22:21). The early Christian writer Tertullian (c. 200), who was among the most important Christian thinkers of the first three centuries, made this position much clearer:

We are forever making intercession for the emperors. We pray for them a long life, a secure rule, a safe home, brave armies, a faithful senate, an honest people, a quiet world, and everything for which a man and a Caesar may pray ... we know that the great force which threatens the whole world, the end of the age itself with its menace of hideous sufferings, is delayed by the respite which the Roman Empire means for us ... when we pray for its postponement we assist the continuance of Rome ... I have a right to say, Caesar is more ours than yours, appointed he is by our God.[11]

This view of Christianity's place vis-à-vis secular authority persisted well after Christianity became the religion of the Roman Empire. Augustine advocated this view in his influential fifth-century book *The City of God*, which suggested that civil government was an independent body and that Christians must obey its laws. Likewise, Pope Gelasius I (r. 492–496) claimed in a letter to the emperor Anastasius that "two there are, august emperor, by which this world is chiefly ruled, the sacred authority of the priesthood and the royal power."[12]

Christian fortunes turned when the Roman emperor Constantine issued the Edict of Milan in 312, which mandated tolerance and freedom for all Christians, restored to the Church all confiscated property, and recognized the Church as a corporate body.[13] The freedoms awarded to Christians had an enormous impact on the fortunes of the Church, and the reign of Constantine is one of the most momentous in Christian history. In 321, Constantine recognized the Church as a valid property holder. Legally regarded as a corporation, each episcopal see was permitted by the Roman state to hold property, and it allowed individuals to bequeath property to the Church. Soon after, it became common for wealthy men and widows to leave one-third of their property to the Church, and landed property quickly became one of the Church's primary sources of wealth. These edicts also had the important effect of lowering the cost of being Christian. It was no longer a social or economic disadvantage to be Christian; believer's property rights were secure and there was no longer a risk of persecution. As a result, the Christian population grew dramatically during Constantine's reign, particularly among the middle and upper classes, rising from 10 percent of the Roman population at the beginning of his reign to 56.5 percent by 350 CE.[14]

Yet, while Constantine and subsequent Christian rulers employed the Church as a legitimizing agent, there were three centuries of doctrine disassociating secular rule from religion that mitigated the Church's capacity to legitimize. This is not to say Christianity could not legitimize political authority – it clearly did during the medieval period – but that Christian doctrine was not as conducive to legitimizing political authority as Islamic doctrine was. In other words, the "rules of the game" were different for Christian and Muslim rulers. Even after Christianity became the dominant religion of Europe, the benefit of religious legitimation was lower for Western European rulers than it was for Middle Eastern rulers. These doctrinal differences are clear in the Bible and the Qur'an as well as in the writings of early Christian and Islamic scholars. While some passages from the Bible do suggest that there is a religious basis for rule (Paul advocated in Romans 13:1 "there is no power but from God: and those that are, are ordained of God"), the separation of Christian religious and secular spheres is clear. On the other hand, there is not even a *concept* of separate spheres of the religious and secular in Islam. There is nothing in Christian doctrine like the Qur'anic and hadith passages explicitly encouraging Muslims to follow rulers who abide by Islamic dictates and rebel against those who do not. Historian Brian Tierney summarizes these differences eloquently (1988, p. 7, italics added):

Most often, as a society grows from primitive tribalism into an ordered civilization, a common religion permeates all its activities and helps to form all its characteristic institutions. The rise of medieval Islam provides a typical example. *In such circumstances the creation of political institutions quite separate from the organization of the accepted religion seems hardly conceivable.* Christianity, on the other hand, irrupted into an ancient civilization that already had its own established hierarchy of government and its own sophisticated tradition of political thought based on non-Christian concepts. In the early centuries, therefore, the Christian church had to develop its own structure of governing offices, *sometimes parallel to but always apart from those of the secular hierarchy,* and from the first there was always the possibility of a conflict of loyalties.

Employing the Framework: Religious Legitimation Over Time

The early histories of Islam and Christianity helped shape the propagating institutions of the Middle East and Western Europe. Due to unique historical circumstances, the institutionalized benefits of religious legitimation were greater in the Middle East because Islamic religious authorities had a greater capacity to legitimize political rule. Since the costs of religious legitimation were similar in the Middle East and Western Europe – costs included tax exemptions, following religious dictates, and financial support – it follows that the ratio of benefits to costs of religious legitimation were greater in the Middle East. One consequence is that Middle Eastern rulers employed the religious establishment to propagate their rule to a greater degree than Western European rulers.

The framework outlined in the previous chapter provides a deeper insight than this simple, static notion of religious legitimation being more important in the Middle East at any one point in time. Because the manner in which rulers receive legitimacy can feed back into the institutions that support the legitimizing arrangements, these differences also had dynamic, long-run consequences. In particular, recall the logic of Testable Prediction #3. Since rulers have little incentive to enforce laws contrary to religious dictates when religious authorities legitimize their rule, citizens have little incentive to transgress religious laws: they face a "double" cost of religious and temporal sanctions. This in turn gives even less incentive for political authorities to introduce laws and policies contrary to religious doctrine in the future. Over time, the institutional arrangement in which political rule is heavily legitimized by religion is never really challenged, and religious authorities are relatively secure from threats to their power. In other words, the institutions are *self-reinforcing* – over time, most players abide by the rules, thus strengthening the incentive for future generations to do so.

The legitimation regime is more likely to unravel when religious authorities are weak legitimizers. This is because rulers stand to lose less from promoting laws and policies contrary to the interests of religious authorities. This puts the religious authority in a no-win situation. They either ignore the fact that the citizens widely transgress their dictates or they update their doctrine, which undermines their hold on "eternal truths." In either case, the religious authority's ability to legitimize is weaker in the future. The more frequently such a process occurs, the less valuable religious legitimation becomes. Eventually, the benefits of religious legitimation do not exceed its rather modest costs, and rulers turn to other sources of propagation.

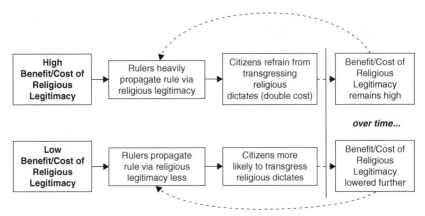

Figure 3.1 Diverging Costs and Benefits of Religious Legitimation Over Time

Figure 3.1 presents a stylized version of this logic. In the top half of the figure, the benefit/cost ratio of religious legitimacy begins at a high level and remains high over time. As the institutionalized benefits and costs of religious legitimacy change little over time, rulers continue to heavily propagate their rule through religious legitimacy (the dashed arrow feeding back into the second box from the left). A different sequence of events occurs in the lower half of the figure, where the benefit/cost ratio of religious legitimacy weakens over time. The change in the benefit/cost ratio feeds back into rulers propagating the rule even less via religious legitimacy, further decreasing the benefit/cost ratio. Ultimately the benefits of religious legitimacy will be so low relative to its costs that rulers will search for alternative means of propagation.

These insights shed light on the institutional histories of the Middle East and Western Europe. The relative importance of political legitimation in early Islamic doctrine created an environment in which religious legitimation was valuable for rulers. This discouraged challenges to religious laws, in turn making religious propagation even stronger in the future. On the other hand, the relative paucity of early Christian doctrine that could legitimize rule placed Western Europe on a different path.

Islamic Legitimation after Muhammad

Muhammad was able to spread Islamic rule in the Arabian Peninsula because he had what Weber called "charismatic legitimacy." That is, he had exceptional personality traits that encouraged people to follow him. His immediate successors could not depend on personality to legitimize their rule. This was problematic, because Muhammad died without a male heir to follow him, and the Qur'an does not formally deal with issues of succession. Periods of succession are precisely the time when legitimacy is the most important, since legitimacy bolsters an individual's right to rule versus the claims of rivals who covet the ruler's position.

Later generations of Muslims solved this problem by using religious clerics as legitimizing agents. Clerics had specialized knowledge of Islam and were independent of the ruler, so their word could bolster the perception of a ruler's right to rule. But in the first few Islamic decades, such agents did not exist.[15] It took time to establish a formal legal system based on Islamic precepts, and it took time to establish institutions for formally training religious scholars. Since there were no independent religious or legal classes to legitimize early Muslim rulers, disputes and civil wars over who was the legitimate ruler were common. Indeed, one of the most important religious schisms in the history of Western religion, the Sunni-Shi'a split, resulted from a dispute over who the appropriate ruler of Muslims was after Muhammad. Sunnis claimed the rightful successor was the most qualified one, whom they believed was Muhammad's father-in-law Abu Bakr, while the Shi'as supported the successor they believed was the most spiritually qualified, Muhammad's son-in-law Ali. Such legitimacy problems manifested themselves in the assassination of three of the First Four caliphs.

Because of these circumstances, the most legitimate rulers of the first Muslim community were Muhammad's Companions – those who interacted with the Prophet. Companions held many of the important governing positions, and the first four Sunni caliphs following Muhammad were Companions. These rulers, known as the "Rightly Guided" Caliphs (632–661 CE), took on both a secular *and* religious role, using their ties to Muhammad to legitimize their rule.[16] Their Sunni successors, the Umayyad Caliphate (661–750), attempted to propagate their rule in a similar manner by giving themselves the religiously charged title "Deputy of God" (*khalifat Allah*).[17]

Combining political and religious leadership into one position gave the early Islamic caliphs tremendous power, since they could claim religious authority and make judicial rulings at their discretion. Having discretion was important, since there are many aspects of Islamic law that are not conducive to ruling, such as laws on taxation, penal law, and the fixing of prices.[18] Yet, this arrangement also presented a legitimacy problem for the caliphs. Legitimizing agents can only propagate authority when they can augment people's belief in the ruler's right to rule. A ruler cannot do this if he is the religious authority – in this case, he has no additional means of strengthening his subject's beliefs.

The early caliphs also faced legitimacy problems in their rapidly expanding provinces. By the time of the Umayyads the Muslim Empire was the largest in world history, but most of the subjects were yet to convert to Islam. In order to establish law and order as well as loyalty to the empire, the caliphs sent "proto-kadis" to the provinces (the term *kadi* is roughly equivalent to "judge"). They were often illiterate and had no legal training, yet rulers still gave them administrative duties such as tax collecting, policing, and adjudicating disputes.[19] The proto-kadis attempted to adjudicate based on Qur'anic teachings and the Sunna (exemplary actions of Muhammad),[20] but they had little specialized religious knowledge and had less religious authority than the caliph did. They were therefore able to provide some level of stability to the provinces but were unable to serve as a source of religious legitimacy.

By the turn of the eighth century, the religious establishment consolidated its base outside the purview of the caliph. As generations after the Companions of Muhammad grew up within empires committed to Islamic ideology, religious study became a much more specialized pursuit. This fostered an environment where the corpus of Islamic law expanded rapidly. The first attempts at expanding Islamic law occurred in the early eighth century, when Sunna based on Muhammad's "exemplary conduct" addressed problems not explicitly covered in the Qur'an. Legal decisions remained somewhat arbitrary, however, as many cases were outside the scope of the Sunna and were left up to subjective interpretation of the jurist as to what Muhammad's exemplary conduct would have been. The adjudication of Islamic law became much less arbitrary over the following two centuries, as hadith became a dominant source of authority, second only to the Qur'an. Hadith attempted to document Sunna as historical fact, and legitimate hadiths could be traced, through transmissions, to one of the Companions of the Prophet.[21] Compiling hadith was a time-consuming process, and since no individual could claim religious authority based on a relationship with Muhammad after the death of the Companions, those that compiled hadith had the best claim to authority. The most widely renowned scholars – those with extensive knowledge of the Qur'an and hadith – used independent reasoning (*ijtihad*) to mold Islamic law in response to new exigencies.[22]

The burgeoning religious establishment served the expanding empire's legal needs, meaning that clerics regularly interacted with the public. This gave them local prestige: they were *elites* who could augment the beliefs of the local population with regard to what "right" actions were. Indeed, the top jurists were often more popular with locals than the caliph was. The wife of the early Abbasid caliph Harun (r. 786–809) noted, upon seeing a crowd gather for the arrival a distinguished jurist, that "true kingship lies in the scholar's hands and hardly with Harun who gathers crowds around him by the force of police and palace guards."[23]

The rise of the religious class altered the "rules of the game" played by Islamic leaders. With a powerful clerical establishment, it was feasible for religious authorities to legitimize political rule. These authorities served as an excellent source of legitimation: Islamic doctrine was highly consistent with legitimation of rule, religious authorities were independent of the ruler, and scholars were widely respected for their religious and legal knowledge. Wael Hallaq (2005, p. 182–3) nicely summarizes this relationship:

[T]he government was in dire need of legitimization, which it found in the circles of the legal profession. The legists served the rulers as an effective tool for reaching the masses, from whose rank they emerged and represented. It was one of the salient features of the pre-modern Islamic body politic ... that it lacked control over the infrastructures of the civil populations it ruled. Jurists and judges emerged as the civil leaders who, though themselves products of the masses, found themselves ... involved in the day-to-day running of their affairs. ... [T]he judges were not only justices of the court, but the guardians and protectors of the disadvantaged, the supervisors of charitable trusts, the tax-collectors and the foremen of public works. They resolved disputes, both in the court and outside it, and established themselves as the intercessors between the populace and the rulers.

The rules of the game therefore stipulated that Islamic religious scholars could augment the beliefs of the citizenry regarding the ruler's right to rule. This was especially true under the Abbasids (750–1258), who overthrew the Umayyads in 750 CE and came to power just as the clerical establishment was strengthening its independent hold on law and religious authority. In order to gain the support of the scholars, the Abbasid caliphs gave out highly lucrative posts to jurists: an average jurist's salary was up to triple the salary of a skilled laborer.[24] Caliphs also gave the scholars some say in state affairs: they always consulted the chief justice of the royal court before making major judicial appointments, and provincial governors sought the guidance of jurists when seeking to find new judges.[25] In terms of the framework laid out in the previous chapter, the costs of religious legitimacy were minimal: rulers had to act in accordance with Islamic law, pay handsome salaries to top jurists, and cede minimal control over state affairs. But the potential benefits of religious legitimation were immense. The clerics conferred legitimacy by associating the ruler with Islamic piety – they mentioned the name of the legitimate ruler in each Friday sermon, supported obedience to the ruler in judicial rulings, accompanied caliphs on pilgrimages, and performed funeral prayers for distinguished caliphs.[26]

Clerics also encouraged rulers to follow Islamic dictates. For instance, the Abbasid caliph Harun consulted a leading jurist when he wanted to buy a slave girl from a man who did not wish to sell her. After a lengthy procedure, the jurist found a way for the caliph to buy the girl according to Islamic law.[27] This procedure was avoidable – the caliph could have easily taken the girl by coercion – but such an action was illegitimate without clerical blessing. Top religious authorities (muftis) also gave advice via fatwas on whether different laws, policies, and behaviors were Islamic. These could range from the mundane – for instance, advice on whether to hold the Friday sermon for slaves – to important actions such as attacking rivals polities or undertaking major reforms.[28] These actions legitimized rulers and their actions by confirming that rulers were abiding by Islamic doctrine and thus were worthy of following. Of course, sometimes acting in accordance with Islamic law meant doing something the caliph would otherwise prefer not to do, but the overall cost-benefit calculation usually weighed in favor of the caliph propagating his rule via religious legitimacy.

Following a significant loss of political power by the Abbasid caliphs in 945 CE, there was an understanding between religious and political authorities that the former would determine the norms of social life through personal, criminal, and civil law while the latter had autonomy in external policies.[29] Just as religious authority reached this powerful position vis-à-vis rulers, Sunni Islamic doctrine consolidated into four schools named after their founders: Hanafi, Maliki, Shafi'i, and Hanbali. Jurists associated with these schools followed a set doctrine and methodology for making legal decisions. Followers of each school considered the founders to be the "absolute *mujtahid*" – one who forged new thought consistent with Islamic ideals for all in his school to follow.[30] All subsequent *mujtahid*s where supposed to follow in the founder's direction. With the consolidation of doctrine into schools complete, juristic ingenuity – which had been so vibrant in the first four Islamic centuries and was responsible for dramatically expanding the corpus of Islamic law – began to slow. A large literature suggests that at some point around the tenth century, an informal consensus arose that independent reasoning (*ijtihad*) – an important method of reinterpretation in the first four Islamic centuries – was no longer an acceptable means of finding truth, and henceforth jurists could only follow precedents.[31] Under this theory, juristic ingenuity was stifled in Sunni Islam after the founding of the four schools consolidated what had been widely dispersed judicial authority. Instead of exercising *ijtihad*, jurists merely accepted previously codified wisdom, which perhaps emerged under very different circumstances. The perceived stagnation in Islamic thought is widely referred to as the "closing of the gate of *ijtihad*." If the gate were indeed closed, this was an important development in Islamic legal and economic history; it meant that new laws and policies could not always be created in response to fundamentally new economic exigencies, since it was not always possible that doctrine created in the past could address such problems.

The history of Islamic doctrine on a host of subjects is consistent with this logic, even though some recent scholarship disputes the idea that the "gate of *ijtihad*" was ever really closed in theory or in practice.[32] For instance, the next chapter overviews how Islamic religious authorities initially relaxed restrictions on taking interest on loans, but reinterpretation of doctrine practically ceased around the tenth century. Timur Kuran (2011) notes in great detail how Islamic laws on partnerships, inheritance, and trusts (*waqf*) remained essentially stagnant after the first few Islamic centuries, and as a result no corpus of law ever emerged that allowed investors to pool their money into large enterprises.

Why did Islamic law stagnate, calcifying around precepts that were relevant for the first four Islamic centuries? The framework presented in the previous chapter provides some answers. To briefly recap the argument of Testable Prediction #4: when rulers rely heavily on the religious elite for legitimacy, they are less likely to adopt changes that threaten the religious elite, and a "conservative" equilibrium can result. In this equilibrium, all nonreligious agents – including the economic elite – have a weak position vis-à-vis rulers in the bargain over new laws and policies. Even as commercial possibilities expand, religious authorities discourage innovations that reduce their power or are contrary to doctrine, which itself was created in an era with different economic and technological possibilities. In turn, religious and secular laws and institutions stagnate; neither is responsive to new exigencies, and rulers address new problems using the old legal and intellectual framework.

This logic provides an alternative explanation for the "closing of the gate of *ijtihad*" to those preferred by Orientalist scholars like Bernard Lewis who argue that the conservatism of medieval Islamic jurisprudence arose due to some ingrained conservatism or an inability to conceptualize change. The problem may lie with the metaphor itself. The framework proposed here suggests that new interpretations of Islamic law were hardly impossible for jurists to conjure: they simply had little incentive to do so because there was little demand for such interpretations. So, perhaps the following metaphor is more appropriate: the "gate of *ijtihad*" may have been closed, but the gate was *not locked*. All that was necessary for the gate to open was for rulers, merchants, producers, or other interested parties to attempt to push it open. Yet, due to the incentives associated with the equilibrium institutions, none of the relevant players had incentive to push the gate open. Observed behavior therefore led to the appearance that the gate was closed and locked – one does not know whether a closed gate is locked until they try to open it. Once this conservative equilibrium emerged around the tenth century, beliefs arose supporting the idea of the gate's closure, which further reinforced the legitimizing relationship between Muslim religious and political authorities.[33]

With the onset of stagnation in Islamic thought and institutions, Middle Eastern economies also began to stagnate just as Western European ones took off. Beginning in the twelfth and thirteenth centuries, the center of trade in Western Eurasia slowly moved from the Middle East to the Italian city-states. This shift was the result of Western European institutions evolving in a manner more conducive to commerce than their Middle Eastern counterparts. But why did Western European institutions change in such a manner?

Christian Legitimation after the Fall of Rome

Following the fall of the Western Roman Empire in the fifth century, Western Europe was an economic, technological, and intellectual backwater. Invaders repeatedly sacked Rome in the fifth century, and the western half of the empire ultimately collapsed (unlike the eastern half, which continued for another millennium as the Byzantine Empire). Barbarian Germanic kings ruled over the remnants of the Roman Empire: the Franks spread over northern Europe, the Visigoths dominated the Iberian Peninsula, and the Ostrogoths overtook Italy and parts of southeastern Europe. These kings propagated their rule via coercion by securing the loyalty of the warrior elite.

The one unifying force connecting the Roman Empire to the Germanic kingdoms was the Church. Large swaths of the Roman Empire converted to Christianity in the fourth century following Constantine's conversion. The Germanic kings were not initially Christian, but they ruled largely foreign populations where Christianity spread under Roman influence. The Church was therefore in a position to serve as a powerful legitimizing agent, if only the kings would adopt Christianity. And adopt Christianity they did. The most important conversion was that of the Frankish king Clovis (r. 481–509) in 496. This was a monumental event in Christian history: prior to Clovis's conversion there was no major ruler anywhere in the Western

Europe who was Christian.[34] Clovis employed Christianity to legitimize the expansion of his rule into Visigoth territory. In 507, upon entering into a war with the Visigoths in southeastern Gaul, Clovis claimed, "I take it very hard that these Arians hold part of Gaul. Let us go with God's help and conquer them."[35] Even more so than the Franks, the Visigoths were foreign, warrior rulers who ruled over a Roman-Christian population in the Iberian Peninsula. Ultimately, the Visigoths converted to Christianity under Recared (r. 586–601), and the Church became an important source of legitimacy until they were overrun by Muslim invaders in 711.[36]

The Germanic kings destroyed most of the institutions that facilitated public order under the Roman Empire. These rulers did not employ anything like the high-functioning Roman administration to collect taxes or provide local order. Because of the destruction of Roman law and bureaucracy, political rule became highly decentralized. There was simply no large centralized state to speak of in the half-millennium following the fall of the Western Roman Empire. Each of the Germanic kings brought their own unwritten set of laws with them, abandoning Roman law for tribal law.[37]

Frequent incursions from Viking, Magyar, and Muslim raiders exacerbated these conditions. Without a centralized government with a monopoly on coercive power to protect the masses, local elites with some access to coercive power provided protection for the masses. The feudal elite provided local law, order, and protection to the peasant masses in return for labor services, but the protection offered only went as far as the lands under manorial control. There was little law or order in the vast lands outside of the manor, making them extremely dangerous for travelers and merchants. Property rights and security were therefore almost nonexistent outside of the confines of small population clusters. The Frankish kings had little access to taxes and could thus do little to protect roads and bridges or provide safe passage for merchants. Other public goods provided by the Roman Empire, such as irrigation systems, deteriorated rapidly in the absence of centralized power. As a result, economic activity was mostly agricultural and concentrated around self-sufficient manors. Urbanization and trade were almost nonexistent except for some small pockets in northern Italy and Flanders.[38] The contrast between early medieval Europe and the Middle East could not be clearer: economies in the latter were ahead of those in the former for centuries following the spread of Islam.

The weakness of centralized political authority in the West between the fall of Rome and the rise of the Carolingian Empire in the eighth century allowed the pope to gain independence and influence that was unattainable under the Roman or Byzantine empires. The Frankish successors of

Clovis continued to use the Church to propagate their rule, gaining religious support by giving the clergy vast properties and privileges, especially to powerful bishops, who became great Frankish landholders. An important consequence of this arrangement was realized during the reign of Pope Gregory I (r. 590–604), who, while deferring to the emperor in the East, established the theory that royal power served the Church in the West.[39] In the mid-eighth century, the papacy formally aligned the fortunes of the Church with those of the Frankish Empire. Both sides stood to gain immensely from this union – the papacy received protection from repeated attacks by the Lombards, while the Frankish king Pepin gained legitimacy for his disputed kingship. Pepin's son, Charlemagne, propagated his rule even more strongly via religious legitimacy. He forced the Saxons to accept Christianity, established episcopal sees in conquered lands, and endowed monastic foundations throughout his empire.[40] Most famously, in 800 CE Pope Leo III and Charlemagne agreed to swear fidelity to each other, as long each recognized the other as the ruler in their respective realm of influence. On Christmas day of that year, Pope Leo and Charlemagne publicized this agreement through a monumental act of legitimation: the papal coronation, where the pope placed the imperial crown on Charlemagne's head. Later rulers of the Holy Roman Empire, including its founder, Otto I (r. 962–973), also felt the need to travel to Rome to be crowned by the pope.

This history suggests the existence of an equilibrium in which European rule was propagated in part by the Church and in part by the highly decentralized feudal nobility, who provided military support and local law and order. This did not necessarily mean that the feudal nobility were in a great bargaining position vis-à-vis their rulers. In the parts of Europe where secular rulers were able to expand their power, coordination was too expensive for the decentralized nobility to organize as a group that could negotiate with rulers. Indeed, the first European parliaments did not arise until the late twelfth century. This left the Church to take on a primary propagating role. It was omnipresent and provided an effective and reasonably inexpensive means of legitimacy.

In the late tenth century, the conditions that supported this equilibrium slowly began to unravel. As the population grew throughout the continent, the land under cultivation also increased. Vast reclamation projects and experimentation with new agricultural techniques permitted a modest agricultural surplus, freeing some of the excess population to seek a living in towns.[41] This sequence of events was not too different from those in the Middle East a few centuries earlier, where the Arab conquests permitted an increased agricultural yield, which in turn encouraged

Table 3.2 *Ten Most Populous Cities in Western Europe around the Commercial Revolution*

Pre-Commercial Revolution: 900 CE		Mid-Commercial Revolution: 1100 CE		Late Commercial Revolution: 1300 CE	
City	Population (1,000s)	City	Population (1,000s)	City	Population (1,000s)
Rome	40	Paris	65	Paris	250
Venice	37	Venice	58	Venice	110
Naples	30	Florence	45	Genoa	100
Laon	28	Milan	45	Milan	100
Trier	25	Salerno	40	Florence	95
Verona	25	Cologne	35	London	70
Regensburg	25	Rome	35	Naples	60
Mainz	25	London	32	Cologne	54
Cologne	21	Naples	30	Siena	50
Paris	20	Regensburg	30	Barcelona	48

Note: Cities conquered and settled by Muslim empires are not included in this table.
Source: Bosker et al. (2013).

urbanization. Northern Italy was the first region to undergo an urban revival (see Table 3.2). The burgeoning city-states of Northern Italy were uniquely suited for commercial expansion, as their proximity and ties to the Byzantine Empire and Muslim North Africa – both of which were far more economically advanced than any place in Western Europe – provided opportunities to engage in long-distance commerce that were unavailable elsewhere on the continent. As the wealth of these cities grew – first in Venice and Amalfi, later in Pisa and Genoa – the political power of the economic elite grew in tandem, independent of any larger political authority. Commerce continued to expand to other parts of Europe, and more independent, commerce-focused cities emerged, especially where centralized political authority was weakest, such as in the Holy Roman Empire, where numerous free and independent cities arose during the Commercial Revolution (a term used for the revival of commerce that spread throughout Europe in the tenth–fourteenth centuries). The merchant elite controlled many of these towns and used the local government to further their interests. The most powerful Italian city-states, especially Genoa and Venice, used their wealth and military power to acquire possessions in regions of strategic advantage to the merchant elite.[42] And success bred even more success. Abundant commercial opportunities encouraged experimentation in financial instruments (e.g., bills of exchange), organizational forms (e.g., the *commenda* and Italian family firm), and double-entry bookkeeping, which made "big business" all the more possible and profitable. By 1300, Venice and Genoa were among the largest and most important cities in the Western world, having acquired numerous territories and housing populations exceeding 100,000. Although religion was important in these commercial city-states, the interests of religious authorities were generally subordinate to those of the merchant elite.[43]

Trade also occurred outside of the city-states and independent cities. As commerce expanded into other parts of Europe, there was more incentive for political authorities to establish boroughs with protections for the property rights of foreign merchants. Merchant guilds (e.g., the German Hansa) negotiated directly with local rulers for protection and property rights, and merchants used their own courts to resolve disputes.[44] In the twelfth through fourteenth centuries, fairs became important meeting places – the most famous and important were the Champagne Fairs – where merchants from all over Europe met and exchanged goods and credit contracts.

The expansion of commerce had clear implications for the legitimizing relationship between European religious and political authorities. The intuition from the previous chapter indicated that increased commercial possibilities had the potential to alter the equilibrium legitimizing arrangement by augmenting the costs and benefits of religious legitimation relative to propagation from other sources. The choice faced by European rulers was simple: they could either continue to employ religious legitimacy, and hence the result of the policy bargain would reflect the Church's interests; or they could give increasing weight to the new commercial classes in the bargain over policy. Testable Prediction #3 provides insight into which option European rulers chose. It indicates that, all else being equal, a medieval European ruler was *more likely* to choose propagation by the economic elite than a medieval Middle Eastern ruler was. Such a choice diminished the role of religious legitimacy, which was less effective in Western Europe than in the Middle East.

There were numerous confrontations between the Church and the European political elite over the Church's role in policy making because of the institutional changes brought on by the Commercial Revolution. As the benefits of religious propagation weakened relative to propagation by merchants and manorial lords, the Church attempted to change the theoretical justification for Christian rule. Throughout the late eleventh and twelfth centuries, the papacy claimed for the first time that the Church bestowed the right of kingship and that the pope therefore had the right to depose rulers. This was a massive change from European justifications for kingship prior to the late eleventh century. Previously, rulers governed

Church leaders in matters of religious doctrine. The Church could anoint a king, but the spiritual authority given to the king as a result meant that it was not the Church's to take away. For instance, in 1067, William the Conqueror asserted that the king had the power to decide whether Norman and English churches should acknowledge the pope and that the king had veto power over ecclesiastical penalties.[45] The Church's gambit ultimately failed. This failure is attributable to one simple fact: unlike the Qur'an, the Bible and other early Christian doctrine established a separate sphere for secular rule, and there was no doctrinal justification for Christian authorities to depose rulers who acted contrary to their wishes.

By far the most important of these conflicts was the Investiture Controversy.[46] This five-decade confrontation between the Church and lay European rulers centered on investiture – the right to appoint clerics. By the middle of the eleventh century, it was common for emperors or kings to select bishops. A newly elected bishop would pay homage to the ruler, who "invested" the bishop with a pastoral staff and ring, along with the feudal estates and jurisdictions associated with a medieval bishopric. Many bishops offered money in return for investiture, a practice known as simony. These practices created internal tensions within the Church; many churchmen considered simony a heinous sin, and investiture diminished the Church's power as Church leaders became increasingly dependent on rulers for their positions.

In 1059, the Church attempted to address these issues at a synod at Rome, which proclaimed a general prohibition on lay investiture. The Church did not enforce this prohibition until 1075, when Pope Gregory VII (r. 1073–1085) put forth a papal decree reaffirming it. The Holy Roman Emperor Henry IV of Germany (r. 1084–1105) quickly ignored this decree. Henry IV was attempting to unify Germany in the face of rebellion – an act that would have been impossible without the ability to appoint and control bishops, who held in fief a significant portion of the Holy Roman Empire. The conflict escalated quickly: Henry IV sought support from his bishops to resist the papal decree, and Pope Gregory VII sought backing from the German princes to depose Henry. Henry attempted to denounce the pope as a usurper, and in response Gregory excommunicated him and deprived him of his royal power. The conflict quickly became one about rulers' rights in a Christian society: Who ruled, king or church?[47]

Henry IV overestimated his position, as the princes of Germany had little desire to submit to an all-powerful centralized emperor. Many of the princes welcomed the battle between Henry IV and the papacy and sided with the pope. As Henry saw his grip on power weakening, he made an infamous appeal to Gregory VII to rescind his excommunication in January 1077, where he stood barefoot in deep snow for three days outside the castle of Canossa in the Italian Alps. Gregory absolved Henry, although he did not offer to legitimize his kingship. This enraged the opponents of Henry, who elected their own king, Rudolph of Swabia. This sparked yet another series of battles among the German princes and, eventually, between Henry and the papacy. Gregory VII sided with Rudolph and re-excommunicated Henry IV, but to no avail. Henry had gained the upper hand in the fighting by this point, and soon defeated and killed Rudolph. With his position secured, Henry did not seek reconciliation with the pope. Instead, he elected his own pope, Antipope Clement III, and installed him by force in Rome in 1084.

The struggle over lay investiture continued well beyond the deaths of Gregory VII and Henry IV and eventually spread into England and France. The struggle culminated in the Concordat of Worms in 1122, a pact that gained for the Church practical independence from royal authority, while stipulating that the king must be present for all ecclesiastical appointments and receive homage from newly elected churchmen. In practice, this gave kings a veto over whom the Church could elect.[48] In England, the conflict between church and state lasted until 1170, when Thomas à Becket was martyred and the crown renounced suzerainty over the English Church.[49]

The century following the Investiture Controversy saw numerous conflicts between the Holy Roman Emperors and the papacy. At stake were two issues: the role the Church played in "making" rulers and who "made" and interpreted the law. On these issues, the differences between Western Europe and the Middle East could not be any starker. In the Middle East, religious jurists interpreted the law. There was only a weak distinction between religious and nonreligious law, and anything covered in the Qur'an or other religious teachings was within the realm of the Shari'a. Following the Investiture Controversy, the Church likewise attempted to establish its own set of systematic laws – the canon law. Through canon law, the Church claimed legal jurisdiction over numerous aspects of life – inheritance, marriage, and even some aspects of finance. But unlike Islamic law, canon law was ultimately unsuccessful in penetrating relations that were not of a strictly religious nature. With the growth of canon law came the concurrent growth of European secular law, which covered feudal and manorial relations, merchant activity, urban-commercial codes, and royal law.[50] Secular law was flexible and offered rulers – kings, manorial lords, and merchant-mayors – the ability to accommodate the exigencies of the day. And while these laws were not devoid of religious overtones – indeed, canon law provided the basis for the different legal codes – the legal pluralism epitomized by the separation of religious and secular law became an integral part of what Harold J. Berman calls the "Western Legal Tradition."[51]

The second issue at stake was the Church's ability to make or depose a ruler. Here too, the contrast with the Middle East was evident. Whenever a usurper attempted to overthrow a Muslim ruler, they usually received permission from an important religious figure in advance. Such power simply did not exist in Christianity. Gregory VII attempted to claim the power to depose emperors at the height of the Investiture Controversy in a 1075 document known as *Dictatus Papae* – the first time a pope made such a claim in Christian history.[52] Henry IV immediately repudiated this claim, arguing that "the emperor can be judged by no man; he alone on earth is 'judge of all men.'"[53] Throughout the twelfth century, churchmen debated whether deposition was a legitimate right of the papacy, or whether consultation with other nobles was necessary.[54] The zenith of papal claims of supremacy was made during the reign of Pope Innocent III (r. 1198–1216), who frequently intervened in political affairs: he claimed the right to decide between two candidates for emperor of the Holy Roman Empire, settled feudal disputes between King John of England and King Philip of France, crowned a king in Bulgaria, and deposed a king in Norway.[55] But stronger Christian rulers who had alternative sources of propagation ignored such papal claims. Indeed, the emperor who Innocent III helped install before his death, Frederick II (r. 1220–1250), ignored multiple excommunications by the papacy and was able to nearly unify Italy despite being in constant opposition to the Church. Instead of deriving legitimacy from the papacy, Frederick II employed coercive agents – Saracen mercenaries – to tighten his grip on power.[56]

After the reign of Innocent III, the capacity of the Church to legitimize rule diminished almost unabated. The rise of the universities in the early thirteenth century provided a means for promoting a theoretical defense of the legitimacy of secular rule using Aristotelian philosophy that was outside the scope of Christian thought. Perhaps the most famous scholastic of the period, Thomas Aquinas (1225–1274), argued (italics added):

The spiritual and the secular power are both derived from the divine power; and therefore the secular power is under the spiritual only in so far as it has been subjected to it by God: namely, in those things that pertain to the salvation of the soul; and therefore the spiritual power is, in such matters, to be obeyed rather than the secular. *But in those things that pertain to civil good, the secular power is to be obeyed rather than the spiritual,* according to the saying in Matthew 22:[21], "Render to Caesar the things that are Caesar's."[57]

One of the clearest manifestations of the Church's decline was the conflict between Phillip IV of France and Pope Boniface VIII over whether Phillip was subject to the demands of the ecclesiastical hierarchy. The nobles and commons wrote letters refusing to recognize Boniface as pope, and in response Boniface claimed the right to depose Phillip. The papacy was ultimately crushed by Phillip, who harassed Boniface's successor, Clement V (r. 1305–1314), into recanting Boniface's claims to papal lordship over France. Afterwards, the papacy fell under the control of the French monarch, and the papal chair moved to Avignon from 1309 to 1377.

Ultimately, the emergence of national kingdoms in England, France, the Iberian Peninsula, and to a lesser extent Italy and Germany further diminished the legitimizing power of the Church. These kingdoms increasingly relied on bureaucracies for justice and finance, mercenaries for military support, and parliaments for legitimacy and law. Parliaments comprised of elites – landed nobility, local churchmen, and urban economic elite – organized themselves in late-twelfth century Spain, thirteenth-century England, France, and Portugal, and soon thereafter in much of the rest of Western Europe.[58] Parliaments legitimized rulers and provided them with financial support in return for some say in policy making. Parliaments eventually became the primary body through which the economic elite gained policy-making influence at the expense of the Church. These changes gave rulers access to vast resources and coercive power. As a result, Western European rulers needed less religious legitimation over time. Unlike Middle Eastern rulers, Western European rulers could choose to ignore the dictates of the leading religious authorities because the Church had a weaker capacity to "make" or "depose" rulers. There was no Christian doctrine claiming that a Christian king had to rule by Christian dictates. The religious and the temporal were two separate spheres, each with rights over their own laws and policies.

Medieval European history is therefore consistent with the framework presented in the previous chapter. The capacity of the Church to legitimize was initially weaker than its Islamic counterparts, and therefore the importance of religious legitimacy diminished over time once commerce revived and secular law emerged in the medieval period. These developments gave rulers an effective source of propagation outside of the Church, and rulers increasingly employed these propagating agents throughout the medieval period.

The Reversal of Fortunes

As recently as 1200, the Middle East was more economically, technologically, and scientifically advanced than Western Europe. At some point a "reversal of fortunes" occurred in which Western Europe clearly took the lead on all of these fronts. This chapter suggests the possibility that the reversal of fortunes arose due to institutional differences that were apparent as early as the turn of the fifteenth century. In Western Europe, the power of the Church to legitimize rulers weakened as secular leaders grew increasingly powerful vis-à-vis the Church. Of course, this is not to say that Middle Eastern rulers were not powerful. Indeed, the Abbasid, Fatimid, Mamluk, and Ottoman sultans were much *more* powerful than their European counterparts. But this is precisely the point. These Muslim rulers were strong, but how they derived their strength was very different from Western European rulers, especially after the Commercial Revolution.

The degree of religious legitimation employed by rulers is not the only thing that matters for long-run economic development. Nor is the weakening of religious legitimation the sole reason why Europe eventually took off. However, it is hard to imagine a world where parts of Western Europe took off – and the Middle East did not – *without* these changes. The institutional changes that reduced the importance of religious legitimation in Western Europe were a necessary but not sufficient condition for certain Western European economies to take off. If this assertion is correct, it also provides an explanation for why Middle Eastern economies never took off to the extent that European ones did, since they never met these "necessary conditions." Chapter 8 supports this assertion; it analyzes the causes and consequences of the lack of political power for the Ottoman commercial classes.

This is also not to say that the organizational structure of Christian and Islamic religious institutions is unimportant. One fact heretofore glossed over is that the Roman Catholic Church is much more centralized and hierarchical than anything that has ever existed in the history of Sunni Islam. These structural differences certainly affected the relationship between religious and political authorities in Western Europe and the Middle East. There was nothing in Middle Eastern history close to a formal military confrontation between religious and political authorities akin to the Italian Wars discussed in the opening of this chapter. But it is unclear how these differences benefited the Western European economic trajectory. It is true that it was easier for a Middle Eastern ruler to find a religious authority that would support its laws or policies, as there were a number of authorities a ruler could choose from. But this also meant that, all else being equal, the Roman Catholic Church was in a *stronger* position to legitimize than any single, decentralized Islamic religious authority. The Church was a pan-European institution; Islamic religious authorities did not have nearly as much breadth of influence. The point here, though, is that *all else was not equal*. Even though the Church's organizational structure gave it a greater capacity to legitimize than its Islamic counterparts, it was still a weaker source of legitimacy due to the weaker doctrinal basis of religious rule in Christianity.

So far, this book has spoken mainly in generalities, laying out a framework for how differing propagating arrangements can lead to different economic outcomes, as well as why these arrangements differed in Western Europe and the Middle East. The histories presented in this chapter are macro-level, overviewing the major events in church-state relations over a millennium or so. One benefit of focusing on macro-historical phenomena is that it provides an opportunity to falsify the testable predictions of the framework: if religious legitimacy became stronger over time in Western Europe but weaker in the Middle East, one could rightfully call the veracity of the framework into question. The relevant macro-history is also important because the "reversal of fortunes" is a macro phenomenon, and this is ultimately what this book attempts to explain. Yet, one major drawback of focusing on macro-history is that it does not allow for an analysis of the micro mechanisms that drive the results predicted by the framework. The next two chapters remedy this problem, analyzing the divergent evolution of two important laws: the legality of taking interest on loans and printing. While the general story of institutional divergence is more important than the divergence of specific laws, these micro-histories highlight in much greater detail *how* and *why* the divergence arose.

PART II

APPLYING THE THEORY: WHY THE WEST
GOT RICH AND THE MIDDLE
EAST DID NOT

4

Bans on Taking Interest

Prior to the 1850s, there was no such thing as a Middle Eastern "bank" that conducted even the most basic of activities we now associate with banking: taking deposits, lending those deposits, and investing in capital markets. There were certainly moneylenders in the Middle East – it is a profession dating well before the advent of Islam – but no complex organizations existed that could readily match capital-needy borrowers and resource-rich lenders. Where money lending did occur, it was generally for small amounts and often between two individuals known to each other.[1]

This imposed impediments on Middle Eastern economic growth. Without a banking system capable of pooling resources, large-scale loans were practically impossible to obtain. Potential entrepreneurs necessarily kept their ambitions small unless they happened to know someone with vast amounts of wealth who was willing to invest in their enterprise. In the absence of fully functioning financial markets, entrepreneurs could not have possibly put capital to anything close to its most efficient use. Multiply this by millions of people over many centuries, and it is not hard to see how the absence of anything close to resembling modern banking had a dampening influence on Middle Eastern economic fortunes.

Why did no indigenous form of banking ever arise in the Middle East? Even when banks did emerge in the Ottoman Empire in the 1850s, Europeans owned them. The contrast with Western Europe is especially relevant. Modern banking arose in Western Europe through a series of innovations – certain forms of partnerships, family firms, branches, bills of exchange, limited liability, and joint-stock companies – during the medieval and early modern periods. Why did these innovations emerge in Western Europe and not the Middle East?

The absence of banks for most of Middle Eastern history was hardly a result of banking being contrary to Islam. In fact, the rise of Islamic

banking since the early 1970s is suggestive that banking can thrive in an
Islamic setting. As of 2016, Islamic banking is a trillion-dollar industry
and is popular in Qatar, Saudi Arabia, Indonesia, Iran, Turkey, and many
other predominantly Muslim nations. Islamic banking borrows many of
its general features from Western banking,[2] but it also contains a number
of unique elements. Islamic banking forbids certain types of "anti-Islamic"
investments. Most famously, loans are "interest free." This is not to say that
lenders give loans free of payment – for all intents and purposes, loans carry
interest but under the guise of some ruse that conforms the transaction to
the letter of the law. And other mechanisms for avoiding interest abound.
For instance, if one wants to obtain the equivalent of a mortgage to buy a
house, an Islamic bank would buy the house and sell it to the "borrower" at
a higher-than-market price, payable in increments. Such a transaction is de
facto tantamount to a mortgage, but it abides by Islamic law de jure.

This chapter provides a partial answer to the puzzling observation that
banking never arose indigenously in the Middle East despite its economic
"head start" during the four centuries following the spread of Islam. The
central claim is that the ultimate complexity of the Western European
financial system relative to the Middle Eastern one was due to the lifting of
bans on taking interest on loans in the former but not the latter.

But the connection between the weakening of anti-interest laws in
Western Europe and the growth of the financial system is not as clear-cut
as it may seem on the surface. It is not simply the case that allowing interest equals financial growth and banning interest equals financial retardation. The connection is complex for two reasons. First, bans on interest do
not mean that people refrain from lending at interest. Humans are smart;
if there is a sufficient demand for some prohibited action, someone will
find a work-around. And indeed, from the early Islamic period we know of
numerous ruses created to simulate lending at interest while following the
letter of the law. The most famous of these is the double sale, in which the
prospective debtor sells to a creditor some commodity for cash, then immediately buys it back for a greater sum payable later. If interest restrictions
were so easily avoidable, it is not obvious they had any practical effect. For
this reason, some scholars have argued that interest restrictions "belong less
to economic history than to the history of ideas."[3]

This chapter suggests that such arguments do not properly account for
the *path-dependent* consequences that followed from the relaxing of interest restrictions in Western Europe and, conversely, the "path not taken" in
the Middle East due to the persistence of formal interest restrictions. Path-
dependent consequences can be difficult to trace because the results are by

definition far removed from the initial causes. This chapter traces out one such consequence: the growth of branching of Western European financial institutions over long distances. Branching is a process by which a central holder of wealth transacts with numerous other offices (i.e., branches) that do business in varied locations; most major modern banks employ this form of organization. Branching emerged in late-medieval Europe *precisely* due to incentives associated with the relaxation of interest restrictions in Western Europe, albeit through nonobvious channels. This was a key development in the growth of Western finance, and it arose because merchants and lenders acted according to the incentives imposed on them by the surrounding institutions. Such an innovation might not have been imaginable in the Middle East, since nothing like the institutional buildup that facilitated branching in Western Europe ever emerged in the Middle East. To be clear, this is not to say that interest restrictions were burdensome because they prevented lending of any type: people in both Western Europe and the Middle East found ways around the restrictions and frequently lent to known relations. The claim here is that the manner in which people found ways around the restrictions precipitated institutional developments associated with larger-scale lending by long-lived organizations – what we now call banking. And as these organizations became more complex in Western Europe relative to the Middle East, organizational differences built on themselves in a path-dependent manner so that, over time, what were once small differences blossomed into very large ones.

Another reason the connection between relaxations of interest restrictions and financial growth is complex is that any explanation must take into account why interest restrictions were relaxed in the first place in Western Europe but not the Middle East. If there were a region in the early medieval period where demand was high for a relaxation of interest restrictions, it was the Middle East, not Western Europe. This is where the framework proposed in Chapter 2 helps guide intuition as to why it was Western Europe, and not the Middle East, where interest restrictions were ultimately relaxed.

Interest restrictions are useful to analyze for reasons beyond their long-run effect on the financial systems of Western Europe and the Middle East. They provide a nice point of comparison between the two sets of economies because they prevailed in *both* Islam and Christianity throughout most of the medieval period. Both sets of restrictions initially emerged for similar reasons, as rulers and religious authorities imposed restrictions in an economic context where most borrowing occurred primarily for consumption purposes. In that environment, borrowers were often poor or recently affected by some negative economic event. They borrowed to prevent starvation in the face of a bad harvest or to ensure enough seed was available for the following year's crop. These borrowers generally faced extremely high interest rates, often leading to lifetime indebtedness or much worse, such as selling one's children into slavery. Since social safety nets were weak and markets for insurance against disaster were missing, religious interest restrictions encouraged interest-free lending among neighbors and discouraged demand for high-interest loans.[4]

Interest restrictions imposed a very different set of hurdles, however, when investment borrowing became feasible. Under such conditions, outright bans on interest prevented mutually agreed-on transactions involving moderate interest and thus inhibited economic growth. Yet, interest restrictions persisted for centuries in both religions in the face of commercial expansion. The persistence of interest restrictions in both religions is a puzzle with no obvious answer. Religious reinterpretations in favor of commerce occurred frequently in both religions, so the answer cannot be some simple appeal to the inviolability of religious dictates or religious hostility to commerce. The questions that need answering are: Why did interest restrictions persist for centuries longer in the Middle East than in Western Europe? Can the political economy framework proposed in the previous chapters shed light on these differences? What was the ultimate economic and institutional impact of these restrictions? This chapter answers these questions. First, however, some historical context is necessary.

History of Islamic Interest Restrictions

Taking interest on loans has always been a sin in Islam. The Qur'an has numerous passages detailing the sinfulness of *riba*, which was a pre-Islamic usurious process in which lenders doubled and redoubled the principal of a loan when the debtor was unable to pay at maturity.[5] This effectively entailed enslavement for debtors, as debts mounted after a single default. Restrictions on taking interest were therefore an optimal response to a situation where extremely high-interest loans created massive social problems. Early Muslims quickly equated *riba* with interest of any kind. Some Qur'anic injunctions against *riba* include:

Those who consume *riba* shall not rise except like the one who has been struck by the Devil's touch. This is because they say that selling and *riba*-making are one and the same thing, whereas God has made selling lawful and has forbidden *riba*. Whoever receives an admonition from his Lord and desists, he shall have his past gains, and his affair is committed to God; but whosoever reverts – those are the inhabitants of the Fire, therein dwelling forever. God destroys *riba* but makes alms (*zakat*) prosper ... O ye who believe! Protect yourselves from God and remit what is left of *riba* if ye be faithful. If ye do not, be prepared for war from God and His Prophet: but if ye desist, ye shall receive back your capital without doing injustice or suffering injustice. If, however, anyone is in difficulties, let there be a delay till he is able to pay, although it is better for ye to remit if ye only knew. (Surah Al-Baqarah ii.274–280)

Believers, do not live on *riba*, doubling your wealth many times over. Have fear of God, that you may prosper. (Surah Al-Imran iii.130)

That which you seek to increase by *riba* will not be blessed by God; but the alms (*zakat*) you give for His sake shall be repaid to you many times over. (Surah Al-Rum xxx.39)

In theory, an absolute ban on interest should have detrimentally affected economic outcomes once investment lending became feasible during the economic expansion of the first four Islamic centuries. In practice, however, the ban hardly meant that capital flows from financier to merchant halted altogether. In such a profitable environment, lenders simply found ways to circumvent interest restrictions. One set of tactics frequently employed were straightforward ruses, known as *hiyal* (singular, *hila*), designed to facilitate evasion of the ban.[6] A famous example of a *hila* is the previously discussed double sale, which worked as follows: Abdul buys a rug from Mahmud for 50 dinars, and Mahmud immediately buys the rug back from Abdul for 55 dinars, payable in a year. The upshot is that Mahmud holds onto his rug, receives 50 dinars from Abdul, and owes Abdul 55 dinars in one year. This is ostensibly a loan at 10 percent interest, with the interest being the difference between the two prices. Yet, because it is not officially a loan but is instead two sales, both of which are legal in Islamic law, the double sale does not violate the letter of the law as long as 50 dinars is a reasonable price for the rug. The double sale was commonplace by the ninth century, and Muslims employed it in Medina as early as the eighth century.[7]

Other forms of circumventing interest restrictions were common. For instance, documents exist showing numerous loans and purchases on credit in twelfth-century Tunisia where lenders made profit by exchanging in different forms of currency.[8] In the Ottoman period (1299–1923), a common form of transaction was *istiğlal*, which involved the debtor giving his creditor a piece of real estate, supposedly as a sale, but actually as a pawn. Such contractual forms were common well before the Ottomans, and *hiyal* became more complicated over time as business transactions became more complex.

Clerics went beyond merely permitting *hiyal*: they actively participated in creating *hiyal*, too. As early as the second Islamic century, clerics wrote treatises recognizing and formulating various forms of *hiyal*.[9] Authorities brought customary commercial law into agreement with Islamic law (Shari'a) in this way. Although the legality of *hiyal* differed over time and place, especially among different legal schools, they usually received stamps of approval from leading jurists.

It is no coincidence that the rise of Middle Eastern economies was also the period of massive reinterpretation of Islamic law via *hiyal*. The flurry of reinterpretation of interest law played a role in permitting commerce to flourish: more transactions occurred, and long-distance trade was common and profitable. In the first four Islamic centuries, legal flexibility was ubiquitous, and economic growth was the result.

This all changed at some point toward the end of the fourth Islamic century. Evidence of further advancements in Islamic law on interest recedes, and as a result, transactions involving overt, guaranteed interest were not a common means of extending commercial credit in medieval Islam. Not coincidentally, this slowdown in reinterpretation of interest law coincided with the proverbial "closing of the gate of *ijtihad*," whereby Islamic reinterpretation of all types of laws slowed immensely. By the mid-twelfth century, contracts stipulating interest existed, but the parties either derived interest from another type of contract or concealed interest in another way.[10] If the parties did not conceal the interest payment, one party could bring the other to court where the transaction was voidable without further legal consequence.

The Ottomans permitted more straightforward interest-bearing lending. For example, the Ottoman Grand Mufti Ebu's-su'ud (c. 1490–1574) permitted lending at moderate interest under the euphemistic designations "transaction" or "legal transaction." He considered charging greater than 15 percent a criminal offense, but he allowed exceptions liberally.[11] Data collected by Timur Kuran (2013) and employed in Kuran and Rubin (2017) indicate that taking moderate interest was normal in Istanbul in the seventeenth and eighteenth centuries – the real interest rate on private loans was around 19 percent – although the contracts usually cite some ruse. Likewise, in a study of seventeenth-century judicial records in Anatolian Kayseri, Ronald C. Jennings shows that lenders regularly charged interest on credit in accordance with Islamic law and "secular" law (*kanun*) and with the consent and approval of the judge's court, religious scholars, and the sultan. But almost all interest-bearing transactions Jennings observes involved some sort of ruse.[12] The same was true in the seventeenth century in the important commercial city of Bursa: interest ranging between 10 to 15 percent was legal, but the parties primarily conducted such transactions via ruses.

It is unlikely that most lenders actually resorted to such ruses. Numerous scholarly works indicate that lip service paid to Islamic law – rather than the actual undertaking of the ruse – prevailed throughout the Ottoman Empire. For example, *waqf* (pious trust) trustees required borrowers to deposit a pledge, suggesting that they lent at interest directly. Courts approved the instruments used by the cash *waqf*s in Bursa, but their relatively constant returns suggest that economic interest prevailed.[13]

It was clearly possible to lend at interest without fear of punishment throughout much of Islamic history. As long as the parties employed a ruse, courts upheld the transaction should the borrower renege. Yet, the mere fact that lending via ruse occurred between two individuals who knew each other does not mean that this was conducive for the growth of larger-scale organizations such as banks. In order for a court to uphold a ruse, the parties *actually had to go through with the ruse*. It might have been possible for friends or neighbors to avoid doing this, since social sanctions provided a strong incentive to pay back loans between two parties that knew each other. The same is not true of bigger organizations like banks, where lenders know prospective buyers much less intimately. Having to actually go through with a ruse with unknown relations for large sums of money makes lending much more risky and costly. It meant a greater outlay of capital in order to conduct the ruse, increased monitoring so that the borrower would not renege before the ruse is complete, and much greater risk of default should the ruse not actually occur. It also made taking deposits and openly paying interest on those deposits next to impossible.

This could not be more contradictory to the essential elements of modern banking. Modern banks engage in some monitoring – they check credit scores – but they have recourse should the borrower renege. Modern banks accept deposits, which are attractive to depositors because of the interest paid, and invest these deposits in more profitable pursuits – often loans at interest to other bank customers. These activities were too risky or costly for a medieval Middle Eastern financier to undertake. Hence, nothing akin to a bank ever arose in Middle East indigenously. Not only were banks capable of pooling resources nonexistent, but there is no evidence from the medieval period that there were individuals whose exclusive occupation was banking. Many of the elements commonly associated with Western banking were simply absent in the medieval and early modern Middle East. In its absence, lenders extended credit primarily via partnerships, which remained small both in terms of size and capital outlay.[14]

The data cited above provide further evidence of the lack of banking. Jennings's Ottoman data suggest that most loans were small, debtors were often poor, and lending was highly decentralized. Neither banks nor a class of big moneylenders existed; individuals incurred 97 percent of all debts and single individuals extended 99 percent of all credit.[15] In Kuran's (2013) Ottoman data set, most loans were small and made either by individuals or cash *waqf*s. The cash *waqf* was an Ottoman institutional innovation that could have substituted for banks – but did not – and it thus warrants further discussion.

The institution of the *waqf*, or pious foundation, existed since the first Islamic century. Originally, the assets of *waqf*s had to be immovable, but this requirement was relaxed beginning in the eighth century and relaxed even further during the Ottoman period in order to permit lending using *waqf* funds.[16] These lending *waqf*s, or cash *waqf*s, functioned primarily in the following way: the *waqf* manager distributed its endowed capital as credit to a number of borrowers and spent the return of the investment on social and religious purposes. The cash *waqf* founder earned returns without violating the Shari'a ban on interest by lending via sleeping partnership or legal ruse.[17]

Leading jurists did not always grant approval of cash *waqf*s. Because they earned income primarily through interest-bearing loans, cash *waqf*s provoked controversy. Yet, as the cash *waqf* became customary and essential to financial dealings, jurists were more willing to accept their validity. An episode known as the "cash *waqf* controversy," which ensued throughout much of the sixteenth century, secured their ultimate acceptance. The controversy reached a peak in 1545 after a jurist issued an opinion opposing the cash *waqf*, which by this time was well established. The Grand Mufti Ebu's-su'ud countered this opinion, and his opinion carried the day. Ebu's-su'ud's ultimate concern was not with juristic texts, but with what was in popular usage and for the welfare of the people, which clearly entailed maintaining cash *waqf*s.[18]

This episode suggests that Islamic law was flexible in responding to overwhelming demand for an "anti-Islamic" action. But this response – the cash *waqf* – is also indicative of the limitations set by the broader political economy equilibrium where religious authorities legitimized rulers. During the reign of Bayezid II (1481–1512), the number of cash *waqf*s in Istanbul increased steadily: in 1505, more cash *waqf*s than land *waqf*s were established, and by 1533, the cash *waqf* became the rule, not the exception.[19] The popularity of cash *waqf*s was due not only to the lack of banks and other alternatives able to meet the demand for interest-bearing loans but also to idiosyncrasies of cash *waqf*s themselves. Where jurists approved them, they allowed moneylenders to operate within Islamic law.[20] On top of the lip service paid to the Shari'a by the *waqf* manager, cash *waqf*s were insulated from the charge of sinfulness though their inclusion in the waqf system, which imbued them with a certain level of sacredness. Yet, this feature also meant they were much more rigid than Western banks, since managers had to spend *waqf* returns on prespecified social and religious purposes. While these investments may have done a great deal of good for society, they forced *waqf* managers to invest funds in an inefficient manner, since they could not reroute funds to the most profitable opportunity. On top of this, *waqf* law prevented cash *waqf*s from expanding their business and branching out, since they were required to spend their proceeds on prespecified purposes rather than reinvesting them in the *waqf*. This meant that a process where growth begat growth was stifled, and cash *waqf*s remained small. Cash *waqf*s therefore never grew into anything remotely resembling modern banks. Such a process did occur in Western Europe, however, due to the different incentives associated with lending at interest that evolved during the Commercial Revolution of the tenth–fourteenth centuries.

History of Christian Interest Restrictions

There are many similarities between Islamic and Christian interest histories. Both religions prohibited interest in the premodern period, although its prohibition was not originally part of Christian doctrine. Prior to the fourth century, the Church had very little to say on the issue of interest.[21] Doctrine espousing the "evils" of lending at interest existed in the early Judeo-Christian tradition, but there was no explicit prohibition of interest in the New Testament. Widespread denunciation of interest commenced in the early fourth century, with a number of Church councils and synods declaring it a mortal sin. Synods in Elvira (306), Arles (314), Carthage (345–348), Laodicea (372), Hippo (393), Arles (443), and Tarragona (516) all prohibited usurious lending by the clergy, although as a general rule it was prohibited to all Christians as a moral duty.[22] The true watershed moment came in 325, when an anti-interest canon was included in the first Ecumenical Council at Nicaea. Unlike smaller synods that only applied to particular regions, this council formulated creeds that were universally binding, thus establishing the sinfulness of taking interest throughout all of Christendom.[23]

Between the fifth-century decline of the Western Roman Empire and the onset of the Commercial Revolution in the late-tenth century, commerce was limited, and most loans were taken for consumption. As a result, there was little need for the Church to reconsider the interest prohibition. Secular authorities – including Charlemagne – generally supported the Church's ban on all forms of interest. The economic environment changed, however, with the onset of the Commercial Revolution. As trade revived in Europe, investment lending became more important: medieval historian Robert S. Lopez suggests that "unstinting credit was the great lubricant of the Commercial Revolution."[24] Much as in the Middle East, this meant that interest restrictions became an impediment to economic growth. Political and religious authorities were thus faced with the conflicting goals of promoting economic development – of which they would certainly take their share – and maintaining legal and doctrinal consistency.

Middle Eastern religious authorities responded to a similar situation in the first four Islamic centuries by permitting evasions that did not conspicuously fly in the face of doctrine. The Church chose the opposite approach, at least initially, by *strengthening* the interest ban in the twelfth and thirteenth centuries. The Church issued decrees at the Second, Third, and Fourth Lateran Councils (1139, 1179, and 1215) that proscribed excommunication for usurers, refused usurers burial in Christian grounds, and interdicted usurers' offerings.[25] The Church strengthened restrictions in the late twelfth century, when Popes Eugene III (1145–1153) and Alexander III (1159–1181) disallowed the mortgage, closing an important loophole used in evading the ban. Alexander III and Urban III (1185–1187) established that it was the intent of the transaction and not its form that determined guilt. In 1234, Pope Gregory IX (1227–1241) issued his *Decretales*, which forever classed usurers as *infames* (making them ineligible to hold public office, honors, or to testify in court), commanded princes to expel usurers from their realms, forbade landlords from renting property to usurers, and invalidated the wills and testaments of usurers.[26] Put simply, throughout the twelfth and thirteenth centuries, the Church's "campaign against usury" crystallized into a staunch prohibition in any form, and the moneylender was linked with the worst type of evildoer.

Despite these condemnations, a growing number of secular rulers permitted moderate interest in the thirteenth century, enacting laws that merely capped the legal interest rate. Several rulers at least partially promulgated these laws for personal reasons. Many needed access to credit, which was often obtained through forced loans. Such loans, which were known in Venice, Genoa, Siena, and Florence since the thirteenth century, were incontestable and received relatively small interest.[27] Larger loans to secular princes were risky and default was common, and this was reflected in the interest rate they received.

Rulers throughout Western Europe granted permission to Jewish lenders and select groups of Christian pawnbrokers to lend at interest. The most famous Christian moneylenders were the lombards, who spread throughout Europe in the middle of the thirteenth century. Being from Lombardy, they were foreigners wherever they practiced and were required to obtain charters from local magnates. In Bruges, the first charters granted to the lombards in 1281 explicitly stipulated that interest was not permitted under the penalty of heavy fines. However, this fine was only payable once a year regardless of the number of transgressions – a clear indication that the grant was permitting, not prohibiting, interest.[28] This stipulation was dropped a mere twenty-five years later; in 1306, municipal accounts stated that lombards were allowed to lend at a weekly rate of 2*d.* a pound per week (43⅓ percent per annum) and not higher. Interest caps of 43⅓ percent per annum were not unique to Bruges, but were ubiquitous throughout Western Europe, including the rest of the Low Countries, Northern France, Western Germany, Castile, and Aragon. Throughout Western Europe, fines paid by pawnbrokers to local rulers turned into regular license fees, which were an important source of revenue that often left moneylenders with little net profit. In return, rulers enforced and upheld the pawnbrokers' monopolies and provided other legal protections and services.[29] Table 4.1 includes a sample of such interest laws from the thirteenth–fifteenth centuries.

Despite being legal in most locales, open lending at interest was still explicitly prohibited by the Church. It is thus not surprising that European lenders, like their Middle Eastern counterparts, found alternative mechanisms for extending credit. Early alternatives arose for legitimate purposes. Examples include partnerships (*societas* or *commenda*) and the *census* (or *rente*), an annuity on a fruitful good. These contracts had features similar to interest-bearing loans and grew deeply embedded in commercial relations.

The *societas* presented the first real problem for Christian bishops and theologians since one could profit from a partnership solely by risking capital. This problem was resolved over a long series of discussions between 1270 and 1450, when the *societas* was justified as legitimate within the context of Christian thought, with risk employed as grounds for the reward. The Church did not extend this justification to interest-bearing loans in general, however; it only accommodated the *societas*, which by this time was essential to commerce. Likewise, the *census* was eventually justified by religious authorities as legitimate within the context of Christian thought. The *census* was like an annuity and was a normal form of long-term investment in landed properties for both nobles and peasants, especially in France and Italy.[30] As the money economy blossomed, borrowers converted

Table 4.1 *Interest Laws in Late Medieval Western Europe*

Location	Date(s)	Law
Legal maxima, general laws		
Catalonia	10th century; 1235	10th century: legal max rate of 12.5%
		1235: Christians permitted to lend at 12%
Venice	12th–14th centuries	Loans at 20% customary, courts enforced rates between 5–12%
England	12th–15th centuries	Only immoderate interest subject to persecution
Aragon	1241	Jews and Moors limited to 20%, Christians limited to 12%
Cordova	1241	Legal max rate of 12.5%
Seville	1250	Legal max rate of 12.5%
Murcia	1266	Legal max rate of 12.5%
Florence	1345–1346	All usury persecution ceased following a financial crash
France	1349	Interest up to 15% authorized for fairs at Champagne and Brie
London	1363	Usury prosecution became sole jurisdiction of civil authorities
Legal maxima, pawnshops		
Milan	End of 12th century	Legal max rate of 15%
Verona	1228	Legal max rate of 12.5%
Sicily	Mid-13th century	Legal max rate of 10%
Modena	1270	Legal max rate of 20%
Genoa	13th century	Legal max rate of 15%
England	13th century	Legal max rate of 43⅓%
Provence	13th century	Legal max rate of 300%
Germany	13th–14th centuries	13th: legal max rate of 173%; 14th: legal max rate of 43⅓%
Bruges	1306, 1404, 1432	Legal max rate of 43⅓%
France	1311, 1361	1311: legal max rate of 20%; 1361: legal max rate of 86%
Lombardy	1390	Legal max rate of 10%
Burgundy	End of 14th century	Legal max rate of 87%
Florence	15th century	Legal max rate of 20%

Reprinted from Explorations in Economic History, Vol. 47, No. 2, Jared Rubin "Bills of Exchange, Interest Bans, and Impersonal Exchange in Islam and Christianity", pp. 213–227, 2010, with permission from Elsevier. Sources for the table are de Roover (1948, p. 104), Lane (1966, p. 61–63), Cipolla (1967, p. 65), Gilchrist (1969, p. 112–113). Grice-Hutchinson (1978, p. 36–41, 48), Helmholz (1986), Le Goff (1988, p. 72), Homer and Sylla (1991, p. 97, 103, 110), and Gelpi and Julien-Labruyère (2000, p. 27).

payments into cash, and the census resembled an interest-bearing loan with rates generally ranging from 4 percent to 10 percent.[31] Pope Innocent IV declared them legitimate in 1251, but the Church did not fully resolve this issue for two more centuries. The Church eventually crafted justifications for its use within the context of Christian thought, although it only applied the justifications to the *census*, which had become so customary that "no one could recall a contrary practice."[32]

The *societas* and the *census* were justified due to their widespread use and their commercial necessity. This does not mean that they were "ruses," like Islamic *hiyal*, employed to deliberately evade the interest ban. These transactions entailed costs and risks that likely eliminated most potential profits for those using them for anything but their natural purpose. Yet the arguments justifying the *societas* and the *census* were important in molding Christian interest theory. The Church later employed these arguments to expand the set of permissible transactions.

As commerce expanded even further in the thirteenth and fourteenth centuries, with Venetian and Genoese merchants conducting business in the Mediterranean and throughout the continent, it was increasingly apparent that the Church's interest restrictions had a practical effect on commerce. This was manifested in the methods employed by lenders to evade the interest ban. Unlike the *societas* and the *census*, which could be employed for legitimate purposes, lenders began employing financial instruments whose main purpose was circumventing the ban. One example is the triple contract, which consisted of three different types of transactions: a contract of partnership (*societas*), insurance on the principal of the partnership, and a contract where one sold an uncertain future gain for a lesser certain gain. Each individual contract was valid, but when combined, simulated a risk-free loan. Other examples include the mortgage, dry exchange, and fictitious sales. These contractual forms were eventually justified by Christian religious authorities, often by resolving them into other, lawful contracts. Churchmen permitted these practices by appealing to theoretical concepts such as *lucrum cessans* (literally "profit ceasing," a pre–Adam Smith term for the opportunity cost of lent money), *damnum emergens* (loss occurring due to not having lent money), and *interesse* (originally a penalty paid for late repayment), all of which quickly gained currency in theological circles and presaged the Church's official relaxation of the ban.[33]

A final blow to anti-usury doctrine occurred at Lateran V (1512–1517), when the Church officially sanctioned the *monte di pietà*, or pious pawn bank. *Montes* were originally charitable, religious institutions, introduced by the Franciscans Perugia and Orvieto in 1462, that collected funds to provide loans to the poor.[34] As public pawnshops, *montes* were fashioned to help the poor gain credit while protecting Christians from the sin of usury, charging interest of up to 15 percent to cover costs. This rate was well below the one offered by other pawnbrokers, but still high enough to receive condemnation from the Church. The *montes* spread quickly throughout much of Europe – there were eighty-seven in Italy alone – before the Church sanctioned them at Lateran V. The *montes*, being the first institutions that lent openly at interest that the Church sanctioned, brought about the virtual disappearance of publicly licensed pawnbrokers and became a vital source of consumption loans for the poor. Indeed, a study by Luigi Pascali (2016) suggests that the increased access to credit afforded by the *montes* had an effect that has lasted to the *present day* – those areas with *montes* in the past currently have more banks per capita and wider availability of credit.[35]

Explaining Differences in Islamic and Christian Interest Restrictions

At first blush, the differences in Christian and Islamic interest restrictions seem rather innocuous. In both Western Europe and the Middle East, lenders were able to get around interest restrictions using ruses or complicated financial instruments sanctioned by religious authorities. But the details of these histories highlight many aspects of the more general differences in the paths these economies took. One obvious parallel is that the early vibrancy of Islamic legal interpretation coincided with the rise of Middle Eastern economies. And, at some later point, both Islamic legal theory and economic performance stagnated. But why were Islamic interest restrictions never fully alleviated? Why did Islamic legal theory on interest stagnate, and what can this tell us about the broader economic performance of the Middle East?

The framework employed in this book indicates that a Muslim lender had to weigh three factors before deciding to transact: the total profit available under each type of transaction, secular penalties (primarily the nonenforceability of the contract), and otherworldly penalties. Given the "double penalty" – worldly and otherworldly – from undertaking any type of transaction that blatantly violated Islamic law, lenders had incentive to incur transaction costs via *hiyal*, which allowed them to cohere to Islamic law. There was little incentive to further push the envelope of what was permissible. In most cases, the additional benefits of lending openly at interest were simply not large enough to overcome the costs of doing so.

There were, therefore, two primary forces affecting the demand for change in interest restrictions. The first consisted of underlying economic conditions: where profitable opportunities for large-scale investment were available, demand for interest-bearing loans was higher, and thus demand for relaxation of restrictions was greater. The second force was the costs – worldly and otherworldly – of lending. The presence of the "double cost" jointly imposed by rulers and religious authorities throughout most of Middle Eastern history dominated the benefits of transgressing the restrictions. The upshot was that there was little demand for changes in anti-interest laws and policies.

Lenders' actions made up only part of the broader equilibrium in which Islamic interest theory stagnated. Another key component was that Muslim rulers had little incentive to permit anything beyond what religious authorities permitted. Muslim rulers faced a dilemma with respect to legalizing interest. On the one hand, they stood to gain if they permitted lenders to openly take interest. More rapidly flowing commerce would increase their tax base, allowing them to propagate their rule while relying less on legitimacy provided by the religious elite. But the cost of openly permitting interest was enormous, since the legitimacy of their rule depended on their compliance with Islamic law. Islamic doctrine states that good Muslims should follow rulers who act in accordance with Islam, and rulers who do not should be overthrown. Hence, rulers were happy to permit actions that did not blatantly violate Islamic law, but not permit anything beyond this. The optimal solution for most Muslim rulers was clear: permit what religious authorities permitted and no more.

Meanwhile, Muslim religious authorities stood to gain from permitting actions that the citizenry frequently practiced. If people viewed the religious elite as ineffectual in their ability to affect lending at interest, this could have spilled over into their ability to dictate views on marriage, inheritance, or political power. Yet, religious authorities stood to lose their power to legitimize if they suddenly and dramatically reinterpreted doctrine: a primary source of authority in both Islam and Christianity is the clerical monopoly on eternal truths. Given these conflicting motivations – one pushing toward reinterpretation and the other toward conserving the past – it was in the religious authority's interest to find some middle ground. And since neither lenders nor political authorities pushed the envelope of what was permissible too far, religious authorities had incentive to permit ruses (*hiyal*) that had become customary, but nothing else. Why would the religious establishment undertake a costly reinterpretation of doctrine when nobody was asking for it?

Put simply, in the absence of a demand for change in interest restrictions by lenders and merchants, rulers and religious authorities had no desire to relax these restrictions. These forces reinforced each other, leading to a situation where none of the relevant parties desired a full relaxation of interest laws. Of course, it was possible that some outside event could have sparked demand for interest-bearing loans among merchants, which would have in turn altered the decision-making calculus of all of the relevant parties. The point, however, is that the self-reinforcing nature of this equilibrium meant that the bar for such an event was high.

The relationship between interest history and the more general economic history of the Middle East is clear. Commerce and trade flourished in the first four Islamic centuries, with Islamic doctrine readily accommodating the pressing needs of the day. The same is true for Islamic interest doctrine. The set of permissible *hiyal* expanded rapidly in the first few Islamic centuries as Muslim clerics accommodated the desires of lenders. At some point, Islamic reinterpretation of interest restrictions slowed without interest ever fully permitted. The stagnation of interest doctrine paralleled the broader stagnation of Islamic thought highlighted by the "closing of the gate of *ijtihad*." The ensuing equilibrium was one that was associated with little endogenous institutional change: religious legitimacy remained vital in most Islamic polities, and endogenous factors were unlikely to undermine the status quo.

These outcomes contrast with those found in Western Europe, where the legitimizing relationship between political and religious authorities changed dramatically in the late medieval period. Perhaps the oddest fact that can be accounted for within this framework is that interest restrictions were maintained in Christianity in the twelfth and thirteenth centuries. On the surface, the rationale for the Church's attitude is not obvious – why would the Church maintain the prohibition just as access to credit was beginning to lubricate commerce?

Prior to the Commercial Revolution, most loans were taken for consumption purposes, and interest restrictions barely hampered the economy. It was only after commercial opportunities began to grow in the late tenth century – and to a much greater extent at the height of the Commercial Revolution in the twelfth and thirteenth centuries – that restrictions on interest became detrimental. The growth of commerce thus changed the incentives faced by Western European rulers. As alternatives to interest became more widely employed, rulers had greater incentive to legalize moderate interest, which they did throughout the continent (see Table 4.1). Unlike in the Middle East, where the benefits to legalizing interest were outweighed by the costs associated with the loss of religious legitimacy, the legitimizing relationship was much weaker in Western Europe. The costs of permitting interest were therefore not nearly as great. Western European rulers responded to the growth of commerce by relaxing interest regulations in spite of religious condemnation.

With so many individuals flagrantly violating the Church's dictates, its capacity to legitimize was undermined. As more profitable commercial opportunities became available, merchants further evaded the Church's dictates and sought further protection from secular authorities. This provided all the more incentive for rulers to legalize interest – and enact other pro-commercial measures – while it further decreased the importance of religious legitimacy. Hence, the Church's loss of power vis-à-vis secular rulers was both *a cause and a consequence* of the rise of commerce and the resulting interactions between the economic and political elite.

The Church's initial reaction to its reduced role in propagating rule was to attempt to change the justification for Christian kingship and thereby reaffirm its role in propagating rule (see Chapter 3). Beginning in the late eleventh century with Pope Gregory VII (r. 1073–1085) and lasting through the middle of the thirteenth century, the Church – for the first time – claimed the rights to bestow kingship and depose rulers. These claims occurred *precisely* at the time the Church strengthened its anti-usury stance. This makes sense in the context of the framework proposed in this book. Since the Church was attempting to bolster its capacity to propagate rule, it would have been foolish for it to simultaneously reinterpret its doctrine. This would have undermined belief in the eternalness of Christian doctrine, which is a key component affecting its capacity to legitimize.

The ultimate failure of the Church to alter the justification for Christian kingship affected its position on lending at interest. The logic of the framework suggests that the Church should have relaxed interest restrictions only *after* its legitimizing power was undermined. And indeed, it was only after the importance of the Church's capacity to legitimize rule eroded in the mid-thirteenth century that political authorities relaxed their restrictions, and the Church followed suit over subsequent centuries. The "campaign against usury" halted in the late fourteenth and fifteenth centuries, and the Church slowly began to permit alternatives to interest thereafter.

In comparison, commercial pressures to relax interest restrictions existed earlier in the Middle East than in Western Europe. Hence, the initial relaxation of interest restrictions happened earlier in the Middle East. Yet, due to the greater importance of religious legitimacy in the Middle East, interest restrictions were never fully alleviated in Islam, and the endogenous processes that eventually undermined both Christian interest restrictions and more generally the Church's capacity to legitimize rulers never occurred in the Middle East.

This logic helps explain why interest restrictions were ultimately relaxed in Western Europe but not in the Middle East. These histories also draw attention to the more general differences in propagating arrangements between the two regions and the resulting economic outcomes therein. It is now worthwhile to turn back to the puzzle posed at the beginning of this chapter: Why did a banking system never arise indigenously in the Middle East? Did the diverging paths of interest restrictions in the Middle East and Western Europe play a role in encouraging banking in the latter but not the former? While it is difficult to imagine a Western banking system without interest, it is also true that interest restrictions were easily evaded in both regions throughout history. So, how did interest restrictions stifle the growth of Middle East banking, if at all?

Path-Dependent Consequences

Ultimately, modern banking and financial operations emerged in Western Europe, while at the same time Middle Eastern lending remained largely confined to known relations. How did it come to this? It is by no means obvious that interest restrictions had anything to do with the divergence in financial institutions in the two regions: lenders easily evaded the restrictions in both regions, and lending at moderate interest was common as long as they employed some ruse. While it is well outside the scope of this book to trace the entire history of modern banking in Western Europe – this would take many volumes – comparing how bills of exchange evolved in the two regions sheds light on some of the dynamic consequences of interest restrictions. Bills of exchange were an important financial instrument in Western Europe – Edwin S. Hunt and James M. Murray describe them as "the most important financial innovation of the High Middle Ages."[36] An instrument very similar to the bill of exchange, the *suftaja* (plural *safatij*), was widely employed in the medieval Middle East. The fact that similar – *but different* – instruments existed in the two regions allows for an analysis of the more general forces affecting the divergence. What were the differences between these instruments? Why did they differ? What effect did this have on long-run economic outcomes, especially in relation to the growth of Western banking?

European bills of exchange were debt instruments issued in one place and remitted in another, in a different currency payable at the market exchange rate quoted in the locale of issue with a stated maturity corresponding to a duration between one and six months. Bills of exchange worked as follows. A lender bought a bill for ready cash from a borrower, who drew on one of his correspondents abroad. At maturity, this correspondent paid an amount in a different currency to the lender's correspondent. They originally emerged to help facilitate trade. They enabled merchants to avoid the costs (armed guards) and risks (robbery) associated with moving specie. Such costs were far from trivial – for example, the charge for moving bullion from Naples to Rome ranged between 8 percent and 12 percent of the cargo's value.[37] Bills of exchange also enabled much quicker movement of funds. For example, it took twenty-one days to deliver coins collected in Rouen to Avignon, whereas a courier could deliver a bill in eight days.[38]

The Genoese used the earliest bills of exchange in the mid-twelfth century, but bills did not become widespread until the following century when merchants at the Champagne fairs began to use them regularly. They became ubiquitous in subsequent centuries, primarily in Italy, evolving into financial instruments that enabled lenders to make profits via differences in exchange rates.[39] Lenders were able to make profits by having their correspondent take the proceeds of a freshly remitted bill and buy a new bill, payable in the lender's homeland, from another borrower. Because the second transaction took place in a distant land, the lender purchased the second bill at a *different* exchange rate than the first one. The rate differential permitted lenders a chance to profit on exchange transactions.[40] To see how this works, consider the following hypothetical modern exchange transaction. Say that a bill purchased in London and redeemable in Florence is available at a rate £1:0.5€, while a bill purchased in Florence and redeemable in London is available at a rate 1€:£3. One could buy a bill in London for £100 and remit it in Florence for 50€, then use this 50€ to buy a bill that yields £150 in London, generating a 50 percent profit. Likewise, one could start by buying a bill in Florence for 100€ and remit it in London for £300 then use this £300 to buy a bill that yields 150€ in Florence – also a 50 percent profit.[41]

Medieval Middle Eastern merchants also employed long-distance credit instruments. These included transfers of debt (*hawala*), orders of payment (*sakk* and *ruq'a*),[42] and bills of exchange (*suftaja*). *Safatij* existed since at least the eighth century CE, well before European used similar credit instruments.[43] *Safatij* were written obligations issued by and drawn on well-known merchants, with the feature (unlike European bills) that repayment occurred in the *same* type of currency paid to the issuing agent.[44] Like European bills of exchange, *safatij* were generally employed in trade but were also used for other purposes. For example, the Abbasid financial administration used *safatij* to transfer funds between provincial treasuries and Baghdad, subjects paid bribes to officials via *safatij*, and tax farmers used *safatij* to pay the royal treasuries. *Safatij* were widely employed and enforced throughout the Ottoman period, where they facilitated transactions between Anatolia, the Aegean islands, Crimea, Syria, Egypt, and Iran.[45]

Unlike European bills of exchange, which involved four parties, *safatij* involved only three parties and worked as follows. *A* lent a sum of money to *B* in return for a *suftaja*, which was given to *C*, who resided elsewhere and paid *A* the same sum in the same currency. A typical *suftaja* read as follows: "Abu Mansur asked me to take from him 25 dinars and 2 qirats, which I did and for which I wrote him a bill drawn on you."[46] *Safatij* were neither transferable nor negotiable and were immediately redeemable upon presentation. The issuer (borrower) charged a fee, which was sometimes significant but could be as low as 1 percent of the *suftaja's* value. If the agent on whom the *suftaja* was drawn delayed payment, he incurred a steep penalty that the *suftaja* holder could claim if not paid via lawsuit in an Islamic court.[47]

Like European bills of exchange, *safatij* were written documents that extended credit and helped merchants avoid risk in transport. However, unlike European bills, *safatij* did *not* involve a currency exchange – the bill merely permitted merchants in one region to make payments in the same currency in another region. While some Muslim jurists permitted *safatij*, they forbade lenders from profiting on the exchange transaction itself.[48] Instead, only borrowers could profit from dealing in *safatij* (through the issue fee).

The bill of exchange differed in the Middle East and Western Europe largely because lending at interest was legal in the latter, even if the Church did not recognize the validity of bills until the fifteenth century. Because Western European lenders could make an enforceable return on exchange transactions, they were encouraged to employ bills of exchange as substitutes for guaranteed interest-bearing loans, in turn avoiding religious and social sanctions associated with manifest usury. Indeed, bills of exchange became a widespread financial instrument in the late thirteenth and early fourteenth centuries, soon after secular rulers relaxed interest restrictions. On the other hand, both rulers *and* religious authorities forbade Middle Eastern lenders from profiting on the exchange transaction itself, and *safatij*, where legal, remained confined to their original purpose: facilitating long-distance transport without the use of specie. While profiting from exchange transactions was legal in Islamic law – otherwise, money-changing would not have been a viable profession – Muslim religious and political authorities forbade profiting from exchange in conjunction with lending.[49] Islamic law considered profit beyond fees stemming from exchange transactions to be usurious. Wealthy lenders could not profit by using instruments similar to European bills of exchange, as such transactions were voidable in Islamic courts.

This raises the question: Why did Islamic religious authorities not create a *hila* by which Muslim lenders could use *safatij* to profit from differences in exchange rates? There are two reasons why jurists never formulated such a *hila*. First, although *safatij* and exchange transactions were both licit, combining them would have entailed the creation of an illicit instrument, as its sole purpose would have been to make a usurious gain. This is different from the double sale, which combined two licit but *separate* transactions. Secondly, one could then ask: Why did Islamic authorities not set up a *hila* that simulated a European bill of exchange yet kept the *suftaja* and exchange transactions separate?[50] If there were differences in exchange rates in places A and B, then this could give a low-risk profit to the lender, as it did in Europe. However, this series of transactions would also have been illicit under Islamic law. The reason is that where clerics permitted the *suftaja*, they permitted it *only* as an instrument of trade.[51] Islamic jurists were suspicious of the *suftaja* due to its usurious nature; hence, they forbade any use of the *suftaja* outside of facilitating trade. Unlike the double sale, which followed the letter but not the spirit of the law by combining two licit transactions, such a transaction would not have followed even the letter of Islamic law, as it would have turned the *suftaja* into an illicit instrument.[52]

The upshot is that the additional element of currency exchange associated with European bills – but *not* Middle Eastern bills – allowed wealthy European lenders to profit from the exchange transaction. Since this profit derived from two transactions that exploited variations in exchange rates in different cities, lenders who purchased bills of exchange were necessarily involved in *interregional* commerce with multiple agents. This seemingly innocuous element of Western European bills had important path dependent consequences for the formation of Western European financial institutions. Specifically, it encouraged the formation of institutions capable of supporting *interregional* finance. For instance, merchants in Florence and Genoa organized fifteenth-century fairs in Lyons and Besançon, respectively, in order to provide opportunities for credit transactions.[53] More importantly, trade in bills of exchange facilitated the formation of interregional organizational forms suited to impersonal lending, a process exemplified by the Medici enterprise.

Headquartered in Florence, the Medici "bank" expanded in the fifteenth century into a decentralized matrix of partnership branches throughout Europe, all dealing to some extent in interregional finance and bills of exchange. The Medici House consisted of a series of partnership branches that were separate legal entities, much like a modern-day holding company.[54] These branches all dealt in exchange operations. For example, in the preamble of the Medici contract with the Bruges branch, which was indicative, the purpose of the partnership was to "deal in exchange and in merchandise in the city of Bruges in Flanders."[55] To take advantage of opportunities afforded by dealing in bills of exchange, branches of the Medici banks acted as both principals and agents of other branches. The Medicis had branches or correspondents in all of the major financial centers of Europe, allowing the network to stay informed of fluctuations in exchange rates and money markets.[56]

The Medici "hub-and-spoke" system emerged as a response to the incentives imposed on those dealing in finance. The profitability of bills of exchange incentivized enterprises like the Medici bank to establish interregional branches to take advantage of exchange rate differences and capital scarcity, while at the same time diversifying portfolios to shield against risk. In an era before credit scores and international finance laws, these complex networks permitted capital-rich entrepreneurs in Italy to invest in all of the major financial centers of Europe. Although the Medicis conducted transactions primarily with semi-personal relations – those known to be good credit risks – the extension of the credit network achieved by the branching system allowed less personal credit relations to arise. From the viewpoint of the primary capital holders (the Medici family in Florence), most financial activities were conducted with unknown relations.

The branching system pioneered by the Medici enterprise was a key step on the pathway to the emergence of the banking system in Western Europe. Through branching, the Medicis focused capital more toward its most highly valued use. If the capital-wealthy Florentine Medicis saw a profitable opportunity for investment in Bruges, branching increased the likelihood that they would invest their money there, since a branch partner could verify the trustworthiness of the potential borrower as well as apply financial sanctions (i.e., cutting off future funds) to a borrower who was late in repayment. Indeed, the branch partner could make the Medicis aware of such an opportunity in the first place. In other words, the advent of branching was a key step on the path to *impersonal* finance – finance conducted with previously unknown relations – which is one of the hallmarks of the modern banking system.

Such institutions simply did not emerge in the Middle East, and most exchange operations remained confined to personal interactions between acquaintances and families.[57] Without the element of currency exchange, there was little incentive for wealthy lenders to employ *safatij* as an instrument of finance. Instead, traveling merchants – not investors – remained the primary lenders, and *safatij* remained relegated to facilitating trade. Foreign agents were unnecessary as long as the borrower-banker had confidence in his business partner, to whom he generally had some social or personal connection. Capital-rich Muslims could not earn returns by buying *safatij*, so there was little incentive to establish networks dealing in *safatij*.[58]

Numerous scholars have employed the widespread presence of interest-bearing lending via ruse in the Islamic world as evidence that the interest ban had no practical effect. The history of bills of exchange suggests, however, that such arguments suffer from focusing on first-order, micro-level observations. It sheds light on an avenue through which religious interest restrictions carried *macro*-level, path-dependent consequences – outcomes that are not observable at any one point in time but can accumulate over time on the margin. Employing Joel Mokyr's terminology, this analysis suggests that the interaction of the unraveling of interest restrictions with Western European politico-legal institutions encouraged a series of financial "microinventions" – marginal changes that led, over time, to very different outcomes in the Middle East and Western Europe.[59]

The history of interest restrictions in Christianity and Islam helps focus attention on numerous aspects of economic development in Western Europe and the Middle East. In many ways, these histories parallel the more general "reversal of fortunes" between the economies of the Middle East and Western Europe that occurred over the thousand years following the advent of Islam. Religious reinterpretation in favor of commerce was much more vibrant in the Middle East than in Western Europe until the tenth century or so, much as Middle Eastern economies were more vibrant than Western European economies. Yet, also like the broader economic trends, Western Europe caught up with the Middle East in relaxing interest restrictions sometime in the thirteenth or fourteenth century and was ahead of the Middle East by 1600.

Interest restrictions form a microcosm of the economic trajectories that evolved in Western Europe and the Middle East in the medieval period.

Although focusing on interest restrictions shades our eyes from many other important historical events affecting the economies of both regions, it brings to light the consequences of one of the primary features dictating medieval political life: the use of religious authority in legitimizing political rule. The rest of this book suggests that interactions between political and religious authorities explain quite a bit more than just the history of interest restrictions, and that these interactions are at the heart of economic success and stagnation.

5

Restrictions on the Printing Press

Around the year 2000, a number of Western entertainment outlets published lists of the "most important people of the millennium." These lists were embarrassingly Western-centric – according to A&E's list, Steven Spielberg was more important than any Muslim and all but one person from China (Mao Zedong) – but almost all of them had one thing in common: Johannes Gutenberg was either the most important person (according to A&E, Life, and the Bio Channel) or among a handful of the most important people. This places Gutenberg ahead of the most influential thinkers (Newton, Darwin, Marx, Einstein), rulers (Genghis Khan, Napoleon, Gandhi), and cultural figures (Shakespeare, da Vinci, Michelangelo) of the last thousand years. Gutenberg was none of these. He was a capitalist inventor known for only one invention: the movable-type printing press.[1]

The consensus on Gutenberg's importance is reflective of the consequences that printing had on European history. Gutenberg invented the movable-type press around 1450 in the German city of Mainz, setting off an information revolution. Much like the Internet in the early twenty-first century, the press was the most important information technology of its day, allowing for an unprecedented rise in the flow of information. Prior to the press, literacy rates were low, books and pamphlets were extraordinarily expensive, and information took weeks or months to reach distant locations. The primary bottleneck was the time it took to produce multiple copies of documents. Small groups of intellectuals in monasteries and universities reproduced longer treatises by a painstaking, labor-intensive process, while hand-copiers reproduced shorter documents such as price listings and short pamphlets. This meant that Europeans did not have a number of things now taken for granted: few had access to books, and new information was often old by the time it reached its recipients. The press helped mitigate these problems, opening up access to ideas to a much larger swath of the population. The economic benefits of the press were obvious, and it consequently spread rapidly throughout Western Europe. By the end of the fifteenth century, most large cities in Europe had at least one press.

The direct economic effects of the spread of the printing press were far from trivial. Jeremiah Dittmar (2011) analyzed hundreds of European cities and found that those that were early print adopters grew much faster than the laggards, all else being equal. Since city growth is a primary indicator of economic growth in the preindustrial world, this indicates that the spread of printing had a positive impact on economic development. But how did printing promote economic growth? For one, it facilitated a much more rapid and widespread publication of price and exchange rate information via news-sheets containing financial information. This resulted in financial integration throughout many of the important economic centers of Western Europe, which in turn facilitated the establishment of new trade routes[2] and the more effective use of financial instruments such as bills of exchange (see Chapter 4). Another link between the spread of the press and economic growth was a rapid increase in the number of books produced. Eltjo Buringh and Jan Luiten van Zanden (2009) estimate that around 12.6 million books were printed between 1454 and 1500, compared to around 10.9 million manuscripts produced in the *millennium* prior to the press.[3] In the century before the press, there was less than one book consumed per 1,000 persons; by the end of the sixteenth century, 29 books were consumed per 1,000 persons. As the numbers grew – by the end of the fifteenth century, the biggest publishers regularly made print runs of around 1,500 copies[4] – their price fell in tandem. On top of the large outward supply shift following the diffusion of the press, technological changes in the paper production process and the use of ink based on oil decreased the price of books around 85 percent.[5] This gave access to books to a much larger part of the population and undoubtedly contributed to the immense increase in European literacy between 1500 and 1800. No nation in Western Europe had a literacy rate above 10 percent in 1500, but by 1800 it was above 50 percent in Great Britain and the Netherlands, and between 20 percent to 40 percent in most other parts of Western Europe.[6]

The story of the spread of printing is interesting in the context of the arguments made in this book due to one fact: despite knowing about the press as early as the 1480s, the Ottomans *did not permit printing in the Arabic script until 1727*. On the surface, it is not obvious why the Ottoman sultan feared the press. Not only was there a potentially important industry in books that was artificially suppressed, but printing could help integrate markets through the spread of price information, spread news of important events to the far-flung reaches of the empire, or spread propaganda favoring the sultan's campaigns. Of course, rebels could have also used the press for propaganda against the sultan, but as long as he had control over the military, this was unlikely. These events raise the questions: Why did the Ottomans forbid printing for so long? What, if anything, were the consequences of the delayed acceptance of the press?

The framework espoused in this book can address both of these questions. To gain insight into why the Ottomans forbade the press, the framework indicates that the following questions need addressing: Who benefited from the suppression of the printing press in the Ottoman Empire? Did they propagate the sultan's rule? Were they important enough pieces of the propagating regime to have their voices heard in the bargain over laws and policies? The "dog that didn't bark" also requires an explanation: if the Ottomans blocked the spread of the press for three centuries, why did European rulers *not* prevent the spread of printing? Were European rulers hapless to prevent the spread of printing? Or were there deeply rooted differences in means of propagation that *incentivized* European rulers to permit the press while *disincentivizing* Ottoman rulers from doing the same? This chapter proposes that such deeply rooted differences were precisely why the two regions reacted differently to the printing press.

Early Printing in Europe

Within five years of Gutenberg introducing his invention, the first major work employing the new technology, the Gutenberg bible, was available for sale. By the end of the fifteenth century, 60 of the 100 largest European cities had a press, and 30 percent of cities with population of at least 1,000 had a press. The press was hardly concentrated in Gutenberg's Germany: nearly every nation had at least one press by the end of the century (see Table 5.1). Perhaps more astoundingly, printers produced more than 27,000 works in this period *that are still in existence*, and the actual number of works produced is likely quite higher.

Gutenberg and his assistants established the first print workshops in Mainz and the surrounding area. They held a printing monopoly for about a decade, before rivals printed a bible in Strasbourg in 1459.[7] The early printers were either apprentices or business partners of Gutenberg in Mainz. Due to the proprietary nature of the technology, there were significant barriers to entry, the largest of which was the acquisition of metal type. The process used to cast movable metal type required a specific combination of alloys that remained a secret among a small group of printers.[8] This meant

Table 5.1 *Number of Cities with Presses and Works Produced*
by 1500, by Country

Current Country	Cities with a Press by 1500	Percentage of Cities with a Press	Works by 1500
Austria	1	11%	84
Belgium	8	20%	808
Czech Republic	6	33%	63
Denmark	2	50%	6
Finland	0	0%	0
France	46	35%	5,766
Germany	51	32%	7,662
Ireland	0	0%	0
Italy	75	37%	9,881
Netherlands	13	34%	1,165
Poland	5	21%	27
Portugal	5	17%	29
Spain	28	30%	938
Switzerland	10	50%	877
United Kingdom	4	6%	398
Total	**254**	**30%**	**27,704**

Sources: Population: Bairoch et al. (1988); Press: Febvre and Martin (1958), Clair (1976), British Library (2011); only cities with population ≥ 1,000 considered.

that the printing "industry" was hardly competitive in its first few decades. The few individuals with the training and knowledge to start a press dominated early printing, and they had their choice of where to establish a press. For these reasons, printing remained almost exclusively German in its first few decades. By the 1470s, a small group of "printer-scholars" – educated laymen who ran printing presses and edited manuscripts – controlled the industry. The printer-scholars were often former priests or university professors. At heart they were capitalists. Most of the early printers readily moved to places where demand for books was the highest: first to major commercial centers and then to university towns.[9] Printing expanded rapidly in the 1470s, particularly in Germany and Italy. Demand was likely the highest in northern Italy, which was Europe's wealthiest region at the time. By the end of the century the press was in nearly universal use throughout Western Europe (see Figure 5.1).

Table 5.1 revealed just how rapidly the press spread throughout Europe in the fifty years after Gutenberg. By 1500, 254 European towns had presses, accounting for about 30 percent of Western and Central European towns with populations of at least 1,000. Presses were most abundant in the

○ Print Cities, Population ≥ 20,000
○ Print Cities, Population < 20,000

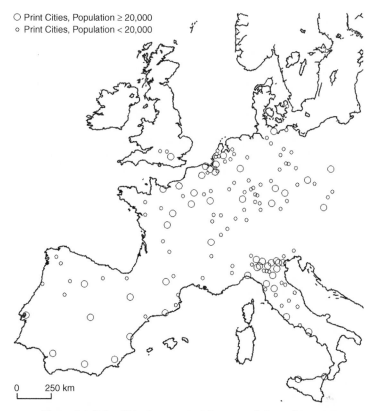

Figure 5.1 Print Cities by 1500 in Western and Central Europe

wealthiest regions of Western Europe – Italy, France (Paris was the largest city in Europe at the time), and the Low Countries – as well as in Germany, which had an ingrained print culture due to its early roots in Mainz and the surrounding area. Even Spain, which had been the wealthiest region in Western Europe while under Muslim rule until being superseded by the northern Italian city-states during the Commercial Revolution, had presses in 30 percent of its cities by the end of the century. Thirteen of the fifteen largest print cities were either big cities by the standards of the day (i.e., had populations of at least 20,000) or university towns (see Table 5.2). These fifteen cities accounted for 71 percent of books that have survived to the present day. Evidently, while printers did spread throughout Western Europe, many of them also concentrated in a few select cities.

Latin was the language of most books printed before 1500 (77 percent), although many were printed in local vernaculars, including Italian

(7 percent), German (4–6 percent), and French (4–5 percent). Religious works were the most popular, making up about 45 percent of all early books published, with the bible by far the biggest seller.[10] This should not be surprising, as most literates of the time were churchmen. The Church was one of the biggest early customers of printing. It used the press to print ordinances, works of popular piety, bulls, propaganda for its anti-Turkish crusade, and indulgences. Local churches also demanded books for church services.[11] Numerous monasteries welcomed printers to their quarters, and printers found a large market for religious works in small Italian cities.

Another important source of demand came from merchants, who desired books of mathematics. The first known printed book of mathematics in the West, the *Treviso Arithmetic*, was printed in 1478, and the works of Euclid first appeared in Venice in 1482.[12] Northern Italians printed most of the early mathematical treatises, as this is where merchant activity was greatest and thus demand for such works the highest. The book dedication of a 1519 Portuguese edition of Euclid reflects the importance of printed works to merchants: "I am printing this arithmetic because it is a thing so necessary in Portugal for transactions with the merchants of India, Persia, Arabia, Ethiopia, and other places discovered by us."[13]

There were some attempts by authorities to slow the spread of printing or control what was printed. In particular, the Church attempted to control the spread of books that challenged its interests. In 1479, Pope Sixtus IV permitted the University of Cologne to censure printers of what they deemed heretical books. This presaged Church policy over the next century: the papacy issued bulls authorizing excommunication and universal censorship in 1487 and 1501, and Pope Leo X issued a bull that forbade the publication of any book without the Church's permission.[14] The Church repressed a number of heretical books during the Spanish Inquisition of the 1490s, and it published the *Index Librorum Prohibitorum* ("List of Prohibited Books") in 1559. It also had French publishers of Protestant literature executed. Monarchs likewise prohibited certain types of books. Henry VIII published a list of banned books as he tried to install the Reformation in England in the 1530s, and in 1538, England prohibited the importation of books written in English. Special interests such as the Stationers in England, to whom the king granted a monopoly on printing throughout the kingdom, were also able to block some aspects of printing, sometimes violently.[15] Yet, printers were easily able to evade most censorship by assuming pseudonyms, falsifying the place of publication, or publishing "pocket books" that were easily concealed from censors. In the end, censorship was rather impotent in Europe, and printers printed books with little fear of retribution.

Table 5.2 *Biggest Print Cities before 1500*

City	Number of Works by 1500	Population in 1500	University by 1500
Venice	3,485	100,000	No
Paris	2,701	225,000	Yes
Rome	1,886	55,000	Yes
Cologne	1,488	45,000	Yes
Leipzig	1,324	10,000	Yes
Lyons	1,320	50,000	Yes
Augsburg	1,195	30,000	No
Strasbourg	1,115	20,000	No
Milan	1,065	100,000	No
Nuremberg	1,017	38,000	No
Florence	765	55,000	Yes
Basel	746	10,000	No
Deventer	598	7,000	No
Bologna	530	50,000	Yes
Antwerp	423	30,000	No
Total	**19,658**		
% of Total	**71.0%**		

Source: British Library (2011).

Printing Regulations in the Ottoman Empire

In 2012, I published two papers with economists Metin Coşgel and Thomas Miceli,[16] which addressed the puzzle posed at the beginning of this chapter: Why did the Ottomans suppress the printing press for nearly 250 years despite knowing about it as early as the 1480s? To understand our answer to this puzzle, some historical context is necessary.

The Ottomans first knew of the printing press during the reign of Bayezid II (r. 1481–1512). According to a widely known, yet debated, version of events, Bayezid II issued an edict in 1485 banning printing in Ottoman Turkish.[17] His son, Sultan Selim I, renewed this edict in 1515. The decree stated that "occupying oneself with the science of printing was punishable by death."[18] The effect of this edict was clear well over a century after its enactment: in the seventeenth century, the Hungarian Ottoman chronicler Ibrahim of Pec explicitly wondered why books in the Arabic and Ottoman Turkish languages were not available.[19]

By all accounts, the ban on printing applied only to Muslim subjects printing in the Arabic script, which was both the official script of all Islamic doctrine as well as the script of the Ottoman Turkish language. Religious minorities were free to set up presses, so long as they printed works on non-Islamic topics and in a non-Arabic script. Thus, the Ottomans allowed Jewish immigrants from Spain and Portugal to establish a press in Istanbul in 1493, and they soon published the Torah and other religious and secular texts in Hebrew characters. Armenians established a press in the 1560s, printing books in the Armenian alphabet with fonts brought from abroad, while a Greek Orthodox monk brought the first Greek printing press to Istanbul in 1627.[20] In 1610, Tunisian Christians in the city of Quzahiya printed the Psalms of the Old Testament in Arabic (using the Syriac type).[21]

It was not until 1727 that an Ottoman sultan gave explicit permission to a subject to establish a press capable of printing in the Arabic script. A Hungarian Muslim convert named Ibrahim Müteferrika went into business with his partner Sa'id Efendi, and they received an edict giving them explicit permission to print in Arabic as long as religious works were not printed. Their first works were practical in nature, including maps, grammar books, and dictionaries.[22] But their press only printed seventeen works in twenty-three volumes, and it closed by 1745, after which printing virtually ceased in the Empire until the nineteenth century. But it is possible to glean some insight from the language used in the edict permitting Ibrahim Müteferrika and Sa'id Efendi's press. It was clear that the sultan was lifting a major restriction. The edict stated that the new technology would be "unveiled like a bride and will not again be hidden."[23] This suggests that the original edicts played some role in suppressing printing in the Arabic script in the intervening two and a half centuries between their original imposition and the explicit permission to establish a press granted in the early eighteenth century.

The Ottomans' failure to adopt the printing press is one of the great missed opportunities of economic and technological history. In Western Europe, the press provided a host of new economic and educational opportunities that were simply unthinkable prior to the press. So why did the Ottomans ban this technology? Two possibilities are immediately discountable as the driving force behind the ban. First, the absence of printed works was not simply a reflection of the peculiarities of the Arabic script. While it is certain that the Arabic script presents greater challenges than the Latin script, Europeans quickly overcame any impediments. By 1530, Venetian printers printed the Qur'an in Arabic, and Italians and Parisians established numerous presses that were capable of printing in Arabic characters long before the Ottomans finally sanctioned the press. Pope Julius II (r. 1503–1513) had a book printed in Arabic on Christian prayer in 1514, and Genoese printers produced an Arabic edition of the Psalms of David in 1516. Both editions were presumably for Arabic-speaking Christian communities. Three noted Arabic publishing houses resided in Italy throughout the sixteenth and seventeenth centuries; one was the Medici press, which published Gospels and grammar books in Arabic.[24] All three of these publishing houses produced works meant for Ottoman consumers. Indeed, until the nineteenth century, most printed works in Arabic were bibles or other Christian literature.[25] In short, it did not take long following the spread of the press in Europe for enterprising printers to overcome any technical difficulties associated with printing in the Arabic script.

Second, it is also untenable that the absence of the Ottoman press was simply due to little demand for printed materials in the Ottoman Empire. It is likely true that the demand for books and pamphlets was smaller in the Ottoman Empire than in Western Europe, and it is quite possible that weak demand dampened incentives for prospective publishers to establish a press. Although there are no reliable estimates, historians generally agree that Ottoman literacy rates were very low in the early modern period: even as late as the early nineteenth century, Ottoman literacy rates were around 2–3 percent, while literacy rates were twice or thrice as high in many parts of Europe as early as 1500.[26] Meanwhile, real wages for both skilled and unskilled workers in Istanbul were only slightly more than half of those for workers in the major European cities in the century following the invention of the press.[27] Since books were a luxury good, lower wages in combination with lower literacy rates must have dampened the demand for books.

But it is simply untenable that demand for printed works in Arabic was so negligible as to make printing unprofitable in the absence of restrictions imposed by the sultan. The European experience suggested that demand for religious texts, especially the bible, was high regardless of the literacy rate or the language of publication. In Western Europe, even illiterates desired owning a bible. The same was almost certainly true for part of the Ottoman population regarding the Qur'an, even those who did not speak or read Arabic. Moreover, Muslim libraries were widespread well before the invention of the press. In the first four Islamic centuries, the Middle East housed some of the world's great libraries. After paper was introduced to the Islamic world in Samarkand in the mid-eighth century (approximately *five centuries* prior to its introduction in Western Europe), paper mills spread rapidly throughout the Middle East and North Africa, and publishing via handwritten copy became an important industry. Copyists doubled as booksellers, and up to at least the thirteenth century, huge bookshops existed in Baghdad, Damascus, Cairo, Granada, and Fez.[28] As a result, mosque libraries grew in cities large and small, and both private and public libraries were widespread. In the thirteenth century, large libraries existed in Baghdad, Damascus, Cairo, Shiraz, Fez, Samarkand, Bukhara, and Cordoba.[29] Although the Mongol invasions destroyed some of these libraries, and it is possible that others fell into disuse as Middle Eastern economies stagnated, it is unfathomable that the printing press would have been unprofitable to an enterprising printer in such a culture. Indeed, Ziauddin Sardar (1993, p. 51) claims that "for over 800 years [prior to the invention of the printing press], Muslim civilization was genuinely a civilization of the book: founded by a book (the Qur'an) … its main preoccupation – while not defending or extending its borders – was the production and distribution of books." True, by the late fifteenth century, the Ottoman and Egyptian Mamluk Empires had different intellectual environments than those present at the heights of the Abbasid Empire, but the importance of books in Islamic culture suggests that there must have been some latent demand for books at the time the Ottomans first heard of Gutenberg's invention.

It is more likely that the relatively low demand for printed works *combined* with restrictions on the press to tilt the prospective printer's cost-benefit calculation away from establishing a press that printed in Arabic. If there were indeed low demand for books, the benefits of establishing a press would have been low enough – although far from zero – to outweigh the potentially large costs of breaking an edict of the sultan. Combined, these forces created a "no printing in the Arabic script equilibrium": demand was positive, but not high enough for any potential printer to take on the large costs of printing.

This insight can also help explain why there is little direct evidence of the ban's enforcement in the 242 years between the enactment of the original edict in 1485 and the ultimate permission in 1727. The secondary literature by and large mentions the original edicts in 1485 and 1515 and then skips two centuries to Ibrahim Müteferrika's press. This literature has not dug up any direct evidence of the Ottoman government denying Muslims trying to establish a press printing in the Arabic script in the intervening period. But this is exactly what one would expect. If the sultan is unlikely to accept a press printing in the Arabic script and demand is low anyway, there is little incentive for an entrepreneur to open a press in the first place. This is an *equilibrium* action. Sometimes, equilibrium actions are difficult to discern in economic history because the action is one of inaction: if no incentive exists to set up a press printing in the Arabic script, we should not see many (if any) edicts explicitly forbidding the press, because such an edict would have been unnecessary. All we have to go by is the language of the 1727 edict that did eventually permit the printing press, which made it appear that this was a major change in Ottoman policy.

Unfortunately for the Ottoman economy, this "no-print" equilibrium carried important dynamic consequences. It is not too much of a stretch to imagine how the introduction of the press could have facilitated a "virtuous cycle" – as it did in Europe – whereby increased literacy resulting from the press would have increased demand for books, which would have caused a supply response, which would have further increased literacy, and so on. As long as there was some initial demand for books, it would have been profitable for at least one firm to enter the printing industry and start the virtuous cycle. But the virtuous cycle could have only commenced if at least one individual had incentive to establish a press. The combination of weak demand and heavy restrictions against printing meant that incentives for any one individual to set such a process in motion were absent.

An important feature of this history is that the Ottoman sultan was not against printing per se, but only against printing in the Arabic script. This gives a clue as to where to look for the reasons for the restrictions on printing. The key is to answer the following questions: To whom was widespread printing in the Arabic script a threat? Was this individual or group powerful enough to convince the sultan to block the spread of printing despite the fact that the sultan was missing out on tax revenue and economic development by blocking this new and important technology?

Why the Ottomans Blocked the Printing Press

In order to uncover why the Ottoman sultans blocked a technology that had such obvious benefits, Metin Coşgel, Thomas Miceli, and I dug into the history of the period. Our main goal was to discover who the press would have hurt and whether they had the power to encourage the sultan to block it. The logic espoused in Chapter 2 suggests that a good place to start looking is the individuals or groups that propagated the sultan's rule.

Like their Muslim predecessors, the Ottomans relied heavily on religious legitimacy to propagate their rule. Although the Ottomans could not claim a bloodline to the Prophet – indeed, they were not even Arab – the legitimizing benefits associated with "acting Islamic" were simply too great for them to dismiss. This was especially true after Mehmed II conquered Constantinople in 1453, an event that reverberated around the entire Muslim world. Halil İnalcık (1973, p. 56) claims:

With the conquest of Constantinople, Mehmed II became the most prestigious Muslim ruler. The Ottomans regarded him as the greatest Islamic sovereign since the first four caliphs, and the Islamic world came to regard Holy War as the greatest source of power and influence. Mehmed the Conqueror saw himself as fighting on behalf of all the Muslims: "These tribulations are for God's sake. The sword of Islam is in our hands. If we had not chosen to endure these tribulations, we would not be worthy to be called gazis (holy warrior). We would be ashamed to stand in God's presence on the Day of Resurrection."

Later, Selim I (r. 1512–1520) conquered the Egyptian Mamluk Empire, which reigned over the holy cities of Mecca and Medina. This further raised the status of the Ottoman sultan as the protector of Islam. These events increased the value of religious legitimacy, which the religious establishment could confer so long as the sultan acted in accordance with Islam. As a result, while Ottoman sultans were often not too pious in their personal lives – many enjoyed alcohol despite its prohibition in Islamic law – they never shied from making overtly religious gestures to give the appearance of acting Islamic. Acts such as attending Friday mosque, punishing those who broke the Ramadan fast, closing taverns and brothels, building madrasas and mosques, and sending yearly gifts of gold to Mecca and Medina were common for fifteenth- and sixteenth-century Ottoman sultans.[30] They were especially prone to emphasizing their religious credentials during times of war against non-Sunnis in order to gain popular support, weaken potential sources of opposition, and curry favor with orthodox clerics. For instance, in the sixteenth-century battles against the (Persian) Shi'i Safavid Empire, the sultan co-opted the religious establishment in order to provide religious justification for a war against other Muslims while portraying the Ottomans as protectors of the orthodox Islamic faith.[31]

The framework established in this book suggests that the religious establishment was therefore in an excellent bargaining position vis-à-vis the sultan. As the sultan's primary source of inexpensive yet highly effective legitimacy, Ottoman clerics had the power to encourage the sultan to block the press should they have desired. But did the religious establishment have any desire to see the printing press blocked? After all, the European experience suggests that the Church was one of the earliest users of the new technology. If the Ottoman religious establishment faced different incentives than the Church, what were they and why?

Even a cursory reading of the relevant history suggests that the Ottoman religious establishment had significant incentive to encourage the sultan to block the printing press – at least those presses printing in the Arabic script. The introduction of the press would have caused it to lose one of its most important sources of influence over the Muslim population: its monopoly over the transmission of religious knowledge. Prior to the introduction of the printing press, the transmission of religious knowledge in the Muslim world was largely an oral process dominated by religious authorities. This was especially true in the Ottoman Empire, where many of the inhabitants – and even the sultans themselves – were not native speakers of Arabic and thus had to rely on others' interpretation of the Qur'an and great Arabic texts.

In the early Islamic centuries, the process of publishing a book was a laborious one controlled by the religious establishment teaching in mosques or madrasas. Clerics produced books in the following manner. First, a well-known religious scholar dictated a book to a scribe, from memory or his own writing, over several weeks or months. Then, the scholar would listen to a public reading of what the scribe had written or he would read it himself, making amendments during the rereading. He would then authenticate it with an *ijaza* (the legal requirement necessary to transmit works), which made it lawful. Once the scholar copied a book, he had the authority to place it in the madrasa curriculum and give others the opportunity to copy it. More often his pupils would commit it to memory; many scholars wrote Islamic texts in rhyme to help facilitate this process. The scholars, in turn, perceived these books as transmitted from him and his predecessors. The *ijaza* document lists the names of all of those who transmitted the book in the past so that the transmission was traceable back to the original author. This created an established line of transmission and authority that only highly trained religious scholars were capable of achieving.[32] Scholars published countless books in this manner, with the oldest existing manuscript published in 874.[33]

The importance of oral transmission in Islam far preceded the Ottomans. Muhammad's companions orally transmitted the hadith, the most important corpus of early Islamic doctrine after the Qur'an. After the companions, an unbroken chain of scholars transmitted the hadith. There is a huge corpus of hadith literature, but only the most trustworthy hadith have become part of the Islamic tradition. A hadith gained trustworthiness only when transmitted by trustworthy individuals – those known for accuracy, dependability, morality, and independence from politics.[34] Hence, in-person, oral transmission played a key role in the development of early Islamic doctrine.

Many of the great pre-Ottoman Muslim scholars traveled across the Muslim world to receive knowledge in person. There are well-known cases of writers traveling around North Africa, Spain, Anatolia, and the Middle East in search of *ijaza*. For instance, the Spanish mystic Ibn Arabi (b. 1165) traveled in search of personal, reliable transmission of Islamic knowledge in modern-day Spain (Murcia, Seville, Almeria, Cordoba),

Tunisia (Tunis), Morocco (Fez), Egypt (Cairo), Israel (Jerusalem), Saudi Arabia (Mecca), Iraq (Baghdad, Mosul), Turkey (Malatya, Sivas, Aksaray, Konya), and Syria (Damascus).[35] The importance of the in-person nature of the *ijaza* is clear in the following tenth-century *ijaza*: "I entrust my book to you with my writing from my hand to yours. I give you authorization for the poem and you may transmit it from me. It has been produced after having been heard and read."[36]

As the proliferation of written texts in the century or two prior to the press threatened to undermine the authority of clerics over the masses, they slowly changed what it meant to communicate and transmit knowledge faithfully to the public. In order to be a legitimate transmitter of knowledge, one had to know the following: the Qur'an (by heart), a vast amount of Arabic literature, the connections of these works to the life of Muhammad (*sunnah*), the interpretations of the Qur'an given by classical jurists, perfect recall from memory of thousands of hadith, and deep knowledge of the science of Islamic law.[37] This helped keep interpretation of religious doctrine solely within the realm of religious jurists – only one who spent a lifetime studying Islamic law and doctrine could hope to qualify as a jurist – while having the negative side effect of making new interpretation (*ijtihad*) difficult to accomplish.[38]

The religious establishment was also able to control information by checking the information of books disseminated in libraries. Although they did not intervene in private libraries, religious authorities scrutinized the contents of libraries the minute one endowed them for public use. The sultan only permitted public dissemination of proper religious books that passed muster with religious authorities. The state sold off all other books to private collectors.[39]

The printing press threatened the religious establishment's intellectual monopoly. Under the pre-printing regime, the only people who had access to Islamic knowledge were those who undertook significant costs – a lifetime of training – to learn and memorize the most important religious works. Any works on nonreligious topics had to make it through the watchful eye of the religious establishment. The *ijaza* was yet another barrier to entry that protected the intellectual monopoly from outside intrusion. Individuals who did not receive an *ijaza* were not legally entitled to teach the text in question. The printing press would have fundamentally altered this dynamic. The press would have substantially reduced the barriers to entry to the intellectual world of Islam. If the press were available, the written word would have been available to the public quickly and cheaply.

Religious authorities were a valuable source of legitimacy precisely because they held control over Islamic wisdom. This explains why the ban on the printing press was only on those works printed in the Arabic script – the script of the language of Islam. The religious establishment was much less concerned with works in other languages – even translations of the Qur'an – as these works did not threaten their stranglehold on Islamic wisdom. Their ownership over this valuable good gave them credibility and importance in the community – it was what made them elite. It thus enabled them, and them alone, to support the sultan's claim to legitimacy by associating his actions with those consistent with Islam. The learned men of the Empire were the only ones who could credibly claim to make such a pronouncement. They dominated the marketplace of ideas, and they had the forum – the Friday sermon – to publicly make these ideas known. This was part of the greater bargain over laws and policies. The sultan gave protections to the religious establishment in return for legitimizing his rule. Both would have lost from anything that threatened to undermine the religious establishment's intellectual monopoly: the religious establishment would have lost their "elite" position as well as all of its associated benefits, while the sultan would have lost his primary source of inexpensive legitimacy.

Put simply, the press would have threatened the religious establishment's role as a middleman between received religious wisdom and its dissemination. With a widespread adoption of the press, Muslims would have been able to receive knowledge directly from books, not the religious establishment. Even though literacy outside of the religious establishment was low, it was not zero. As events in Europe eventually proved, it did not take a large literate population for the printed word to facilitate the rapid spread of ideas, since ideas could spread quickly and cheaply by literates reading printed works aloud in public spaces (see Chapter 6).

Why Did the Press Spread Quickly in Europe?

The Ottoman suppression of printing raises the question: Why did Western European rulers by and large permit the press? Did European propagating arrangements play a role in permitting the press much like Ottoman propagating arrangements played a role in preventing its spread? By now, it should be clear that Western European rulers were engaged in very different propagating arrangements than their Ottoman counterparts by the era of Gutenberg. The Church was a much weaker source of legitimacy for rulers in Western Europe than the religious establishment was in the Ottoman Empire. Although there was heterogeneity throughout Europe, Church leaders began to lose their ability to confer legitimacy beginning in the thirteenth century, and their capacity to legitimize weakened further in the fourteenth and fifteenth centuries.

Many factors encouraged the spread of printing in Western Europe but not in the Ottoman Empire. All of these factors were either a *result* of differences in propagating arrangements or *exacerbated* by differences in propagating arrangements. Take, for example, one of the distinguishing features between the Ottoman religious establishment and the Church: unlike Ottoman clerics, the Church lacked a monopoly on educational and intellectual institutions in the fifteenth century. This was not always the case. Prior to the late thirteenth century, men of the Church produced most European manuscripts. Indeed, the primary determinant of how many books a region produced in this period was the number and size of its monasteries.[40] This was especially true in the tenth–twelfth centuries, after the Cluniac reforms led to an explosion of monasteries in Western Europe.

Beginning in the late thirteenth century, two intertwined events helped shift the center of book production away from the monasteries: the growth of cities and the emergence of secular universities. The new urban elite were an important source of demand for printed works. Merchant manuals, books on arithmetic, and price sheets were among the early works published by European presses. This source of demand played an important role in encouraging the creation of printed works outside the control of the Church.

More importantly, the weakened role of the Church as a legitimizing agent meant that secular rulers desired justification for their rule that was outside, but complementary to, the religious justification provided by the Church. They found this in the doctors located at the most prestigious universities. The doctors formulated theories of the state based on Aristotelian foundations – not Christianity – in return for the ruler's financial support for the university. Such tracts were discouraged, and sometimes banned, when the Church dominated the universities prior to the late thirteenth century.[41] But the secular wings of universities (i.e., everything outside of theology) grew rapidly beginning in the late thirteenth century, and even many of those universities previously controlled by the Church had control wrestled away by secular rulers.[42] Political support for universities continued unabated throughout the remainder of the medieval period. For instance, during the Hundred Years' War, both the French and the English founded universities to promote patriotic feelings. Meanwhile, Florence established a university in order to repopulate after a plague, and numerous other cities solicited universities in order to establish a new source of income.[43] Associated with these movements was a growth in lay collections of nonreligious books.[44]

An unintended consequence of the weakened importance of religious legitimacy in general and the rise of the universities in particular was that universities established a separate sphere of book production.[45] Evidence collected by Eltjo Buringh and Jan Luiten van Zanden (2009) indicates that while monasteries were the driving force behind manuscript production in the early medieval period, the center of manuscript production slowly moved to cities and universities in the latter half of the medieval period. This provided a setting in which there was widespread demand for books over which the Church did not hold a monopoly.

As a result, the Church would not have been able to stop the spread of the press had it desired. And it is not even obvious that the Church desired to stop the spread of printing. It was one of the big early users of the press, which it used to print papal bulls, indulgences, and religious texts. But this is not prima facie evidence that the Church would have favored printing had it been in the position to oppose its spread. It simply reflects the Church's optimal response to the broader economic and institutional realities it faced. Surely, given the press's potential to undermine the existing social order, the Church would have preferred a world where the press did not exist. In fact, the next chapter shows that such fears were justified – the press played a key role in the Reformation, which was the biggest threat to the Church's religious hegemony in more than 1,000 years. But the simple fact is that the Church was in no position to stop the spread of the printing press. Indeed, the Church's actions during the Reformation are telling: it attempted to place prohibitions on many "heretical" works – often in the form of mass book burnings – but it never suggested an outright ban on printing, probably because it would have been futile.

The different reactions to the printing press in the Ottoman Empire and Western Europe were therefore not simply the result of differences in the preferences of Christian and Muslim religious authorities. Although oral transmission was much more important in the Islamic tradition than in medieval Christianity, there was an immense downside to permitting the press for religious authorities in both religions. The rapid transmission of ideas threatened both, since ideas could quickly escape their control. Thus, the key difference between Ottoman and Western European religious authorities was not their preferences, but their influence with rulers. The Ottoman religious establishment played an important enough of a propagating role that it could convince the sultan to prohibit printing in the Arabic script, but the Church was in no position by the end of the fifteenth century to do anything similar with Western European rulers. And since the Church was helpless to prevent the spread of the press, it might as well have reaped the benefits of having access to rapidly reproduced works.

It is also possible that Western European rulers would have been unable to prevent the spread of printing even had they wanted to. Unlike the Ottoman Empire, Western Europe was highly fragmented, with numerous rulers presiding over relatively small territories. This meant that if one ruler suppressed printing, printers could simply go to a neighboring state and print there. And since printed works were often small and easily concealable, it was not difficult to smuggle printed works into the prohibited region. This, in fact, happened in sixteenth-century France, where the Crown banned many Protestant tracts. Printers subverted these prohibitions by printing in nearby regions with Protestant sympathies – the Netherlands and the western part of the Holy Roman Empire – and as a result, Protestant literature was available to the French Huguenots.

It is undeniable that fragmentation played some role in the spread of printing in Western Europe. It certainly would have been easier for the Church to negotiate with one centralized state to suppress printing rather than numerous, decentralized, competing states. But fragmentation alone cannot be the sole reason for the spread of printing in Europe. It must have worked in tandem with the weakened role of the Church in legitimizing rule. To see why this is true, imagine a world where the Church was the most important propagating agent of every European state in the latter half of the fifteenth century. In such a circumstance, the Church should have been able to prevent the spread of printing. If the Church were to enact an edict prohibiting the printing press, how would rulers react? Sure, one enterprising ruler might permit the press, thereby attracting printers, the associated tax revenue, and other efficiencies enabled by the press. But they also would have been taking the chance of losing one of their primary propagating agents. In a situation where many rival states were waiting for any sign of weakness to appear before attacking – as was largely the case for the thirteen to fourteen centuries following the fall of the Roman Empire – it is possible that a set of fragmented states would have been even *less* willing to adopt the press, as it would have weakened the propagation of their rule relative to their rivals. So, while it is probable that fragmentation played a positive role on balance in facilitating the spread of printing, it did so only in the context of a Western Europe that had become less reliant on religious propagation of rule.

Unforeseeable Consequences

History is full of missed opportunities. Rarely do missed opportunities have persistent long-run consequences; long-run trends tend to overwhelm the idiosyncratic choices made by rulers or other important decision-makers.[46] Yet, sometimes missed opportunities initiate path-dependent processes that push history in a very different direction than it would have taken had someone seized that opportunity. Was the Ottoman failure to adopt the printing press an example of such a missed opportunity? What were the consequences of two and a half centuries of Ottoman printing restrictions?

Like restrictions on taking interest, Ottoman restrictions on the printing press serve as a useful tool to highlight the mechanisms at the heart of the framework proposed in this book. The relationship between rulers and their propagating agents was different in Western Europe and the Ottoman Empire in the fifteenth century, and as a result, rulers enacted different policies regarding the press. And like restrictions on taking interest, there were significant long-run, *unintended* consequences of the Ottoman suppression of the printing press. This chapter does not address these consequences, and the argument presented here does not imply that the press was directly responsible for the long-run divergence in economic fortunes between Western Europe and the Middle East. Sure, improvements in literacy and better access to price and exchange rate information had a positive effect on long-run economic outcomes in Western Europe. But these direct effects of printing pale in comparison to the unforeseeable, path-dependent consequences that arose following the spread of the press in Western Europe. The most important of these consequences was that the press permitted dissent to spread rapidly, making it much more likely that the existing political order would at some point be undermined. The next chapter proposes that this is precisely what occurred within a few decades of the entrenchment of printing throughout Western Europe. Specifically, the next chapter details how the press was instrumental in the spread and success of the Protestant Reformation, an event that completely upended propagating arrangements in large parts of Western Europe. Such a rapid and fundamental change never occurred in the Middle East, in no small part due to the absence of an information technology like the printing press that permitted dissent to spread rapidly and outside the hands of the existing elite. The ultimate upshot, detailed in Chapters 7 and 8, is that by the end of the sixteenth century, the manner in which rule was propagated was vastly different in the Middle East and Western Europe (especially Protestant Europe), and the resulting laws and policies favored commerce to a much greater degree in the latter. *This* is the reason that economic success ultimately occurred in parts of Western Europe but not the Middle East. The printing press did play a key role in the long-run divergence between the two regions, but only through a path-dependent sequence of events far removed from the initial causes of the divergence. The next chapter takes the first step at tracing this path, employing empirical evidence to support the connection between the spread of the printing press and the subsequent spread of the Protestant Reformation.

6

Printing and the Reformation

The previous chapter began by noting the widely perceived importance of Johannes Gutenberg, who ranked as the most important person of the last millennium by a number of popular press publications. Not far behind Gutenberg on all of those lists was a man who was born 15 years after Gutenberg's death in a city about 250 miles from Gutenberg's Mainz. This man, Martin Luther, set in motion a sequence of events in 1517 known as the Protestant Reformation. The Reformation was the most crippling blow to the religious hegemony of the Roman Church since it became the established church of the Roman Empire in the fourth century. Within just a decade, new religious groups formed that forever split from the Church, and Protestants would ultimately count Baptists, Lutherans, Calvinists, Presbyterians, Methodists, Anglicans, and many more among their ranks.

Why were Luther and his Reformation so important to world history? It is one thing to suggest that the Reformation was one of the most important religious events of the last millennium, and it certainly was. It is quite another to claim that the consequences of the Reformation extended beyond the world of religion. Yet, this book has thus far suggested that religion – specifically, the role religion plays in propagating political rule – can have far-reaching implications for a region's economic performance. It is natural, therefore, to ask whether the Reformation had any impact on the development of Western European economies.

There is a long line of scholarly work suggesting that Protestantism did indeed have a positive impact on European economic development. The most famous thesis making this connection is Max Weber's (1905 [2002]) classic *The Protestant Ethic and the 'Spirit' of Capitalism*. In this text, Weber argued that the Calvinist doctrine of predestination inspired some Protestants to work hard to show that they were one of the "elect" selected for paradise after death. According to Weber, the ethic encouraged by this doctrine motivated Protestants to succeed at their "calling": they could earn salvation through hard work. This work ethic was therefore consistent with capitalist growth. Protestants worked harder because it was their calling from God to do so, and Protestant economies grew as a result.

Weber's hypothesis has been subject to immense scrutiny in the century since he initially laid it out. One of the most obvious critiques cites the simple fact that capitalism predates the Reformation. Merchants built the Catholic Italian city-states of the late medieval period in order to conduct merchant activity, and a "capitalist ethic" imbued nearly every aspect of their social and economic life. Indeed, the most powerful of the city-states, Venice, was still one of the most important and wealthiest states in Western Europe during Luther's lifetime. Put simply, it is a stretch to claim that Protestants had any *unique* capitalist work ethic.[1]

While Weber was almost certainly wrong about the causal connection between Protestantism and economic success, this does not mean that the correlation he tried to explain was nonexistent. Weber came upon his idea about the connection between Protestantism and economic growth in part due to the conditions that surrounded him in Prussia in the late nineteenth and early twentieth centuries. A number of Prussian cities were primarily Catholic and many others were primarily Protestant. One could see during Weber's time that Protestant towns were better off than Catholic towns. Sascha Becker and Ludger Wößmann (2009) confirmed the possibility that this was due to something about Protestantism – and not something correlated with Protestantism – in a carefully identified study. Using the 1871 Prussian census, Becker and Wößmann found that Protestants had significantly higher incomes than Catholics did.[2]

The positive correlation between Protestantism and economic success extends well beyond the borders of Prussia. Consider Figure 6.1, which shows the "welfare ratios" of skilled workers in seventeen European cities from the sixteenth through the nineteenth centuries.[3] A welfare ratio is the ratio of one's real wages relative to how much it costs to buy a subsistence basket of goods. A welfare ratio of 1 means that workers are just at subsistence, while a ratio of 2 indicates that workers can buy twice the level of goods necessary for subsistence. This figure is divided into the six Protestant cities for which Allen (2001) gives data (Amsterdam, London, Strasbourg, Augsburg, Leipzig, and Hamburg), and eleven cities which remained Catholic (Antwerp, Florence/Milan, Naples, Valencia, Madrid, Paris, Munich, Vienna, Gdansk, Krakow, and Warsaw), and the welfare ratios are weighted by the city's population.[4] The trend is clear: beginning in the seventeenth century, skilled workers in the Protestant cities started to do

Figure 6.1 Welfare Ratios of Skilled Workers in Protestant and Catholic Cities, 1500–1899
Source: Welfare ratios – Allen (2001); Population – Bairoch et al. (1988); a city is considered Protestant if its population was largely converted by 1600.

significantly better than their Catholic counterparts. This trend begins *prior* to the Industrial Revolution and persists after industrialization. Although this pattern "proves" nothing in itself, it suggests that Weber's observation regarding the difference between Protestant and Catholic areas had some foundation.

This correlation is still apparent today. Figures 6.2–6.4 plot real per capita GDP against the percentage of Protestants, Catholics, and Muslims in 182 countries for which there were data in 2010. For all the limitations of these figures, they make apparent a Weberian connection. A country made up of only Protestants is $13,406 wealthier per person (in 2010 U.S. dollars), on average, than a country with zero Protestants. There is a positive effect for Catholicism, but it is weaker: a country made up of only Catholics is $3,900 wealthier per person than a country with zero Catholics. The effect is negative for Islam, even after accounting for the oil-rich nations of the Persian Gulf: a country made up of only Muslims is $7,509 poorer per person than a country with zero Muslims.

These data show that a *correlation* exists – and has existed since at least the seventeenth century – between Protestantism and wealth. This says

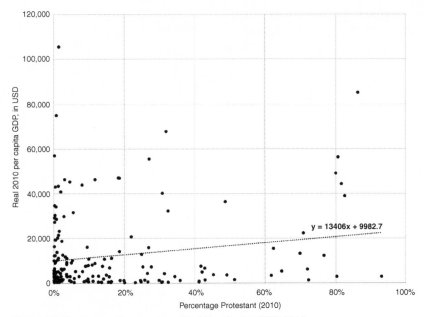

Figure 6.2 Percentage Protestant vs. Real Per Capita GDP, 2010
Sources: GDP – IMF (2012); Religion – Johnson and Grim (2008).

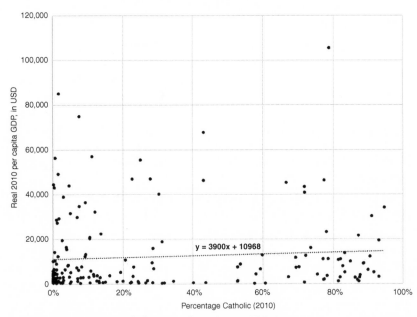

Figure 6.3 Percentage Catholic vs. Real Per Capita GDP, 2010
Sources: GDP – IMF (2012); Religion – Johnson and Grim (2008).

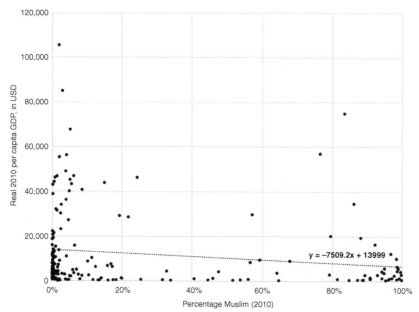

Figure 6.4 Percentage Muslim vs. Real Per Capita GDP, 2010
Sources: GDP – IMF (2012); Religion – Johnson and Grim (2008).

nothing about whether this relationship is *causal* or not. Can it possibly be a mere coincidence that the regions that dominated the world economy since the Reformation – first the Dutch Republic, then England, then the United States – were all predominantly Protestant? Of course this is a possibility, but this chapter argues that this was no coincidence, and there is indeed a causal connection between Protestantism and economic success. The reasons underlying the causal connection are found in the history of the Reformation: what it was, how it spread, and how it upset the prevailing political-economy equilibrium that dominated Western Europe since the fall of Rome.

To begin to address this history, a little context is necessary. The century between 1450 and 1550 is arguably the most important one in the post-Roman history of Europe – even more important than the onset of industrialization from 1750 to 1850. Many of the institutional and technological features that eventually pushed Western Europe onto the path of economic success came to fruition in this century. A far from exhaustive list of important events in this century include the "finding" of the New World, the Copernican revolution, the Ottoman conquest of Constantinople and sieges of Vienna, the Renaissance, the Protestant Reformation, and, of course, the invention and spread of the printing press. These events marked the end of the medieval period and the onset of a new era that culminated in Western European world hegemony. Indeed, many economists and historians have pointed to at least one of these events as heralding the "rise of the West."[5] The problem is disentangling them. Which events resulted from other historical events, and, more importantly, which events were the true "prime movers" of this momentous period of economic history?

The previous chapter focused on one of these events – the spread of the printing press in Western Europe and its absence in the Middle East. Certain effects of the spread of printing are unsurprising: literacy rates rose substantially in Western Europe, cities with presses grew, and books became much less expensive. Perhaps more important were the indirect, *path-dependent* effects of the spread of printing. The press facilitated an information and communication revolution that went well beyond books. It allowed new ideas to spread much faster than ever before. This meant that anti-authority ideas could spread fast enough to become entrenched before authorities crushed them. This is analogous to the twenty-first-century spread of the internet and social media – arguably the most important information and communication technologies since the printing press. Websites like Facebook and Twitter allow people to organize quickly and spread new ideas almost instantaneously. For this reason, autocratic regimes susceptible to revolution (e.g., North Korea, Iran, China) do everything they can to suppress these sites. Their fear is rational: social media websites facilitated the toppling of autocratic regimes during the Arab Spring.

Around the time Gutenberg invented the movable-type printing press, the Catholic Church was, like those autocratic regimes, particularly vulnerable to dissent. For a couple of centuries, it increasingly engaged in worldly pursuits far removed from its original mission of salvaging souls. Practices such as simony (buying or selling of ecclesiastical privileges), selling prayers to alleviate the suffering of loved ones in the recently invented purgatory, and the selling of indulgences (a "get out of Hell free" card purchasable for the right price) were all rampant in the late medieval Church. This created displeasure with the Church among both churchmen and the laity. In such a circumstance, a revolt against authority was possible so long as it could spread before the Church and its allies suppressed it. The printing press enabled the spread of such a revolt, and the result was the Protestant Reformation.[6]

This chapter details the connection between the printing press and the Reformation. This connection is a classic example of a *path-dependent* series of events. Johannes Gutenberg had no intention of undermining the Church or of creating a technology that could possibly undermine the existing political equilibrium. He was a capitalist who figured out the key ingredients to making movable-type printing feasible, and he used this knowledge to print books. But what makes the press arguably the most important invention of the last millennium are the unintended and unforeseeable consequences that the spread of printing had on Western European political development. As this chapter documents, the press allowed the Reformation to spread rapidly enough that it became too entrenched for the Church to suppress it outright. Such a rapid spread of ideas would have been impossible to imagine in a pre-printing world. Indeed, many attempts at reforming the Church failed prior to the spread of the press. More importantly, where the Reformation became entrenched, the reformers generally removed the Catholic Church from power. They kicked churchmen out of town and confiscated the Church's possessions. This was the final death knell to the Church in these regions – and its capacity to legitimize political rule. In England, Henry VIII confiscated Church lands, forbade all appeals to the pope on religious or other matters, claimed for the monarch all of the powers over the Church once held by the pope, and removed all abbots from the House of Lords. In the Dutch Republic, the reformers stripped the clergy of practically all their political power. In Sweden, the crown confiscated much of the land donated to the monasteries and claimed authority over the Reformed church. In the northern German independent trade cities, reformers removed churchmen from city councils and Church land was confiscated. And so on.

This was the most important consequence of the Reformation on the economic fortunes of Protestant nations. Where the Church ceased playing a role in propagating rule, the economic elite, organized in parliaments, often stepped in to take their place. Their interests aligned more closely with laws and policies that facilitated broader economic success, and the laws and policies they helped enact reflected this. *This* is why Weber observed a connection between Protestantism and economic success – he was wrong in his causal argument, but there is indeed a reason the two were often connected.

The economic consequences of the spread of printing and the Protestant Reformation raise another important question: What did the *absence* of the printing press mean for the economic and institutional trajectory of the Middle East and, in particular the Ottoman Empire? If the spread of printing were so important to the success of the Protestant Reformation, is it possible that the delayed acceptance of the press prohibited a similar change from occurring in the Islamic world? This chapter answers this question in the affirmative. This is among the primary reasons why the spread of printing was important. Where it spread, religious authorities were more likely to be undermined; where it did not spread, the status quo was more likely to hold.

The framework established in this book therefore suggests that whether a region adopted the printing press was both a *cause* and a *consequence* of the strength of the legitimizing relationship between political and religious authorities. In other words, the absence of information technology strengthened the legitimizing relationship, while a strong legitimizing relationship was the very thing that supported the suppression of printing.

The Spread of the Protestant Reformation

On October 31, 1517, Martin Luther nailed his Ninety-Five Theses to the door of the All Saints Church at Wittenberg, unwittingly sparking what would become the Protestant Reformation.[7] Luther was concerned with what he viewed as theological errors, such as whether salvation could come through faith alone. He also condemned abuses of Church power such as the use of indulgences, relic cults, clerical privileges, clerical concubinage, and simony. Although Luther's complaints initially focused on reforming the Church from within, lay and clerical interests throughout northern Europe quickly echoed his complaints.

The Reformation initially spread in what was a highly fragmented Holy Roman Empire. Cities such as Nuremberg accepted the Reformation, with powerful friends of Luther appointing preachers sympathetic to reform ideas. A contemporary movement emerged in the Swiss confederation, where Huldrych Zwingli (1484–1531) espoused similar principles and preached to Zurich congregations in the vernacular. A hybrid Luther-Zwingli message caught on in the 1520s in many of the free cities of southern Germany, such as Strasbourg and Constance.[8]

The Reformation usually took hold in a city through the efforts of a small cadre of learned, literate priests and scholars who took it upon themselves to spread Luther's or Zwingli's message. Most of these reformers had positions in the established Church and could address the masses directly from the pulpit. They fervently and aggressively questioned congregations about the nature of worship and the practices of the Church hierarchy and the pope. These preachers were particularly effective in Saxony and Central Germany in the 1520s, where they spread the Reformation to towns such as Altenburg, Eisenach, and Zwickau. In the late 1520s and 1530s, reforming preachers helped convert larger towns such as Strasbourg and Lubeck, with numerous Baltic cities following suit. Many major south German cities, such as Augsburg, converted in a similar manner in the 1530s.[9]

The message of the Reformation also spread from city to city through broadsheets and pamphlets, most of which were written by the lead reformers, especially Luther. Although most people were illiterate in this period, oral communication was the primary way the printed word spread, and Reformers wrote pamphlets in such a manner that literate sympathizers could read them aloud in public meeting places. For example, Luther's pamphlet in response to a papal bull of condemnation was addressed to "all who read or hear this little book."[10]

In many of the cities that accepted the Reformation, such as Strasbourg and Ulm, city councils took charge of installing the Reformation by bringing in preachers sympathetic to reform ideas. This is a primary reason that historian A. G. Dickens (1974) put forth the thesis that the Reformation was an "urban event." There is evidence to suggest that there is validity to this hypothesis: fifty of the sixty-five imperial cities of the Holy Roman Empire either permanently or periodically accepted the Reformation. The close proximity of urbanites to each other, greater levels of wealth and literary awareness, and their relative political sophistication and freedom compared with the closed, autocratic regimes of the princes were are all reasons why the Reformation took off in many of the free cities of the Holy Roman Empire. In the northern Hanseatic cities, it was largely the middling bourgeoisie – who were wealthy but had little political power within the cities – who encouraged the adoption of the Reformation as a means of confronting the established powers. Some of the members of these councils sought economic gains, such as confiscation of Church property, while others undoubtedly felt the pressures for change arising from preachers and the masses. Once the Reformation was accepted by a town, it generally followed that the old privileges and status of the priesthood and hierarchy were removed, followed by the confiscation or destruction of the Church's material wealth.

In the territories of the princes, fear of imperial retribution discouraged the introduction of the Reformation for at least a decade after its initial spread. Ultimately, the houses of Saxony, Hesse, Braunschweig-Lüneburg, Anhalt, and Mansfield all adopted the Reformation in the late 1520s. This was an important event in the early history of the Reformation because it gave the movement support from lay authorities. Their support helped the Reformers confront the existing governance structure of the empire, in which the Church played an important role. In 1530, many of the Protestant cities and princes signed the Augsburg Confession, despite condemnation from the Reichstag, which contained twenty-two articles stating the Lutheran message. In 1530–1531, a number of Protestant electorates formed an alliance known as the Schmalkaldic League. By 1535, many of the important Protestant independent cities joined the League, which provided mutual defense against Catholic invasion. Denmark quickly joined the league; it had adopted the Reformation in the 1520s under the imperial edicts of kings Frederick I (1523–1533) and Christian III (1533–1559). The defense provided by the League permitted a truce for over a decade. Eventually, the Emperor crushed the League in the Schmalkaldic War (1547). This did not end the conflict between Protestants and the emperor, however. It was not until 1555 that the Augsburg Reichstag put most disputes to rest by permitting sovereign princes and lords of the Holy Roman Empire to determine the faith of their subjects.

The time of the Reformation was also the height of Ottoman power. The fact that the Habsburg Holy Roman Emperor Charles V – who, as Holy Roman Emperor as well as king of Spain, received propagation by the Church like no other monarch in Europe at the time (see Chapter 8) – did not quickly crush the Protestant alliances was in part a consequence of Ottoman incursions into central Europe. The Ottomans conquered much of southeastern Europe by this time (Hungary, Bulgaria, Romania, Greece, Bosnia, and Serbia) and were pushing toward central Europe. They made it as far as the gates of Vienna, the capital of the eastern portion of the Habsburg's vast European holdings. Murat Iyigun (2008, 2015) points out that the Catholic powers therefore had a much more pressing threat on their hands than the religious heresy of the Reformers. The Ottoman threat diverted resources that could have fended off the Reformation, and when the Ottoman threat was starkest, conflict between Catholics and Protestants was rare. The Ottoman threat was therefore important to the ultimate success of the Reformation because it allowed the Reformers to gain traction with the wider populace and local rulers before the Church and its allies could suppress it.

The printing press was important to the ultimate success of the Reformation for precisely the same reason: it allowed the Reformation to become entrenched enough to pass the point of no return. And indeed, what needs explaining is the initial spread of the Reformation in the Holy Roman Empire. What mechanisms allowed the Reformation to spread unlike previous movements against Church power, which usually ended up violently suppressed?

Connecting the Spread of the Printing Press to the Reformation

"[The printing press is] God's highest and ultimate gift of grace by which He would have His Gospel carried forward." – Martin Luther (quoted in Spitz 1985)

Is it merely coincidental that two of the most important events in the Western world of the last millennium – the spread of the printing press and the Protestant Reformation – sprouted 250 miles apart in the Holy Roman Empire? Is it merely coincidental that the Reformation commenced soon after the press became entrenched throughout Europe? Probably not. Mark U. Edwards (1994, p. 1) begins his book on Luther and the printing press by noting that "the Reformation saw the first major, self-conscious attempt to use the recently invented printing press to shape and channel a mass movement." Indeed, can it possibly be a coincidence that the Reformers employed, in the words of Lucien Febvre and Henri-Jean Martin (1958, p. 288), the "first propaganda campaign conducted through the medium of the press"?

The classic connection made between the printing press and the Reformation is a supply-side one, focusing on the role that the new information technology played in spreading Lutheran ideas. There are a number of factors supporting the supply-side theory. Most importantly, the press allowed for the spread of pamphlets to literate preachers who brought the Reformation into cities and villages. High transport costs and lack of copyright meant that printers did not often ship printed works to distant locations. Instead, works more frequently spread through reprinting. Hence, those living in cities with presses or close to presses had much greater access to inexpensive pamphlets, and traveling preachers were more likely to be effective in these areas.[11]

It is also possible that the printing press affected demand for the Reformation. Elizabeth Eisenstein (1979) argues that print culture transformed cities, in some cases elevating the desires of the bourgeoisie and middle classes to greater social importance. This in turn could have made print cities more receptive to the Reformation, as the rising bourgeoisie had incentive to undermine the old order dominated by the Church and landed interests. Eisenstein (1979, p. 132) also suggests that the demand for the Reformation could have been enhanced by the press in a more subtle way:

[W]hile communal solidarity was diminished, vicarious participation in more distant events was also enhanced; and even while local ties loosened, links to larger collective units were being forged. Printed materials encouraged silent adherence to causes whose advocates could not be found in any one parish and who addressed an invisible public from afar.

Yet, it is unlikely that the press facilitated the spread of the Reformation solely by affecting the demand for reform. Numerous pre-Reformation heresies indicate that there was plenty of demand for reform prior to the Reformation – indeed, prior to the spread of the printing press. Some pre-Reformation Church leaders attempted to strip power from the pope and reduce the pomp associated with the Church hierarchy, pushing instead for the transfer of power to Church councils. Jean Gerson (1362–1429) was the leading proponent of this "reform from within" and was an important influence on Luther's writings. Gerson wrote at a time of schism within the Church, with two rival popes making claims from their seats in Avignon and Rome from 1378 to 1418. This schism helped inspire the conciliarism movement, which claimed that the pope did not hold supreme authority within the Church; instead, the Ecumenical Council (a conference of top Church leaders and theologians) held authority within the Church. Church leaders attempted such reform – unsuccessfully – at the Councils of Lyons (1274), Vienne (1311–1312), Constance (1414–1418), Pavia-Siena (1423–1424), and Basel (1431–1439).[12] In fact, much of the support for the anti-papist agenda at Basel originated from those free cities of Switzerland and southern Germany that were so important to the spread of the Reformation eighty years later. Even on the eve of the Reformation there was considerable pressure to reform the Church from within, but attempts made at the Fifth Lateran Council (1512–1517) were unsuccessful.

Other heresies abounded in the centuries prior to the Reformation. In fifteenth-century England, the Lollard movement spread the ideas of John Wyclif (d. 1384). Like Gerson, Wyclif wrote during the Great Schism between Avignon and Rome. Wyclif was a supporter of the rights of lay rulers over the papacy – he claimed that lay lords had the right to take the property of undeserving clergy – giving him significant influence with poorer parish priests. Wyclif went as far as to attack the doctrine of transubstantiation, a key point of doctrinal attack for the Protestants. The Church brutally suppressed the Lollard movement that Wyclif inspired in the half-century after his death. Their predecessors, the Waldensians, met a similar fate in the twelfth and thirteenth centuries. The Waldensians, who took a vow of poverty, rejected open displays of Church wealth and the worldly lives of churchmen. They gained some measure of influence in France, Spain, and Italy, but the Church and its allies suppressed them wherever they arose. In 1192, they were ordered in France to be put in chains; in 1194, they were banished from Aragon and the populace was forbidden to furnish them with shelter or food; and a decree of death by burning was enacted against them at the Council of Gerona in 1197.[13]

Perhaps the most serious challenge to the Church came from the Prague preacher Jan Hus (c. 1372–1415), who led the anti-Church movement that bore his name in the early fifteenth century. Hus challenged the rights of sinful churchmen to keep their positions and wealth, denounced the morality of what he perceived to be a corrupt clergy and pope, and translated Wyclif's heretical writings into Czech. For this the Church excommunicated Hus in 1410, although he continued to speak out against church abuses such as the offering of indulgences to anyone who supplied funds for a crusade against the king of Naples. These positions ultimately caused the Church to burn him at the stake in 1415.[14] The Hussite movement that followed over the next century established rival churches throughout Bohemia based on the denial of the Roman hierarchy. The Roman Church was able to limit the spread of the Hussite movement – going as far as to send a crusade to Bohemia – and Hussite influence never extended beyond Bohemia. The Hussites simply never gained much traction outside of Bohemia because the Church was quickly able to levy punishment against anyone that showed Hussite sympathies.

It is striking that the Church rather easily suppressed all of the attempts at reform prior to the invention and diffusion of the printing press. A. G. Dickens (1968, p. 51) explicitly makes this contrast between these movements and the Reformation: "Unlike the Wycliffite and Waldensian heresies, Lutheranism was from the first the child of the printed book." But disentangling the role the press played in the spread of the Reformation from other causes is no small task. For example, is it possible to separate the role of the press from, say, the increased selling of indulgences? In order to make a *causal* claim connecting the spread of printing to the Reformation, it is necessary to dig deeper. I did just this in a 2014 article in which I collected and analyzed city-level data on printing presses, Reformation status, and economic characteristics. The following section provides a brief overview of that analysis.

Testing the Effect of the Printing Press on the Reformation

The central focus of the analysis conducted in Rubin (2014b) is confined to the Holy Roman Empire, which was the birthplace of both printing and the Reformation.[15] It is useful to concentrate on the Holy Roman Empire because this is where the Reformation initially spread. The most important aspect of the Reformation to analyze is its initial spread, because so many other previous attempts at reform were never able to get off of the ground. Once the Reformation spread throughout the Holy

Roman Empire, it took on a life of its own elsewhere. Henry VIII was able to bring the Reformation to England to suit his own dynastic and financial purposes (see Chapter 7). Like Henry VIII, the Swedish King Gustav I (r. 1523–1560) confiscated land from the Church during the Swedish Reformation. In France, Calvinist churches rapidly spread in the west and south in the 1550s. The French monarch violently suppressed these Protestants, known as Huguenots, until they agreed on a series of peace edicts in the 1570s–1590s. Similar movements occurred in the Low Countries, where William of Orange co-opted the new religion in part as propaganda favoring the Dutch Revolt from Spanish rule (see Chapter 7). In each of these cases the Reformation spread for reasons that had little to do with the reasons for its emergence. But this is precisely the point: without the initial spread of the Reformation, Henry VIII, Gustav I, William of Orange, and their Protestant counterparts would never have had such an opportunity.

For the sake of statistical analysis, studying the Holy Roman Empire is also convenient because there was substantial variation in religious choice within the empire. Without any variation in religion, it is difficult to discern what the driving factors in adoption were; how do we know what convinced a city to adopt the Reformation if all (or none) of them did so? The variation in the Holy Roman Empire thus allows one to test the importance of various factors that could have caused a city to adopt the Reformation. Table 6.1 provides initial evidence; it lists cities in the Holy Roman Empire with populations of at least 20,000, along with their religious affiliation in 1600 and whether the city had a printing press by 1500. It is immediately noticeable from this table that a majority of the larger cities in the Holy Roman Empire had printing presses. This is not surprising. Printing spread outward from Mainz soon after its invention in 1450, and printers generally moved to large population centers where demand for printed works was greatest. This is the primary reason why A. G. Dickens's (1974) oft-cited claim that the Reformation was an "urban phenomenon" might be a spurious connection. If the printing press were indeed a significant causal factor in the adoption of the Reformation, then cities that were likely to adopt the Reformation were *also likely to be large*, since large cities were more likely to have a press.

More than population must be considered to understand the connection between the printing press and the Reformation. For example, a quick glance at Figure 6.5 indicates that proximity to Wittenberg played a role in a city's likelihood of adopting the Reformation.[16] It is also possible that cities that housed universities were more likely to reject the Reformation – many universities were church strongholds – but also adopt the press early due

Table 6.1 *Cities in the Holy Roman Empire (Population ≥ 20,000)*

Cities (with population ≥ 20,000) *with* Printing Presses by 1500			Cities (with population ≥ 20,000) *without* Printing Presses by 1500		
City	Population (in 1500)	P/C (by 1600)	City	Population (in 1500)	P/C (by 1600)
Prague	70,000	C	Tournai	35,000	C
Ghent	55,000	C	Lille	26,000	C
Cologne	45,000	C	Mechelen	25,000	C
Nuremberg	38,000	P			
Bruges	35,000	C			
Brussels	33,000	C			
Augsburg	30,000	P			
Antwerp	30,000	C			
Breslau	25,000	P			
Lübeck	25,000	P			
Regensburg	22,000	P			
Strasbourg	20,000	P			
Vienna	20,000	C			

Note: Population data from Bairoch et al. (1988); P/C indicates whether a city was Protestant or Catholic by 1600.

to their scholastic nature. Indeed, Hyojoung Kim and Steven Pfaff (2012) argue that university students were important links connecting pro- and anti-Reformation ideas from the universities to the broader spread of the Reformation. They find that cities housing numerous students from the universities at Wittenberg and Basel (Zwingli's intellectual home) were more likely to adopt the Reformation, while cities housing students from Cologne and Louvain (Catholic strongholds) were less likely to adopt the Reformation.[17] Table 6.2 also suggests this possibility; it lists the eleven cities in the Holy Roman Empire that housed a university by the time that Gutenberg invented the movable-type press in 1450. All six of the university towns that also housed a bishop or archbishop remained Catholic. Meanwhile, four of the five university towns that were not bishoprics or archbishoprics adopted Protestantism. This suggests a dual effect of universities on adoption of the Reformation: those in Catholic strongholds may have been more able to fend off the Reformation, while those not in Catholic strongholds were more likely to view the Reformation positively. Of course, this is hardly concrete evidence for such an effect – it is evidence from only eleven cities – but it does indicate the need to take a number of factors into account before making a causal claim connecting the spread of printing to the Reformation.

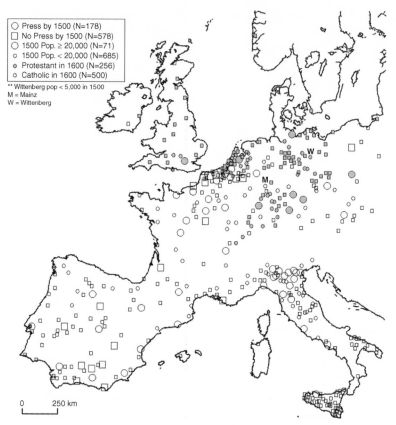

Figure 6.5 Printing and Protestantism in Western and Central Europe
Sources: Reprinted from Jared Rubin, "Printing and Protestants: An Empirical Test of
the Role of Printing in the Reformation," *The Review of Economics and Statistics,* 96:2
(May, 2014), pp. 270–86. © 2014 by the President and Fellows of Harvard College and
the Massachusetts Institute of Technology.

Fortunately, social scientists have a method called *multiple regression
analysis,* which allows one to address these problems. In a nutshell, multiple regression analysis provides a best-fit prediction for how one variable
affects another while holding all other variables constant. In other words,
the results could tell us: Given that a city has population X, has a university,
is home to a bishop, and many other things,[18] what is the average probability
that this town adopted the Reformation if it had a press? What is the average probability that it adopted the Reformation if it did not have a press?

These questions are answerable even if non-observable features might
affect a city's likelihood of adopting both the printing press and the

Table 6.2 *Cities in the Holy Roman Empire with Universities by 1450*

City	Population (in 1500)	Bishopric	P/C (by 1600)
Prague	70,000	Y	C
Cologne	45,000	Y	C
Vienna	20,000	Y	C
Erfurt	19,000	N	P
Leuven	17,000	N	C
Leipzig	10,000	N	P
Rostock	10,000	N	P
Heidelberg	8,000	N	P
Trier	8,000	Y	C
Würzburg	7,000	Y	C
Dôle	5,000	Y	C

Note: Population data from Bairoch et al. (1988); P/C indicates whether a city was Protestant or Catholic by 1600.

Reformation. For instance, literacy rates are unknown for the period prior to the spread of printing, especially in small towns. But pre-press literacy might have affected the adoption of the press *and* the adoption of the Reformation. More literate towns were more likely to adopt the press, and it is quite possible they also had a greater desire for the Reformation, due possibly to greater engagement in humanist philosophy or greater awareness of church corruption. Alternatively, more literate towns might have been Catholic strongholds due to many churchmen being literate, meaning that such towns were less likely to adopt the Reformation. Either way, it is possible to disentangle the connection between the spread of printing and the Reformation without any concrete evidence on pre-press literacy through an econometric technique known as two-stage least squares regression analysis (2SLS). This technique permits the separation of the two effects by first estimating the features that affected whether a printing press was present in a town, then using this information to estimate the effect of the printing press on the likelihood of a town adopting the Reformation.[19]

The 2SLS regression analyses employed to test the connection between the press and the Reformation provides very strong results. They indicate that the mere presence of a printing press prior to 1500 increased the probability that a city would become Protestant in 1530 by 52.1 percentage points and Protestant in 1600 by 29.0 percentage points, all else being equal. These results far surpass the "95 percent confidence threshold"

Table 6.3 *2SLS Regression Coefficients – Effect of City Characteristics on the Reformation*

	Did a city adopt the printing press by 1500?	Did a city adopt the Reformation by 1600?
Printing Press by 1500	–	**29.0%**
Log Distance to Mainz	–19.2%	–
Log Distance to Wittenberg	8.8%	–34.3%
Log Population in 1500	12.7%	–4.3%
Free Imperial City	–	30.8%
University Town	36.5%	–
Bishopric	21.4%	–11.9%

normally considered necessary for a result to be statistically significant, indicating that there is a strong relationship between the spread of the printing press and the spread of the Reformation. Table 6.3 lists some of the other regression coefficients that are statistically significant with at least 95 percent confidence (it lists only statistically significant coefficients). These coefficients can be interpreted as follows: if a city had a characteristic in the leftmost column (i.e., it had a printing press, was a free imperial city, had a university, or was a bishopric), its probability of adopting the printing press or the Reformation was affected, all else equal, by the corresponding number. Likewise, one can multiply a city's log distance to Mainz or Wittenberg or its population by the number in the corresponding column to see how these variables affected the likelihood of press or Reformation adoption. As expected, being further away from Wittenberg made adoption of the Reformation less likely, university towns were much more likely to adopt the printing press than non-university towns (by 36.5 percentage points, although they were not clearly more or less likely to adopt the Reformation), and bishoprics were also more likely to adopt the press (by 21.4 percentage points) than non-bishoprics while they were less likely to adopt the Reformation (by 11.9 percentage points).

While no counterfactual history exists to indicate whether an event like the Reformation would have occurred without the press, these results suggest that the printing press was necessary for the Reformation to occur when and where it did. Consider again the fate of previous attempts at reforming the Church. The Church rather easily and brutally suppressed the Hussite movement, Lollards, Waldensians, and others. The presence of these movements indicates the possibility that the seeds of discontent existed for centuries. The primary difference between Luther's movement and his predecessors is that *Luther had the press.*

The deleterious effect of the Reformation on the legitimizing power of the Church raises the question: Who replaced the Church in propagating political rule in Protestant states? Rulers must have looked elsewhere for propagation. Who did they turn to, and what effect did this have on laws and policies?

Propagation by the Economic Elite: A Protestant Phenomenon?

The decline of religious legitimacy following the Reformation paved the way for different propagating agents to increase their say in governance. The agents in the best position to replace the Church were the economic elite that comprised parliaments – merchants, urban commercial interests, and the landed elite. Protestant rulers ended up turning to these elites more frequently following the Reformation than their Catholic counterparts.

The economic elite provided one of the most important – and most expensive – alternatives to religious propagation. Elite support was especially important during times of war, when kings needed both money and loyalty. Indeed, a growing literature suggests that beginning in the seventeenth century, the need for defense against increasingly large and well-organized states created a common interest between rulers and the economic elite to provide greater provision of public goods, especially defense, which in turn required greater access to revenue.[20]

While protection against foreign invasion may have provided some of the initial impetus for the growth of large-scale fiscal institutions, the economic elite also wished to receive other things which improved their economic standing. In some cases, this meant investment in naval protection, which increased trade and prevented attacks from outside forces, or investment in poor relief, which reduced vagrancy and other social ills. If the elite were powerful enough or if the ruler were weak enough, they could ask for the biggest prize of all: secure property rights and freedom from arbitrary encroachment on those rights. When a weak ruler refused these rights, the elite were sometimes powerful enough to revolt. This occurred numerous times in medieval and early modern Europe – the English Baron's Revolt of the early thirteenth century (which culminated in the Magna Carta), the Spanish *comuneros* revolt (1520–1521), the Dutch Revolt of the 1570s, and the English Civil War of the 1640s are cases in point.

Jan Luiten van Zanden, Eltjo Buringh, and Maarten Bosker (2012) argue that the precarious position of medieval European rulers is precisely why parliaments formed when they did. In the twelfth-fourteenth centuries, as the power and wealth of the economic elite in the cities grew to rival that of the nobility and the Church, the city leaders, nobility, and clergy formed parliaments in order to collectively bargain with the king. In return for tax revenues, kings agreed to constrain themselves – that is, they agreed to not arbitrarily encroach on property rights and would only ask for tax revenue during times of war or fiscal crisis.[21] The first parliaments arose in Spain in the late twelfth century after the *Reconquista* of parts of Spain from the Muslim Umayyads. King Alfonso IX (r. 1188–1230) called the first parliament (Cortes) in León. He called for a meeting of the impor-tant citizens – nobility, bishops, and elected citizens – in order to stabi-lize his regime, which had low legitimacy due to the fact that the citizens were newly conquered and owed no allegiance to him. Parliaments consist-ing of Church leaders, nobles, and city leaders quickly spread to England, France, and Portugal in the thirteenth century and the rest of Europe soon after, helping rulers gain a consistent stream of tax revenue in return for limited rights, including veto power over new taxes. This "king and coun-cil" template was the dominant form of governance in almost all parts of Western Europe until 1800.[22] Roger Congleton (2011, p. 192) notes that "the paucity of governmental alternatives analyzed by enlightenment schol-ars shows how narrow the range of governance was in Europe in the late-medieval and early-modern periods. Neither Hobbes, Locke, Montesquieu, Rousseau, Kant, nor von Humboldt took the time to analyze representa-tive or parliament-dominated systems fully, in large part because they had never seen one operate."

Where kings had weak religious legitimacy or had limited control over the military, they had to give up more in the quid pro quo with the economic elite. For example, in Alfonso IX's call for a Cortes to stabilize his weakly legitimized regime he laid out a host of promises: he offered to administer justice impartially, refrain from acting arbitrarily, and guaranteed the secu-rity of persons and property.[23] Rulers often called parliaments soon after they came to the throne in order to stabilize and legitimize their rule. van Zanden et al. (2012) calculate, for instance, that between 1307 and 1508 the English Parliament met much more on average in the first few years of a king's reign than they did later in his reign.

Propagation by parliament was clearly a *substitute* for religious legiti-macy. Where one was more expensive or less effective, it was more worth-while to use the other. Once a ruler adopted the Reformation, he could no longer turn to the Church to propagate his rule. There was, therefore, stron-ger incentive for Protestant rulers to turn to parliaments than for Catholic rulers and certainly more than for Middle Eastern rulers, who did not have to contend with institutions similar to European parliaments. With religious legitimacy weakened, Protestant rulers had to give the elite even more rights and privileges than they had in the past in order to incentivize them to act in accordance with their wishes.

The importance of parliament in a given time and place is highly correlated with how frequently it was called in session. Typically, it met only when called into session by the ruler, who could disband it at will. Meanwhile, members of parliament only had collective power vis-à-vis the king when in session. Kings therefore called parliament into session when they could not meet their fiscal needs.[24] An increase in the frequency of parliamentary sessions was therefore generally the result of two different, mutually compatible events: increased royal expenses or lower revenues. In an ideal world for the king, he would be able to cover all royal expenses with streams of revenue that did not come from parliament, since obtaining funds from parliament meant giving up rights in return.

After the Reformation, there was a much greater use of parliaments in Protestant regions than in Catholic regions. Figure 6.6 confirms this point by showing the average number of times rulers called parliament into session in all regions that converted to Protestantism by 1600 and those that did not. The Protestant regions include England, Scotland, the Netherlands, different parts of the Holy Roman Empire, and the Scandinavian countries. The Catholic regions include Spain, Portugal, Ireland, the Italian states, France, Belgium, Poland, Bavaria,[25] and Austria. Prior to the Reformation (twelfth-fifteenth centuries), parliaments were more frequently called in regions that remained Catholic. Economically advanced Spain and the Italian territories called the most parliaments in this period. It was only after the Reformation commenced in the sixteenth century that Protestant rulers called parliaments in greater numbers.[26] While this trend reflects partly the fact that rulers called parliaments in the sixteenth century in order to deal with the Reformation, the difference between Catholic and Protestant regions was even greater in subsequent centuries. In addition to the Protestant English and Dutch parliaments – discussed in detail in Chapter 7 – the first meeting of the Swedish Riksdag occurred in 1527 in order to establish the Reformation, and it met every three years after 1527 – a very high rate relative to the rest of the continent. The Swiss parliament also met frequently in the fifteenth and sixteenth centuries, and from the 16th century onward it had the highest meeting rate in Europe.[27]

Figure 6.6 only provides motivating evidence. There was a clear shift toward Protestant parliaments propagating rule following the Reformation.

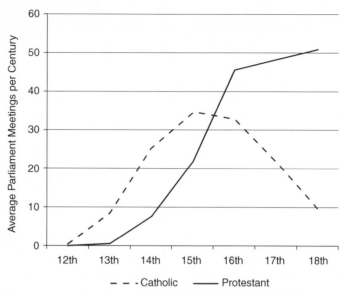

Figure 6.6 Average Parliament Meetings per Century, Protestant and Catholic Territories
Sources: Data from van Zanden, Buringh, and Bosker (2012).

This did not occur in the Catholic lands; if anything, parliaments became less important in the seventeenth and eighteenth centuries. This was clearest in France, where the Catholic Bourbon kings Louis XIII (r. 1610–1643), Louis XIV (r. 1643–1715), and Louis XV (r. 1715–1774) had sources of revenue outside the scope of their parliaments, such as the *taille*, and were otherwise highly legitimate. As a result, they were able to avoid calling the Estates-General for 175 years (1614–1789).

But did this institutional shift have any economic consequences? If not, then the rise of parliaments in the Protestant lands is nothing more than an interesting historical footnote. The remainder of this book suggests that this shift toward parliaments did indeed have a fundamental effect on the policies Protestant rulers pursued. These policies were much more in line with economic success than were previous policies or policies enacted in Catholic or Muslim regions.

A comparison of the propagating arrangements that persisted in the Ottoman Empire to those in the Protestant lands further amplifies the effect of the Protestant shift away from religious legitimation. It is in this comparison that this book's broader arguments begin to take shape. The Reformation was possible in Western Europe in large part due to the spread of the printing press, the absence of which made such an event less likely in the Ottoman Empire. The spread of printing in Western Europe but not in the Ottoman Empire was itself a consequence of the marginally weaker efficacy of religious legitimation in Western Europe. It is possible to trace these differences back even further to the formation of Islam and Christianity. In other words, differences in legitimizing arrangements in early Christianity and Islam had long-run, *path-dependent* effects on eventual economic outcomes. Each link of the argument makes sense taken in isolation, but the connection between the first link and the last link is far less obvious.

Summary: Explaining the Diverging Institutional Paths

Why did the Middle East and Western Europe, particularly Protestant Europe, undergo such divergent institutional histories? Part of the answer has to do with the presence of printing in Europe, but much more important was how the spread – or absence – of printing *reinforced* or *undermined* the relationships between political and religious authorities.

Prior to the spread of the press in Western Europe, heretical movements such as the Hussite and Lollard movements arose but did not spread far. It was only after the press was widespread that a movement like the one started by Luther could succeed. The absence of the printing press in the Ottoman Empire meant that even if such anti-authority thoughts did exist, they were unlikely to spread.[28] This meant that Ottoman institutions were self-reinforcing (see Figure 6.7). The high degree of relatively inexpensive legitimacy bestowed by religious authorities discouraged the Ottoman sultan from permitting the spread of printing in the Arabic script. And it follows that the absence of the printing press was *the very thing* that prevented alternatives to religious legitimacy from emerging. And it was not simply the case that there was little opposition to the Ottoman religious establishment – mystical and dervish anti-Ottoman orders abounded even at the height of Ottoman power, especially among the tribes in the provinces. The Ottomans crushed the most famous of these movements, the Kizilbash movement, in the mid-sixteenth century – incidentally, right around the time of the Reformation.[29] As was the case with rulers in pre-Reformation Europe, the Ottomans were able to quash any religious dissent from spreading too far before it was out of their control. While it is impossible to know whether these mystical movements would have been more successful had they had access to the press, the European experience suggests the possibility. After all, Jan Hus, John Wyclif, Jean Gerson, and other pre-Reformation reformers also lacked the press – and met similar fates.

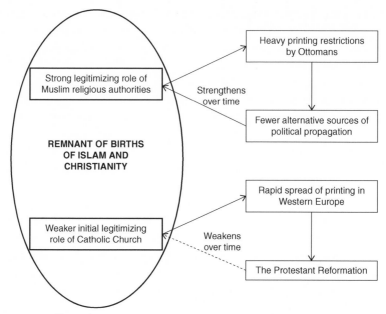

Figure 6.7 Self-Reinforcing Institutions and the Absence of an "Islamic Reformation"

The (Eventual) Rise of Ottoman Printing

In our 2012 articles,[30] Metin Coşgel, Thomas Miceli, and I addressed one final puzzle: If religious legitimacy were so important to the Ottoman sultan, why did the Ottomans eventually relax the ban on printing in the Arabic script? Sure, it took 242 years for the Ottomans to permit a press printing in the Arabic script, but time alone is not an explanation. If it were indeed the fear of losing religious legitimacy that encouraged the sultan to enact the ban in the first place, then something must have changed in the period between the initial ban and the eventual acceptance of the press. There must have been a rise in the demand for printed works, a change in the manner in which the Ottomans propagated rule, or some combination of the two.

It is possible that the demand for printed works increased between the fifteenth and eighteenth centuries. Yet, Ottoman literacy was around 2–3 percent at the beginning of the eighteenth century, and real wages were *lower* in the latter half of the eighteenth century than they were in the latter half of the fifteenth century.[31] It is therefore unlikely that demand conditions were so different in the eighteenth century as to incentivize the formation of the printing industry in the presence of restrictions imposed by the sultan. The "virtuous spiral" that propelled literacy in Western

Europe – printing decreased the cost of books, which increased access to books, which increased literacy, which increased demand for books, which triggered a supply response, and so on – never occurred in the Ottoman Empire prior to the nineteenth century.

This is not to say that there was no demand for printed works in the nineteenth century, but simply that the demand was not much greater than it had been in centuries past. In fact, the publication industry performed well enough in the nineteenth century to indicate that a market for mass printing in the Ottoman Empire was possible in the absence of restrictions by the sultan. The Ottomans eventually lifted the ban on printing on Islamic topics in 1802, and printers adopted the lithographic press soon after its invention in Germany. In 1831, the publisher Takvimhane-i Amire printed the Ottoman Empire's first official newspaper. Six new presses appeared in the ensuing decade, publishing 278 books. Publishers launched thirteen new presses in the 1840s, altogether publishing 394 books.[32] The industry was well established by the mid-nineteenth century, and the state actively supported the printing of schoolbooks, official newspapers, and administrative publications.

The spread of printing presses capable of printing in the Arabic script corresponded with two parallel developments. The first was a change in the internal organization of the religious establishment in the seventeenth century. Over the course of the century, it increasingly became the case that a cleric's connections and wealth, rather than his merit or seniority, determined whether he received a promotion within the religious hierarchy. This allowed prominent families to dominate the highest ranks over several generations. Institutionalized privilege was the norm: twelve of the forty-two Grand Muftis in the seventeenth century came from only five families. The proportion rose in the eighteenth century, with half of the fifty-eight Grand Muftis appointed between 1708 and 1839 coming from eleven families.[33] This resulted in a misalignment of incentives between the top of the mufti hierarchy and the rank and file. The latter, who were the primary conduit between the religious establishment and the people, had little incentive to publicly support the ruler, since doing so did not improve their possibility of rising in the ranks. The growing resentment of the lower members of the hierarchy therefore undermined the capacity of the hierarchy as a whole to legitimize the sultan. This altered the sultan's decision-making calculus with regards to how best to propagate his rule. With the efficacy of religious legitimacy weakened, other propagating agents became relatively more attractive sources of propagation.

The weakening of the religious establishment allowed alternative agents to increase their role in governance. Prior to the sixteenth century – an age of Ottoman expansion – the most obvious alternative was the military elite. The sultan was able to control the military by giving soldiers tax farms in newly conquered territories under the *timar* system, a system where the military elite gained wealth and power in return for collecting taxes and supporting the sultan. But once the Ottoman Empire began to contract in the late sixteenth century, the military elite were no longer a good alternative, as it was increasingly expensive to win their loyalty. Instead, the group in the best position to replace the religious establishment were the notables (*a'yan*) – local elites who were eminent tribal leaders, owned land or resources, belonged to a prominent family, or possessed other sources of social, economic, or political power. They were often the descendants of Janissaries (military elite) stationed in the provinces, and they owed their position and wealth to their heritage as well as their ability to maintain law and order.[34] Prior to the seventeenth century, the Ottomans were able to limit the power of the notables by controlling the provincial military through the *timar* system. With this option for controlling the notables no longer feasible, the Ottomans instead bargained directly with the notables to control the state's relationship with the local population, collect taxes, mobilize troops, represent local interests, maintain public order, and manage civil disputes.[35] Chapter 8 further discusses the economic consequences of this transition to propagation by the notables.

With respect to the sultan's decision to permit the printing press, the rise of the notables at the expense of the religious establishment meant that there was a fundamental change in the costs and benefits of permitting printing in the Arabic script.[36] While the notables were not necessarily beneficiaries of the printing press, its spread also did not harm them. The ability of the notables to propagate the sultan's rule depended on their capacity to provide representation and local public goods, not on a monopoly over the transmission of knowledge. Hence, the shift from propagation by the religious establishment to propagation by the notables meant that mass printing was less of a threat to the sultan. In other words, while the benefits of permitting the press did not change much between the fifteenth and eighteenth centuries, the costs of removing the restrictions – that is, the loss of religious legitimacy – decreased substantially. The sultan's actions indicate that the benefits of permitting presses printing in the Arabic script outweighed the costs, and the Ottomans consequently lifted restrictions on the press.

This history permits a brief foray into a speculative, counterfactual history of Ottoman institutional development. The rifts between the Ottoman religious elite and the rest of the religious establishment in the seventeenth and eighteenth centuries bear resemblance to the dissension within the Church at the time of the Reformation. It stands to reason that the printing press could have facilitated movements against the upper echelons of the Ottoman religious hierarchy. While we will never know the counterfactual – what *would* have happened had the Ottomans never banned the press – it is still instructive to analyze what happened with the establishment of the Ottoman printing industry in the middle of the nineteenth century. Is it possible that this was just the thing needed to provoke increased opposition to religious authorities in a manner akin to the Protestant Reformation?

In fact, soon after the printing press spread across the Islamic world in the nineteenth century, modernist thinkers proposed the first real calls for a "reform of Islam." Reforms of Islam did not aim to change the fundamental tenets of the religion, but instead reform the control of the clerical class over religion. In many ways, the reform movements resembled the Reformation. In fact, Sunni and Shi'a Muslim thinkers from the Ottoman Empire, Iran, Egypt, India, Russia, and beyond explicitly invoked Luther as a liberalizing force. For example, the renowned Indian reformer Muhammad Iqbal (1877–1938) suggested that "we are today passing through a period similar to that of the Protestant revolution in Europe, and the lesson which the rise and outcome of Luther's movement teaches us should not be lost on us."[37]

Why did a widespread call for an "Islamic Reformation" occur in the late nineteenth century rather than centuries before? Many of the grievances of the would-be reformers were applicable to the Ottoman religious hierarchy for at least a couple of centuries. There is not one simple explanation for the timing of these events, and there were multiple, mutually compatible reasons the late nineteenth century saw the first large-scale push toward a "reformation of Islam." For one, the growth of secular education in the nineteenth and early twentieth centuries provided a large base of individuals outside of the religious establishment with the human capital necessary to challenge the legitimacy of political authority. Educational reforms began throughout much of the Ottoman Empire under Selim III (r. 1789–1807) and continued throughout the nineteenth century.[38] Prior to this period, education was almost exclusively available to the religious and political elite. The spread of education to a larger part of the population broke the monopoly of religious authorities over education, especially in bigger cities such as Istanbul and Cairo. The first Ottoman secular military and bureaucracy schools opened in the early nineteenth century, and foreign language and secondary schools followed a few decades later.[39] This permitted, in the words of Felicitas Opwis (2004, p. 30), an "intellectual atmosphere that perceived traditional religious law and its exponents largely as obstacles to progress and as antithetical to modernization. Enlightenment ideas, reason, and the rational sciences were held in high esteem, while adherence to traditional authority that could not stand the test of reason were rejected as obsolete." This situation was not too different from Western Europe at the time of the Reformation, where most scholars were educated at universities, and humanist ideas permeated a new intellectual atmosphere.

A second explanation is that the Islamic world had clearly fallen behind economically by the end of the nineteenth century. Within the Ottoman Empire, foreigners and non-Muslims monopolized numerous markets, and trade capitulations given by the Ottoman government to foreign merchants further disadvantaged Muslim commerce.[40] Because of this, the relative decline of the Islamic world was a common theme in the calls for reform. For example, the noted Iranian reformer Sayyid Jamal al-Din al-Afghani (1838–1897) called for a reformation similar to Luther's so that Islamic societies would "succeed someday in breaking its bonds and marching resolutely in the path of civilization after the manner of Western society."[41] Other reformists saw the relative decline of the Islamic world as a reason to call for a return to the fundamentals of early Islam, in a manner not too different from calls by twenty-first-century groups like the Taliban.[42]

Most importantly, the spread of the printed word aided nineteenth-century Islamic reform movements. Until the 1860s, most printed books in the Islamic world were secular, and those that were religious were mostly reprints of classic texts. This meant that the flow of religious information and ideas remained monopolized by the religious establishment, who had incentive to maintain this monopoly in order to maintain their grip on their primary source of influence. This situation changed in the mid-nineteenth century. The Ottoman government set up the first permanent press in Damascus in 1865, and the Egyptian newspaper market boomed under the reign of Isma'il (r. 1863–1879).[43] This had the important effect of taking religious thought out of the hands of religious scholars. For the first time in the history of the Islamic world, the religious elite were not sole producers, interpreters, or transmitters of intellectual and religious thought. The printing press made legal, political, and religious knowledge open to interpretation by any literate person. This point is made clear by Francis Robinson (1993, p. 245):

[Printing did] serious damage to the roots of the [religious scholar's] authority … they were no longer necessarily around when the book was read to make up for the absence of the author in the text; … their monopoly of the transmission of knowledge was broken. Books … could now be consulted by any Ahmad, Mahmud or Muhammad, who could make what they will of them.

These three features – the spread of education, the relative economic stagnation of the Islamic world, and the spread of the printing press – helped establish an environment in which calls for Islamic reform were common.[44] It is unlikely that such calls would have had any impact in a previous era, even if Muslims desired such reform. The works of those who did call for reform in earlier periods are prima facie evidence of this. For example, the famous Islamic scholar Taqi ad-Din Ahmad ibn Taymiyyah (1263–1328) called extensively for reform, although, ironically, present-day conservative Islamists consider him a champion. But the impact of his calls on mainstream thought were limited, since the transmission of ideas in his day were dependent on traditional channels, particularly the madrassa system.[45]

Although some of the background and institutional details were similar, it would be a mistake to claim that the calls for an Islamic Reformation followed the same path as the Protestant Reformation. Many of the Protestants' complaints were against the practices of the pope and the centralized Church, giving the Protestants a concrete target against whom to voice their displeasure. This was not the case in the Islamic world, and for this reason the messages underlying the calls for Islamic reform did not focus on one particular body. It would thus not be wise to take the analogy between the "Islamic reform" movement and the Protestant Reformation too far, but it is still instructive to draw comparisons between the two. Both movements called for a revolt against traditional authority and institutions far removed from their initial purpose and message. In the case of the Reformation, practices such as the selling of indulgences and simony were merely the tip of the iceberg highlighting just how far removed the late medieval Church was from its origins. Islamic reformers had different types of grievances, although they similarly rejected traditional authorities. One important example was their desire for independent reasoning (*ijtihad*) to be widely practiced. While there were certainly recent precedents for the use of *ijtihad* and the "gate of *ijtihad*" was not closed in theory or in practice (see Chapter 3), the reformers believed that the opposite of *ijtihad* – following old opinions without knowledge of the bases from which it was derived (*taqlid*) – dominated discourse. Reformers such as Muhammad Abduh, Jamal al-Din al-Afghani, Rashid Rida, Sayyid Ahmad Khan, and Muhammad Iqbal blamed *taqlid* for the stagnation of the Islamic world, claiming that wider use of *ijtihad* would make Islamic law more adaptable to their present-day problems.[46]

The practical intention of both movements was to modernize religion. Although the theological arguments made by the Protestants pointed to reverting to the "original Church," in practice the Reformation's most important adherents were merchants, princes, and bourgeoisie who saw it as an opportunity to rid society of the archaic and economically detrimental institutions of the Church. Likewise, Islamic reformers such as the famous Iranian Ali Shari'ati (1933–1977) argued that Islam was "living at the end of the Medieval period," and would follow a path similar to the Protestants who "found their new destiny by destroying their old faith, and transforming traditional Catholicism to a protesting, world-minded, political, and materialist Protestantism." He went on to urge Muslims to embrace "an Islamic Protestantism similar to that of Christianity in the Middle Ages, destroying all the degenerating factors which, in the name of Islam, have stymied and stupefied the process of thinking and the fate of the society, and giving birth to new thoughts and new movements."[47]

What Could Have Been?

It is easy to ask "what could have been" when reflecting on history. What could have happened had Ottomans subjects had the ability to quickly spread the printed word centuries earlier than they actually did? It is certainly possible that local notables or other well-connected economic elite could have encouraged movements to reduce the legitimizing power of religious authorities. Had this occurred, the world would likely be a very different place today, and it is possible that an Ottoman economic resurgence could have taken place in a manner similar to what occurred in early modern England or the Dutch Republic.

Such a sequence of events never occurred. Does this mean that the Islamic world was doomed from the dawn of Islam to long-run economic stagnation? The answer is an unqualified no. It is true that the path that some European countries took was less likely to emerge in the Islamic world, although it was hardly impossible for the Ottomans, or any other Muslim polity, to follow this path. Moreover, it is also true that the path that Western Europe took to economic success is by no means the only path. Yet, this does not mean that it is useless to ignore the path that the successful Western European economies *did* take. The following two chapters take on this task, showing how two Protestant nations – England and the Dutch Republic – chartered the path to economic success, while one Catholic nation (Spain) and the Ottoman Empire lagged behind.

7

Success: England and the Dutch Republic

In the first half of the sixteenth century, Western Europe seemed primed for a takeoff. The recently discovered New World promised untold wealth, large centralized states controlled an increasingly large fiscal apparatus, and a larger portion of its population lived above subsistence. Throughout the continent, skilled workers were able to feed and clothe their families at about 1.5 to 2 times the amount necessary for subsistence, and even unskilled workers were at or slightly above subsistence in most cities. This was not destined to last, however. Over the next two to three centuries, living standards plummeted throughout most of the continent; by the late eighteenth century, even skilled workers could barely afford a subsistence-level basket of goods in most of the continent, and unskilled workers almost everywhere made below-subsistence wages.

What happened? The most accepted explanation is that European wages were artificially high in the fifteenth and sixteenth centuries because of the ravages of the fourteenth-century Black Death.[1] After one-third to one-half of the European population died in the span of a half-century, those that survived were in a good position in the labor market. Workers were scarce, and the value of labor consequently increased. This upward pressure on wages lasted for centuries; the European population did not recover back to the pre–Black Death levels until sometime in the latter half of the sixteenth century – allowing Europe to escape the "Malthusian trap" for about two centuries. In a Malthusian trap, population growth eventually wipes out economic gains from temporary shocks such as demographic or technological change. People are better off for a while – the production and consumption of goods and services per capita increases – but because they are better off, they also feel that they can have more children. Eventually, these extra mouths eat up all of the gains reaped from the initial shock, and people only stop having excess children when they near subsistence

Table 7.1 *Population-Weighted Welfare Ratios for Skilled Labor,
by Current Country*

	1500–1549	1700–1749	Change	Religion
England (UK)	2.19	2.21	0.02	Protestant
Netherlands	2.02	2.02	0.00	Protestant
Germany	1.56	1.06	–0.49	Mixed
Austria	1.87	1.33	–0.54	Catholic
Belgium	2.41	2.23	–0.18	Catholic
France	1.44	1.26	–0.18	Catholic
Italy	1.82	1.38	–0.43	Catholic
Poland	1.69	1.64	–0.05	Catholic
Spain	1.79	1.71	–0.08	Catholic

Sources: Welfare Ratios – Allen (2001); Population – Bosker et al. (2013).

income.[2] This is what purportedly happened in much of Europe beginning around the late sixteenth century. European populations eventually reached their pre–Black Death levels, at the cost of lower wages for workers.

But this is not the entire story. While real wages certainly decreased throughout most of the continent, northwestern Europe was largely able to escape this fate. The welfare ratios for skilled laborers in London and Amsterdam barely changed between the first half of the sixteenth century and the eve of industrialization (see Table 7.1). Welfare ratios remained around 2 for skilled workers up through the eve of industrialization in both cities, meaning that the average worker could afford around twice the amount necessary for subsistence. While this might not seem like a positive thing – after all, this indicates that real wages stagnated for *two centuries* in England and the Dutch Republic – these figures stand in stark contrast with the rest of Western Europe, where welfare ratios fell precipitously.

Meanwhile, the urban population of England and the Dutch Republic sky-rocketed, while it rose slowly elsewhere in Western Europe (see Table 7.2). This is yet another indicator that something was different in England and the Dutch Republic. Urban populations were among the best markers of economic success in the preindustrial world. Higher populations meant that there was the capacity to feed the urban population, and urbanites were generally engaged in the production of luxury goods or trade. Yet, premodern cities were notoriously unhealthy places to live, with death rates much higher than birth rates. Evidently, rapid immigration – driven by higher wages – was the main driver of growing urban populations. So, while England and the Dutch Republic were hardly "taking off" in the

Table 7.2 *Total Population (in 1,000s) of Ten Largest Cities, by Current Country*

	1500	1700	1800	Per annum % Change 1500–1700	Per annum % Change 1500–1800	Religion
England (UK)	88	736	1,539	1.07%	0.96%	Protestant
Netherlands	136	500	474	0.65%	0.42%	Protestant
Germany	251	368	623	0.19%	0.30%	Mixed
Belgium	275	369	357	0.15%	0.09%	Catholic
France	583	992	1,216	0.27%	0.25%	Catholic
Italy	707	1,078	1,369	0.21%	0.22%	Catholic
Spain	376	527	756	0.17%	0.23%	Catholic

Note: Only countries with at least ten cities by 1700 included.
Source: Bosker et al. (2013).

manner that the industrializing nations did after the Industrial Revolution, they *were* able to maintain the artificially high wages that followed in the aftermath of the Black Death. Of course, these wages were no longer artificially high; they became the norm, and increased even more dramatically following the onset of industrialization.

The previous chapter proposed a reason why England and the Dutch Republic were able to escape the negative economic fate that much of the rest of Europe suffered in the sixteenth and seventeenth centuries: they both adopted the Reformation, and their political institutions changed as a result. By the end of the sixteenth century, the religious elite had little capacity to legitimize rule in Protestant Europe. In order to propagate their rule, Protestant rulers turned to other, more expensive means of legitimacy. Meanwhile, in Catholic Europe and the Ottoman Empire, religion and religious institutions remained important sources of legitimacy. This is not to say that Protestant rulers refrained from cloaking their dictates in the context of religion; Queen Elizabeth I was famous for doing just this. Yet the Reformation diminished the efficacy of religious legitimation. In Protestant countries, this affected the cost-benefit analysis associated with the choice of propagating agents. While religion remained the least costly option for legitimizing rule, the Reformation dramatically reduced its benefit. Hence, Protestant kings and queens transitioned to alternative means of propagating rule.

This chapter traces these changes and their long-run economic effects. Its primary implication is that *it matters who propagates political rule.* Where propagating agents had incentives consistent with economic success, economic success was more likely to follow. Conversely, insecure property rights and minimal investment in public goods were the norm throughout much of history, because the groups that historically propagated rule – especially the religious establishment and militaries – were not overly concerned with them. This changed following the Reformation. In Protestant states, the religious establishment's loss was the economic elite's gain; the latter saw its political influence soar following the Reformation.

The remainder of this chapter overviews the consequences of these changes in the two Protestant nations that were the most successful in the post-Reformation period: England and the Dutch Republic. As late as 1500, neither one would have been an obvious candidate for an economic takeoff. England was just getting over a bloody, prolonged civil war (the War of the Roses) and was behind the Southern European powers and possibly even the Ottoman Empire in terms of military power, technology, and economic development. The northern Netherlands (modern-day Netherlands) was in a much better position to succeed than England was, but was well behind the southern Netherlands (modern-day Belgium). The great merchant and finance centers of northwestern Europe at the turn of the sixteenth century were located in Antwerp and Bruges, not Amsterdam. The southern Netherlands, which remained Catholic, was clearly in a better economic position than the northern Netherlands was. Why, then, was the seventeenth century the "Dutch century," and why did modern economic growth begin in England? How did England and the Dutch Republic escape the Malthusian pressures that ended up crushing many European economies throughout the early modern period?

Post-Reformation England

England adopted the Reformation in the 1530s under Henry VIII (r. 1509–1547). After a brief spell at attempted reconversion to Catholicism under the Catholic Queen Mary I (r. 1553–1558), England permanently adopted Anglicanism under Queen Elizabeth I (r. 1558–1603). There are some idiosyncrasies in England's history that do not generalize to all Protestant nations, but analyzing the changing church-state relations in England is especially important given its eventual economic and technological dominance.

Prior to the Reformation, English monarchs propagated their rule by two sources: the Church and Parliament. These were sometimes overlapping classes, with churchmen holding numerous seats in the House of Lords. The term "parliament" first appeared in the 1230s, and the first parliaments propagated the king by providing him tax revenue. In return, members of Parliament were able to conduct trials by their peers and had the right to reject future tax increases. Parliament consisted of three groups – the clergy, nobility, and economic elite – with the slowly growing commercial cities having their first representatives as early as 1275.[3] The role of the thirteenth-century Parliaments was limited to local tax collection. During the fourteenth and fifteenth centuries, both houses attained a legislative role as kings increasingly gave concessions in order to fund long and expensive wars. By the time that the first Tudor, Henry VII (r. 1485–1509), ascended to the throne, Parliament was a taxing, legislative, and consultative institution. The king could not make, amend, or repeal laws or impose taxes without the consent of Parliament.[4]

The Church was also a key player in the propagation regime prior to the Reformation. The importance of religious legitimation dates back at least to William the Conqueror (r. 1066–1087), who conquered England with the support of a papal blessing and a consecrated banner that gave William's conquest the aura of a religious crusade. Henry II (r. 1154–1189) secured a similar blessing for his proposed conquest of Ireland a century later. King John I (r. 1199–1216) went even further, appealing to the Church to protect him from his angry barons and agreeing to surrender his crown to the pope – with the pope returning it to John as a fief – in return for papal support. Indeed, the Church was England's only pre-Reformation organization with enough wealth and power to place it beyond the control of the monarch.[5] As the primary landholder in England, owning around 30 percent of all English land at the time of the Reformation, the Church had incentive to propagate any ruler who established law and order and protected the Church's right to its vast properties.

The Reformation came to England in part due to the idiosyncratic desires of Henry VIII, who sought a divorce from Catherine of Aragon, which the pope did not grant. Henry VIII instituted the English Reformation from the top. Unlike in the Holy Roman Empire, where political considerations mixed with local economic and religious preferences to determine whether a city adopted the Reformation, Henry VIII pushed his own brand of Protestantism through Parliament. The printing press played a relatively muted role in the spread of the Reformation in England, but this does not undermine the broader argument made in the previous chapters. By the time Henry VIII brought the Reformation to England, the press already played its role in starting a movement the Church could not stop. Henry VIII merely used it opportunistically to further his own dynastic ambitions. The unintended and unforeseen consequences of this decision are of concern here.

The Reformation permanently altered the capacity of the religious elite to legitimize the English monarch's rule. Henry VIII confiscated all Church lands and neutered the power of any churchmen who did not accept the new world order. When Henry VIII married Anne Boleyn following his divorce from Catherine, she was visibly pregnant with Elizabeth. This was a clear indication that Henry VIII believed that "the English king could determine and legitimize the future of its monarchy without authorization from Rome. [Henry] set out to rewrite history by replacing the Spanish queen with the English Anne, transferring the Tudor succession from Princess Mary to Anne's as-yet unborn baby."[6]

After Henry VIII voluntarily undermined one of his primary legitimizing agents, he turned to other agents to propagate his rule. Parliament was a natural alternative to the Church: it previously helped legitimize the Crown's controversial policies by giving them the blessing of Parliamentary authority. Consequently, Henry VIII used Parliament to legitimize his Reformation. During the 1530s, Henry VIII pushed through Parliament a series of reforms that increased both monarchical and Parliamentary power at the expense of the Church. The Ecclesiastical Appeals Act of 1532 forbade all appeals to the pope on religious or other matters,[7] the 1534 Act of Supremacy claimed for the monarch all of the powers over the Church once held by the pope,[8] the Dissolution of the Monasteries Acts of the late 1530s permitted a massive confiscation of Church property, and abbots were removed from the House of Lords in 1539–1540.[9]

These changes had enormous consequences for the types of laws established by Parliament and the Crown. One important and immediate consequence was the decade-long debate over English land and property right law. This debate centered around two acts: the Statute of Uses (1536) and the Statute of Wills (1540).[10] The nature of the debate over these laws is important, since it sheds light on the changing dynamic between the Crown and Parliament. The basis of the debate was that Henry VIII, starved for funds, sought to end a major loophole in property law that allowed property holders to avoid feudal dues. This loophole – the use – worked as follows: individual A gave "use" of his land to a trusted accomplice, individual B, who would in turn allow those designated by A to enjoy the fruits of the land upon A's death. This allowed landholders to evade feudal dues owed to the king. Under feudal law, one's heirs owed dues to the Crown for all of the land that the deceased held at the time of death. If the deceased placed his land in a use, he did not officially hold it at his death, so his heirs owed the Crown nothing.

Henry VIII wanted to stamp out evasions of feudal dues facilitated by uses. Since the landowners in the House of Commons and Lords were among the primary beneficiaries of uses, Henry VIII was unlikely to succeed by merely asking them to remove this loophole. So Henry used his influence with the courts to secure a ruling declaring that land was not devisable and that the Crown had full rights over all land.[11] This could have been disastrous for the landed elite, many of whom already had their land in use. So Henry VIII suggested a compromise: the Crown offered legislation that would once again make the use legitimate, and in return the beneficiaries of the use were subject to feudal taxation. This law passed as the Statute of Uses in 1536.

What happened following the passage of the Statute of Uses reveals just how much the Crown-Parliament dynamic changed in the years following the Reformation. After the passage of the Statute of Uses, Henry VIII faced a near-revolt by the landed elite in Parliament, who felt that Henry transgressed their rights as property holders.[12] Henry was in no position to put up a fight – Parliament was an important propagator of the Tudor line – so he relented on many of the concessions he won in the Statute of Uses. The result was the Statute of Wills (1540). This statute made land devisable by will and restricted the king's rights to one-third of the estate rather than the entire estate, as was the case under the Statute of Uses.[13] This was a monumental advance for the property rights of landholders. For one, it provided the death knell to the system of primogeniture by allowing landowners to bequeath their land to anyone they desired by writing a will. More importantly, the Statute of Wills provided an unprecedented strength and clarity to property rights. Landholders henceforth had the ability to will their land to whomever they pleased with minimal interference from, or payments to, the Crown. In the context of the Crown-Parliament relations, this was a harbinger of things to come. With the Crown relying all the more heavily on Parliament for revenue and propagation of its rule, the Crown had to cede more rights, most of which favored the economic interests of members of the House of Commons.

Greif and Rubin (2015) argue that the shift toward legitimation by Parliament persisted throughout the Tudor era, in part due to the unique circumstances in which Henry VIII's three children came to the throne. Edward VI, Henry VIII's infant son, took over the throne in 1547. As both a child and the first English monarch born a Protestant, he did not have the traditional means of legitimacy available to previous adult male heirs of the English throne. The situation was even worse for his two older sisters, Mary I and Elizabeth I. Mary I intended to reimpose Catholicism on England – often violently, hence her nickname "Bloody Mary" – while Elizabeth I intended to reintroduce Protestantism. Making matters even more difficult for them was the fact that there were open questions about their legitimacy when they came to power. Their father, Henry VIII, had both sisters officially labeled as bastards by separate acts of Parliament in 1533 and 1536,[14] which made them ineligible to inherit the throne. Henry had Mary declared a bastard when Anne Boleyn ascended to the throne in order to make way for Elizabeth, while he had Elizabeth declared a bastard after he had Boleyn's head removed. Although the Third Succession Act of 1543 revoked their status as bastards,[15] there were open questions about their rights to the throne. Both Mary I and Elizabeth I felt the need to have Parliament officially confirm the legitimacy of their title to the crown once their reigns commenced. The names of these acts were revealing: the Legitimacy of the Queen, etc. Act of 1553 and the Queen's Title to the Crown Act of 1558.[16]

The three post–Henry VIII Tudor monarchs thus came to the throne under unique circumstances. Edward VI, Mary I, and Elizabeth I lacked two of the conventional means of legitimacy that many of their predecessors had: being an adult male heir and support from the Church. In these circumstances, the Tudor monarchs attempted to claim the "divine right of kings" (or queens) to propagate their rule, but their weakened legitimacy meant that they could not rule absolutely without the support of Parliament.[17]

Members of Parliament did not support the Tudors out of the kindness of their hearts, of course. Parliamentary support of the Tudor regime came at a cost, particularly in the House of Commons. Henry VIII, Edward VI, and Elizabeth I made concessions that gave a major voice to property holders in Parliament at the expense of the religious establishment. Unlike the religious establishment, many members of Parliament had a stake in securing property rights, promoting trade, making internal improvements, and promoting general economic well-being. Under Elizabeth I, hundreds of bills concerning industry, poor relief, and agricultural use were passed. Important bills included the Statute of Artificers (1558–1563), which gave the English state many of the rights previously held by guilds; the reinstitution of usury laws, which allowed interest up to 10 percent[18]; and the 1601 Poor Law. The last of these provided a social safety net unlike any other in Europe at the time, and the economic elite strongly supported it in order to reduce vagrancy. Avner Greif and Murat Iyigun (2013) suggest that the Poor Law was essential to the long-run prosperity of England, as it gave inventors incentive to take on the risks associated with inventive activity by providing a safety net in case of failure.

Despite these concessions to the House of Commons, Elizabeth I had independent sources of revenue available to her, which gave her some leverage vis-à-vis Parliament. The most controversial of these revenues was the sale of monopolies, which gave the Crown funds at the expense of producers. Elizabeth also sold off 25 percent of the Crown's land to finance the war with Spain.[19] As long as the Crown had these independent sources of revenue, there was less incentive for it to negotiate with the House of Commons. But the problem with selling monopolies and land is that they do not provide infinite streams of revenue. Once the Crown ran out of industries to monopolize and land to sell, it went back to Parliament for funds.

Although Elizabeth I maintained some power independent of the House of Commons, Parliament clearly became a more important legitimizing, revenue-generating, and legislative institution in the course of the sixteenth century. Parliament could threaten to revoke either legitimacy or revenue if the Crown did not implement its desired laws and policies. More importantly, Parliament's increased political power and organizational capabilities permitted it to credibly threaten to revolt against any monarch who attempted to undermine it.[20]

Research that I have conducted with Avner Greif (2015), which picks up where the arguments presented in this book leave off, suggests that the change in the balance of political power following the Reformation was the source of the multiple institutional and policy changes in the seventeenth century. Specifically, our analysis suggests that the Civil Wars of the 1640s and the Glorious Revolution of 1688–1689 were conflicts over Parliament's role in legitimizing the Crown.[21] Besides providing revenue, Parliament played a key role in determining the law – that is, which actions were legitimate for the Crown to take. As long as the king followed the rule of law, as determined by Parliament, he was legitimate. We suggest, therefore, that when the Stuart kings of the seventeenth century attempted to reestablish the legitimizing power of the Catholic Church – Charles I married a Catholic princess and James II's wife birthed a Catholic heir weeks before Parliament kicked him out – Parliament had no choice but to revolt. Otherwise, the gains in wealth and propagating power they achieved under the Tudors would have been undermined.

When the dust settled in 1689, Parliament had the upper hand against a severely neutered Crown. The upshot of Greif and Rubin's analysis is that the new institutional framework imposed after the Glorious Revolution settlement enabled the Crown and Parliament to cooperate in advancing their common interests. The new institutional arrangements depended much more on the rule of law than before, with the rule of law being dictated by Parliament. This, in turn, encouraged the formulation of pro-commerce policies and laws. For instance, Greif and Rubin document how naval and trade policy reflected commercial interests during the Interregnum (1649–1660), when Parliament held executive power. In this decade, Parliament passed the Navigation Acts, ordered convoys to protect Levant Company shipping, and engaged in wars over commercial policy (the First Anglo-Dutch War [1652–1654] and the Anglo-Spanish War [1654–1660]).[22] After the Glorious Revolution, pro-growth policies were all the more evident. Dan Bogart and Gary Richardson (2009, 2011) show how Parliament reorganized land rights throughout the eighteenth century in order to make land transfers, improvements, and enclosures much more efficient and less costly, while Bogart (2011) shows that the clarity of rules and protection of property rights for those who undertook transportation improvements improved after the Glorious Revolution. This was in stark contrast to the prevailing, pre–eighteenth century property rights regime, where numerous inefficiencies existed: owners were limited in how they could exploit and improve their land, localities were inhibited from providing basic public goods, and the process of changing property rights was costly and time consuming.

The English civil wars and Glorious Revolution were not the first instances where an English monarch faced revolt from within. Just two centuries prior, the houses of Lancaster and York fought over rival claims to the throne in a series of battles known as the War of the Roses. What differentiated the Glorious Revolution and, to some extent, the civil wars from previous attempts to overthrow the Crown was that they accomplished more than the replacement of one ruling family with another. There were no real institutional changes resulting from the War of the Roses; a king with power over the economic elite replaced a different king with power over the economic elite. By contrast, the Glorious Revolution resulted in a new institutional structure. After 1689, Parliament reigned supreme over the Crown, and its interests dominated English economic and foreign policy.

The broader takeaway highlighted in Greif and Rubin is that these events were the result of a long historical process that began with Henry VIII's Reformation. It was the search for alternative sources of legitimacy under the Tudors that led to a rise in the power and wealth of Parliament, which in turn *aligned the incentives* of major governmental stakeholders with laws and policies conducive to economic success. When Parliament became supreme vis-à-vis the monarchy, it established and enforced new laws that were consistent with its own economic interests. Since these interests were also consistent with broader macroeconomic success, England was well positioned to succeed by the turn of the eighteenth century. It is not coincidental that this is precisely when and where the modern economy – and the Industrial Revolution – soon emerged.

The Reformation, the Dutch Revolt, and Economic Success

The Netherlands provides perhaps the most straightforward example of how movements away from religious legitimation can encourage economic growth. A broad overview of the history of the Dutch Revolt against Spain (1568–1648) and the shift toward Calvinism in the 1570s is strikingly consistent with the arguments made in this book. Prior to the Revolt, the Netherlands was already one of the most advanced economies in Europe. However, the center of economic activity was in the southern Netherlands – present-day Belgium – in cities such as Antwerp and Ghent. These territories remained Catholic under Spanish rule after the Revolt. Yet, soon after the Dutch States General (i.e., parliament) adopted the Reformation in the northern Netherlands, the locus of economic activity moved north to present-day Netherlands, initiating the Dutch "Golden Age." Over the ensuing century, the Dutch Republic became a superpower deeply entrenched in the political spats and colonization efforts of the other European powers. Dutch wealth, urbanization, energy consumption, population, wages, and industry all grew immensely in this period in both absolute and relative terms. Between 1550 and 1675, the fraction of the Dutch population living in urban areas increased from 24 percent to 45 percent, and a gap in real wages opened between Holland – the most economically advanced province in the Dutch Republic – and England.[23] The Dutch also took the lead in science and art; Dutch economic success provided an atmosphere in which important scientists such as Huygens and van Leeuwenhoek and artists such as Rembrandt and Vermeer thrived.

How could such a small nation become a world superpower? A number of institutional and historical features combined in this period to propel the Dutch economy. First, the Dutch had a "head start" prior to the Reformation. By 1500, the Low Countries were more highly urbanized than the rest of Europe, with a much greater portion of their workforces employed outside of agriculture. This was in part a result of progress made in Dutch agriculture in the late medieval period. Sophisticated drainage techniques and the concentrated use of manure resulted in excess food that fed the urban population.[24] In the cities, the wages of laborers and craftsmen rivaled, if not exceeded, those in England and were higher than wages in the rest of Europe.[25] Clearly specified and enforced property rights supported vast capital markets, Dutch ships and merchants dominated Baltic trade, and nonagricultural activities were almost completely oriented to international markets.[26]

There were many reasons for these developments. For one, the Burgundian rulers of the Low Countries historically discouraged monopoly privileges as well as guild and trade restrictions, all of which were drags on medieval European economies.[27] Perhaps more importantly, feudalization was less present in the Low Countries than elsewhere in medieval Europe. As early as the twelfth and thirteenth centuries, land reclamation and colonization of new areas encouraged wealthy lords to free the peasantry from feudal ties, incentivizing them to farm the new land by leasing them small farms.[28] It is true that a small feudal elite of nobles dominated political life in the late medieval period, but their small size and the relative lack of centralized authority allowed the urban economic elite to gain a larger say in government than elsewhere in Europe.[29] The result was that by 1500, the Dutch commercial cities were politically and economically important.[30]

The Dutch "head start" meant that a Golden Age may have occurred in the sixteenth and seventeenth centuries even if the Reformation had not taken hold in the Netherlands. However, other facts suggest that the Golden Age was by no means a sure thing. First, and most importantly, it was the southern Netherlands where the head start was most apparent, yet the actual Golden Age occurred in the northern Netherlands. Prior to the Golden Age, the "rich trades" in textiles, spices, metals, and sugar, which eventually dominated the economic life of the Dutch Republic in the seventeenth and eighteenth centuries, were centered in the Flemish and Brabant towns of the southern Netherlands. The northern Netherlands was not involved in the rich trades; its trade consisted of less valuable bulk goods such as fish, grains, and timber.[31] The southern Netherlands thus provides the relevant counterfactual. It hardly became an economic laggard at the time of the Dutch takeoff, and it ended up being a relatively early adopter of industrial technologies in the nineteenth century. But, unlike its northern neighbor, it was far from an economic leader in the early modern era. This result was far from preordained, and as late as the mid-sixteenth century, the southern Netherlands was in a better position to succeed than the northern Netherlands was. Is it coincidental that the Dutch shook off Spanish and Catholic domination while the southern Netherlands remained Catholic under Spanish Habsburg rule? Is it a coincidence that the Dutch Golden Age occurred in the century following the major institutional changes brought on by the Reformation and the fight for independence from Spain?

The framework laid out in this book suggests that these were not coincidences, although the framework applies differently to the Dutch case than to the English one. One difference between the two was that the Dutch Republic was not a monarchy. The Dutch states shared power; there was no central ruling apparatus. The provinces had a chief executive, the *stadhouder*, but by design he was weak relative to the provincial parliaments. Another important difference was that the power of the Dutch urban economic elite grew relative to the rural lords and Church leaders in the two centuries prior to the Revolt, as urban wealth and economic activity became an increasingly important part of the Dutch economy.[32] The pre-Reformation "players" were therefore the same in Dutch politics as they were in England, even if their relative strengths were different; in both, power was split between the Church, landed nobility, and urban economic elite.

The Dutch political situation changed dramatically during the early stages of the Revolt. The Revolt particularly affected the States General, a legislative body similar to the English Parliament, which brought together urban, noble, and religious elite from the various Dutch states. The States General originated in 1406, but it was relatively inactive under the Habsburgs prior to 1572, meeting at most for sixty days a year. Under the Habsburgs, issues of religion, military, and foreign policy were not within its purview. In 1572, however, the Revolt spurred activity in the States General. From that point on, the States General met on average around 200 days a year, and after 1593 it remained in a permanent, unbroken session.[33] The States General formalized its role in 1579, when it reestablished itself under the Union of Utrecht as a coordinating institution for the new coalition of provinces that participated in the Revolt.[34] Although the Union of Utrecht was a defensive alliance, it ended up cementing the States General's role as an exclusively Protestant coordinating and legislative body for the newly formed Dutch Republic. This gave it the power to negotiate with foreign powers, conclude treaties, mint its own coins, draft a war budget, and specify central government expenditures.[35]

The spread of the Reformation played a pivotal role in the early stages of the Revolt.[36] The Reformation took hold in the Low Countries as early as the 1520s. By this time, printing spread to most cities in the Low Countries – Antwerp was arguably the leading print city in Europe – and Protestants printed their propaganda locally. Like in much of the Holy Roman Empire, the Reformation spread via the printed word largely from the ground up, rather than from above as in England. But the Spanish violently suppressed the Reformation for decades following its initial spread. Charles V, who served as both king of Spain and Holy Roman Emperor, prohibited books, sermons, and Lutheran writings,[37] ordered hundreds of book burnings, established a state-run inquisition in 1522, and burned to death the first Protestant martyr in the world in Brussels in 1523. In all, the Spanish executed at least 2,000 Protestants.[38]

These events were important precursors to the events of the latter half of the sixteenth century. By the 1550s, various wars placed the Spanish kingdom in a tight fiscal situation despite all of the gold and silver flowing in from the New World. In response, they turned to the Netherlands for additional revenue, increasing taxes and failing to pay back loans. Not surprisingly, this fomented the seeds of dissent. Further calls by Philip II, Charles V's son, to persecute Calvinists and ban Calvinist worship helped ignite the first stage of the Revolt in the 1560s. The Catholic Church sided with the Catholic Spaniards – who claimed to be the "protectors of the true Catholic religion" – and it was thus easy for those with an economic interest in the Revolt to paint the Church as an instrument of economic and religious repression. Consequently, the expulsion of the Church and the confiscation of its wealth was one of the first actions taken in the early years of the revolt in the northern Netherlands. Bursts of anti-Catholic violence were common, and rioters destroyed Catholic relics seen as superstitious. But the Catholics were not the only group harmed by the Revolt. Many of the nobility and the guild-protected industries also threw in their lot with the Catholic Spanish regime – to their ultimate detriment.[39]

Urbanites were the driving force behind the Revolt, and they benefited from freedom from Spanish rule for many reasons. First, Protestantism spread rapidly among the merchant community in the southern Netherlands, so many of the southern merchants moved to the northern Netherlands in order to avoid repression and confiscation of their property. Second, Spanish policy toward Protestants threatened relations with foreign merchants who had Protestant sympathies. Third, city leaders had a direct monetary incentive to support the Reformation: with its success, the cities and provinces received vast clerical properties. Fourth, once the Revolt began, the urbanites' privileges of citizenship and economic autonomy were at stake if the Revolt failed. Fifth, and most important, the Revolt gave the urban elite the political upper hand within the States General.

The Reformation provided the impetus, grievances, and propaganda opportunities necessary for the urban economic elite to rise against the old guard of the nobility and the Church. Over time, religion played a relatively smaller role in the Revolt; once the initial struggle with the Spanish succeeded, economic and political motives were more important.[40] Yet, as in England, the institutional changes resulting from the Reformation were important in the long run. These events *dramatically and permanently* shifted power away from the religious establishment toward the economic elite. The consequences were even starker in the Dutch Republic than in England. Unlike in England, where the landholding nobility held onto much of its power after the Reformation, the Dutch nobility lost most of its power following the Revolt. The ultimate success of the Revolt thus meant that the Dutch economic elite gained political power that was unmatched elsewhere in Europe. To this point, Jan de Vries and Ad van der Woude (1997, p. 165) argue that the Revolt

resulted in a transformation of political representation in the provincial states from one where before the Revolt the cities had to share power with the nobles and (usually) the clergy, to a situation in which the Revolt had removed the clergy from formal political power and the nobles (many of whom remained loyal to Crown and Church) had lost much of their influence.

De Vries and van der Woude (p. 168) go on to suggest that these changes were a direct result of the Reformation coming to the Dutch Republic:

[W]ithout the Reformation political relationships would not have shifted so strongly in favor of the cities. And this shift in political constitution undergirded a state in which dynastic goals would ordinarily be subordinated to those of an urban regental elite, which never lost entirely its sensitivity to economic interests.

These dynamics were strikingly clear in the Dutch state of Zeeland, where de Vries and van der Woude (p. 507–8) point out:

[B]efore the Revolt the States of Zeeland consisted of three orders – the abbot of Middelburg, the Zeeland nobility, and the cities – each entitled to a single vote. The Reformation removed the abbot of his franchise. Since most Zeeland nobles had chosen the cause of Philip II, they, too, were stripped of their right to participate in the provincial States … [The cities of Zeeland] were the great winners in this process.

The rise of the urban economic elite after the Revolt changed the way the government financed itself. Soon after the States General held their first "free" session in 1572, the dominant urban interests imposed a fairer share of the tax burden between different industries and between urban and rural areas. Prior to 1574, urbanites paid most taxes and only a few commodities faced taxation, such as beer, wine, and peat.[41] In 1574, the number of commodities taxed expanded, and urban and rural interests paid a more even share of the tax burden. This is not surprising, given that the urban economic elite in power previously footed a disproportionate amount of the federal tax bill. The economic ramifications of the broadened tax base were immense. The Dutch government was able to collect much more tax revenue per person following the Revolt using small, highly decentralized tax farms, with the average tax burden rising from 6 percent of income at the start of the Revolt to 20 percent by 1630. Given that both the population and per capita GDP were rising, total tax revenues exploded in this period.[42]

Increased tax revenues allowed the Dutch government to borrow at lower rates, since investors felt more secure that the government had the capacity to repay them. Hence, a positive feedback loop emerged. The increased fiscal capacity of the Dutch government allowed for more revenue extraction, and this revenue further stimulated commerce. Greater commercial revenue, in turn, further expanded the tax base and lowered borrowing costs. These features fed into each other, allowing the Dutch Golden Age to persist until the end of the seventeenth century.

There were aspects of the Dutch case to which the framework elaborated in this book does not apply. There was not really a centralized Dutch "king"; the *stadhouder* hardly had the power of the English, French, or Spanish monarch. But the primary ideas spelled out in previous chapters remain true: it was the relative power of the economic elite versus the religious establishment, landed nobility, military, and other sources of power that matters. In the English case, the relative power of the economic elite mattered because they were part of the coalition that propagated the monarch, incentivizing him to exercise executive power in a manner that was consistent with their interests. The improved position of the English economic elite following the Reformation indirectly improved commercial outcomes, since this process worked through the change in incentives faced by the monarch. In the Dutch case, the amalgam of religious, military, economic, and landed elites combined to share executive power, so the increased power of the economic elite at the expense of the religious and landed elite led to a more direct improvement of economic outcomes.

The book's framework suggests that the transition to increased political power for the economic elite should have led to laws and policies that increased the level of commercial activity. Perhaps the most famous example is the establishment of the United East India Company (VOC) and the West India Company (WIC) by the States General. These were chartered joint-stock companies with the strong backing of the state – a revolutionary organizational form at the time. The charters of the VOC and WIC envisioned massive trading and military enterprises aimed at expanding Dutch economic and military power throughout the world. While these companies maintained some freedom, they were heavily dependent on the States General to conduct diplomacy, sign treaties, make alliances, provide arms, and build fortifications.[43] Shares in these companies facilitated the creation of a huge secondary market, which in turn helped make Amsterdam one of the leading capital markets of the early seventeenth century.[44] The first "modern" market for futures and options developed in Amsterdam in the early seventeenth century in response to the availability of VOC and WIC shares.[45]

The economic elite also dominated local politics, where individual cities were free to pursue policies that benefited commerce. Most cities invested in public goods such as canals and other inland transport. By the 1660s, the Dutch had the fastest and most efficient inland transportation in Europe. Although private parties sometimes funded these goods, the States General played a key role in their supervision. Improvements in transportation had the important effect of placing the Dutch Republic, and particularly Amsterdam, at the center of seventeenth-century international trade.[46] The cities also took control of poor relief, providing assistance to the working poor and seasonally unemployed. Numerous visitors to the Dutch Republic in the seventeenth century remarked on how efficient and humane the Dutch systems of poor relief and charity were relative to the rest of Europe.[47] The Reformation also affected labor markets in a more direct way: the Calvinist churches abolished all of the old saint's days promoted by the Catholic Church, extending the work year by 15 percent.[48]

Because of these initiatives, the Dutch economy took off following the Revolt. Real wages grew much faster in the Dutch Republic than in the rest of Europe. Real wages did not converge between the Netherlands and even the relatively well-off southern parts of England until the early nineteenth century. The Dutch population more than doubled in this period, with urbanization rates increasing from 31–32 percent in 1525 to 45 percent by 1675. In the two most urban provinces, Holland and Zeeland, numerous cities had growth rates over 1 percent per annum during the entirety of the Revolt, an extraordinary number in premodern times and an indicator of the high wages available in most Dutch cities (see Table 7.3). By 1600, one-quarter of the Dutch population lived in cities of at least 10,000; even in England, the number at the time was less than one out of ten.[49] It was not until the mid-nineteenth century that England reached the urbanization rates of the Golden Age Dutch Republic.

This rapid increase in real wages was in large part due to improvements in productivity. Indeed, the Republic was the most productive European economy for most of the seventeenth and eighteenth centuries.[50] During the revolt, Dutch cities actively recruited highly skilled workers from the southern Netherlands who fled the south for the relatively safer havens of the Republic. Emigration brought the "rich trades" to the Dutch Republic; a substantial portion of Flemish tapestry weavers and masters emigrated to Amsterdam, Leiden, Gouda, Middelburg, and Delft to rebuild their manufacture. The "new draperies" they produced were one of the staple industrial products of the Dutch Golden Age.[51] Protestant Germans also fled to the

Table 7.3 *Urban Population Growth during the Dutch Revolt in Holland and Zeeland, 1570–1647*

	1570	1647	Per annum % Change
Amsterdam	30,000	140,000	2.02%
Leiden	15,000	60,000	1.82%
Haarlem	16,000	45,000	1.35%
Middelburg	10,000	30,000	1.44%
Rotterdam	7,000	30,000	1.91%
Delft	14,000	21,000	0.53%
Dordrecht	10,000	20,000	0.90%
Enkhuizen	7,500	18,000	1.14%
The Hague	5,000	18,000	1.68%
Gouda	9,000	15,000	0.67%
Hoorn	7,000	14,000	0.90%

Source: Israel (1995, p. 328).

Dutch Republic during the violent Thirty Years' War (1618–1648), further increasing the stock of skilled workers. The Dutch excelled in other areas, too. Dutch hydraulic engineering and fortification and harbor construction were the envy of Europe in the seventeenth century, due in no small part to the unique geography of the Low Countries and the increased demand for land and defense.[52]

The Golden Age also saw the emergence of Dutch dominance in international markets for commodities and factors of production. Capital was abundant and interest rates remained low, stimulating Dutch industry and business organization. Property rights allowing easy alienation and transfer of property buoyed Dutch labor markets and facilitated mobility in a manner unseen even in England.[53] By the end of the Golden Age, the Dutch Republic was also a leading financial center, with Amsterdam serving as the primary European clearinghouse for bills of exchange. The Republic's centrality in trade and finance made it a hub of information flows, which in turn reinforced its central economic position.[54]

Yet, Dutch success was not destined to last forever. The mechanisms that led to an economic takeoff would not necessarily allow the takeoff to persist. The Golden Age lasted a little over a century, after which England surpassed the Dutch Republic. After the 1670s, urbanization and population growth stagnated or regressed, as did per capita income – although they remained high relative to the rest of Europe. The Netherlands was even late to industrialize; Belgium, which fell behind its northern neighbor after the Dutch Revolt, industrialized early and eventually surpassed the Netherlands in terms of production and wealth.[55] One reason for the Netherlands' relatively slow industrialization was that it was a victim of its own success; during the century of the "Golden Age," economic special interests emerged. This resulted in industrial regulations that raised obstacles for newcomers, protective measures that reduced access to foreign markets, oligarchic ruling elites cut off from other social groups, and an antiquated tax system that served the interests of a narrow swath of tax collectors.[56] While these interests served the Dutch economy well in the early part of the Golden Age, they had incentive to block creative destruction caused by industrialization.

Yet, the growth of the Dutch economy during the Golden Age placed the Netherlands in a position where, though it lagged in industrializing, it remained the most productive economy in Europe as late as the late eighteenth century and compared favorably with other industrialized economies by the end of the nineteenth century.[57] More to the point, the fact that the Netherlands was late to industrialize does not contradict this book's primary arguments. This book focuses on the various institutional mechanisms that made modern economic growth and industrialization either *possible* or *unlikely* in parts of Western Europe and the Middle East. By the seventeenth century, the Netherlands was clearly on a path where modern economic growth was possible, and this opportunity arose due to the vast changes to Dutch institutions following the Revolt and the Reformation. Why the Dutch did not see this path to fruition is a subject for an entirely different study.

Precursors of the Modern Economy

In 1500, it was far from obvious that the economic world of the next four centuries would find its locus in two small nations in northwestern Europe. But the sixteenth century was one of massive institutional change in England and the Dutch Republic. Both adopted the Reformation – in England, Henry VIII imposed the Reformation for dynastic reasons, while the Dutch Reformation was deeply entwined with the revolt against Spanish rule. Although there were differences in the specific histories of the two nations, there was one crucial similarity: in the post-Reformation world, the economic elite gained political power at the expense of the Church. The resulting institutional arrangements fostered an environment where pro-commerce policies were the norm. In England, economic interests in Parliament had more say in policy-making vis-à-vis the Church and the Crown, while in the Dutch Republic, the urban economic elite were increasingly among the most important political decision-makers at the national and local levels.

By 1600, this institutional shift affected laws and policies in England and the Dutch Republic. Sure, battles remained in both nations to ensure that the shift would last – in England the civil wars and the Glorious Revolution in 1689; in the Dutch Republic the Eighty Years' War with Spain. And the institutional shift hardly secured permanent economic dominance: the Dutch lost their worldwide economic lead to England in the eighteenth century, and England lost its lead to the United States in the twentieth century. But that is not the point. Unlike other nations that once dominated the world economy, the economic world ushered in by the Dutch Republic and England was distinctly modern, with power over laws and policies increasingly concentrated in a decentralized matrix of economic and political elites rather than religious and military elites. Understanding how this came about is a worthy undertaking, because the ultimate result was the modern economy: an economy that reduced poverty, increased the standard of living for people of all classes, and fostered an environment where sustained institutional and technological change was the norm rather than the exception.

It is one thing to analyze the histories of successful states to see what went right; it is quite another to analyze those that were once successful but ultimately stagnated. Analyzed in isolation, it is far from obvious that the path-dependent series of events that were so important to the ultimate successes of England and the Dutch Republic were as important as they were. It is just as necessary to understand why similar institutional changes did *not* occur in many parts of the world – especially those that were at one point in time in an economic position where such change was feasible. The arguments made in this book suggest that the importance of religious legitimation in the Islamic world – and, to a lesser extent, the post-Reformation Catholic world – discouraged the type of pro-commerce changes seen in England and the Dutch Republic. Given the greater weight placed on religious legitimation, it would have been unnecessary and costly for Muslim or Catholic rulers to cede rules and rights to the economic elite. The next chapter suggests that this logic sheds a great deal of light on the institutional and economic fortunes of Catholic Spain and the Muslim Ottoman Empire – two states that, as of 1500, rivaled northwestern Europe in economic and military might.

8

Stagnation: Spain and the Ottoman Empire

If one asked a knowledgeable person living in the middle of the sixteenth century which nation would be the first to undergo rapid and sustained economic growth two centuries hence, she almost certainly would not have guessed England, and although she might have guessed the Netherlands, she would have identified the locus of growth as modern-day Belgium. The Low Countries were Spanish territories anyhow, so much of the wealth would have accrued to Spanish coffers. Indeed, two very reasonable guesses, based on geopolitical power, would have been the Spanish and Ottoman Empires. These two empires were arguably the two strongest political entities of the sixteenth century. The Spanish Empire became one of the largest the world has ever known, including much of the modern United States, Mexico, Central America, numerous Caribbean islands, the western half of South America, the Philippines, southern Italy, the Low Countries, and parts of Morocco (see Figure 8.1). At its peak, the Spanish Empire covered 13.9 percent of the world's inhabitable land – the largest empire of the time and trailing only Russia and ultimately the British Empire in the early modern period (see Table 8.1). Gold and silver flowed in from the Spanish colonies in the Americas, and its territories in the Low Countries were among the world's economic powerhouses. Meanwhile, the Ottoman Empire expanded throughout the century and eventually ruled most of the North African coast, the Arabian Peninsula, the Balkan Peninsula, and most of the Middle East. These territorial gains allowed the Ottomans to control the important commercial links connecting east and west – including the Red Sea and parts of the Persian Gulf – as well as the eastern Mediterranean and Black Sea. Why shouldn't the Spanish or Ottomans have been able to turn their territorial and trade advantages into a long-run economic advantage? From the perspective of the sixteenth century, the answer to this question was far from obvious.

Table 8.1 *World's Largest Empires in the Early Modern Period*

Empire	Peak Area (Million km²)	% of World's Habitable Land
British	36.6	26.8%
Russian	22.8	16.7%
Spanish	*19.0*	*13.9%*
Qing	14.7	10.8%
French	11.2	8.2%
Portuguese	10.4	7.6%
Ming	6.5	4.8%
Ottoman	*5.6*	*4.1%*
Mughal	4.0	2.9%
Maratha	2.5	1.8%
Inca	2.0	1.5%
Lithuania-Poland	1.1	0.8%

Sources: Turchin et al. (2006); www.mtholyoke.edu/acad/intrel/empires.htm.

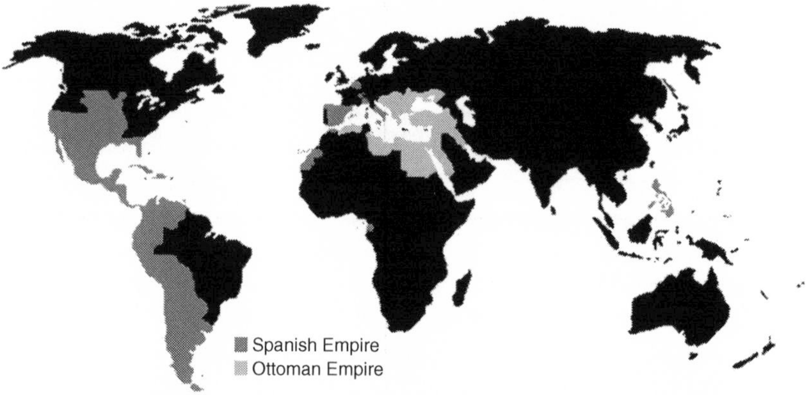

Figure 8.1 Spanish and Ottoman Empires in the Sixteenth Century

It was hardly preordained that success for both of these empires would be fleeting. As of 1500, Spanish per capita GDP was slightly higher than England's, on par with the southern Netherlands (modern-day Belgium), and trailed only the northern Netherlands and northern Italy among the European powers (see Table 8.2). Even as late as 1570, Spanish and English per capita GDP were similar, even if Spain fell behind the rest of the economic leaders. Over the next 180 years, however, Spanish per capita GDP stagnated – dropping slightly – while the wealth of the other Western European powers steadily increased (save Italy, which began the early modern period with a head start). By the end of the early modern period – and,

Table 8.2 *Per Capita GDP in Five Western European Countries, 1500–1750 (Netherlands 1750 = 100)*

Year	Spain	England	Netherlands	Belgium	Italy
1500	46–51	46	62	49	71
1570	46–51	46–48	62	59	69
1650	41–51	57	101	56	64
1700	41–47	73	100	59	61
1750	43–44	89	100	65	65

Source: van Zanden (2009, table 10).

importantly, *before* the onset of industrialization – Spanish per capita GDP was less than half of England and the Dutch Republic, and it was only around two-thirds that of Belgium and Italy.

The Ottomans underwent a similar economic degeneration. At its height in the sixteenth century, the Ottoman Empire threatened the great powers of central and southern Europe – Spain, Venice, and the Holy Roman Empire. Its incursions into Europe, while primarily military in nature, also threatened important European trade and commercial centers. Yet, by the end of the seventeenth century, the Ottomans had offered trade capitulations to many of the European powers, giving the European economic elite customs relief, legal jurisdiction, and freedom from prosecution within the empire. These capitulations were merely one of the more overt symptoms of the greater divergence that occurred between the Ottoman Empire and the leading Western European states prior to industrialization.

What happened? Why did two states that seemed at least as primed for takeoff as, say, England fall behind while Protestant northwestern Europe surged ahead? This chapter proposes that underneath the geopolitical expansion of these empires were inherent economic weaknesses traceable to the institutions that propagated political power. It was no coincidence that neither Spain nor the Ottoman Empire experienced a fundamental institutional change akin to those that occurred in Protestant nations. The mechanisms through which the Spanish and Ottoman propagated rule allowed them to ignore the economic elite, and this in turn had a detrimental effect on their long-run economic fortunes. The deterioration is explicable through the arguments made in earlier chapters. The histories of the Spanish and Ottoman Empires provide a telling counter-story to the histories of England and the Dutch Republic. In all four histories, the same message holds: *it matters who propagates political rule.* Unlike England and the Dutch Republic, however, the identity of the Spanish and Ottoman propagating agents mattered for the types of laws *not* passed.

Ironically, the strength of the Spanish monarchs and Ottoman sultans was the long-run undoing of both of their economies. Because these rulers were so strong, they did not have to bring the economic elite to the bargaining table, and they consequently never enacted the types of laws that facilitate long-run economic growth. This was the key similarity between the Spanish and Ottoman Empires that was not present in early modern England or the Dutch Republic: the Spanish monarch and the Ottoman sultan were *too* legitimate. In other words, there is some optimal middle ground for a ruler's legitimacy: a weak ruler will not have people follow him, and the benefits associated with centralized governance will be lost, while a strong ruler does not have to negotiate with the economic elite in order to propagate rule. Early modern Spain and the Ottoman Empire had the latter problem, while the relatively weak (though not too weak) legitimacy of rulers in England and the Dutch Republic fostered a situation that eventually enabled prosperity.

Long-Run Economic Stagnation in Spain

Like elsewhere in Western Europe, the propagators of the Spanish king placed constraints on what he could do and encouraged him to adopt policies to their benefit. In the language of economics, Spanish rulers faced a constrained optimization problem – they chose the best option they could given their own desires and the constraints they faced. The key point of this chapter is that the constraints faced by the Spanish Crown were fundamentally different than those faced by Dutch and English rulers. These constraints did not emerge out of thin air; they were the path-dependent results of the histories of these regions that emerged over centuries. By the sixteenth century, and especially after the Reformation, these differences were large enough that the rulers of England and the Dutch Republic were "solving" a very different problem than the Spanish Crown was. But what were these differences? Why did they emerge in the first place? What were their consequences?

Answering these questions requires historical context. Religious conflict, primarily between Christians and Muslims, was among the most important legacies of Spain's medieval history. The relevant history commenced in 711, when Muslim Umayyad warriors first entered the Iberian Peninsula. The Umayyads conquered most of the peninsula and inhabited some of the most important and wealthiest towns of the period, including Seville and

Valencia. Over the following six centuries, Christian forces slowly took back parts of the peninsula. The legacy of the reconquest established a religious dynamic in early modern Spain that existed nowhere else in Western Europe.

The manner in which the Iberian Peninsula was reconquered played a major role in structuring the institutions of Spanish government. Spanish rulers gave loyal members of the military tracts of land within recently conquered towns as a reward for their service. Since rulers relied on these newly urbanized nobles for military support, the towns gained a much greater say in governance than anywhere in Europe at the time. These events presaged similar events in northern Europe by at least two centuries. Indeed, the first European parliaments (Cortes) arose in Spain. The earliest known Cortes was in Léon in 1020, and the first one where towns had a voice was the Cortes of Burgos in 1169. The Cortes's power increased over the twelfth and thirteenth centuries, and by the reign of Ferdinand IV (r. 1295–1312) they were meeting once a year – a development that did not occur elsewhere in Europe for centuries. The Cortes of Castile – by far the most economically important region of Spain – formed in this period and consisted of the nobility, clergy, and "commons," much like the parliaments of England.

It is impossible to discuss the propagation of medieval Spanish rule while ignoring the role of religion. This is even more true of the "Catholic monarchs" Isabella of Castile (r. 1479–1504) and Ferdinand II of Aragon (r. 1479–1516). Their reign was important for numerous reasons. First, by uniting the crowns of Castile and Aragon, they mobilized enough resources to finalize the reconquest of Spain. They finished the Reconquista on January 2, 1492 with the capitulation of Granada, the last Moorish kingdom on the Iberian Peninsula. The papacy supported the Reconquista: it funded around three-quarters of the fight against Granada, and the pope crowned Ferdinand and Isabella the "Catholic Monarchs" in 1494.[1] Granada gave the Spanish crown an additional 300,000 subjects, an important new source of wealth, security on the southern coastline, and perhaps more importantly an invaluable source of prestige in the broader European "fight against Islam."

The Catholic Monarchs bolstered their religious credentials through the establishment of the Inquisition. Spain was easily the most religiously diverse region of Western Europe at the time, with hundreds of thousands of Jews and Muslims, and perhaps even more recent converts (*conversos*) intermingling with millions of Catholics. The expressed purpose of the Inquisition was to create a "unity of religion." The pope thus gave the crown the authority to root out heretics in 1478. The Inquisition terrorized Jews and *conversos* for decades, and later terrorized Muslim converts (*moriscos*), causing the death or expulsion of thousands of religious minorities.[2]

The brutal persecution of religious minorities during the Inquisition is prima facie evidence that religious legitimacy was important to the Spanish crown. This was a *costly* policy – not only in terms of establishing the institutions of the Inquisition but in the loss of human capital and labor of those who were either murdered or fled Spain as a result of persecution. But the Crown must have considered the benefits of the Inquisition greater than its costs. Such persecution could have only been beneficial for the Crown if there were something tangible to gain by tying itself to the Church. There were less expensive ways to gain religious legitimacy – endowing churches, enacting religion-friendly policy – but even a costly policy like the Inquisition still might have been optimal from the Crown's perspective if the perceived benefits were great enough. Indeed, Anderson et al. (2016) find that the persecution of Jews in medieval and early modern Europe (and especially Spain) was much more likely when weather was unseasonably bad and crops more likely to fail – precisely the type of precarious circumstance under which a ruler would want to secure as much legitimacy as possible.

The nobility also benefited from the reconquest of Spain, amassing vast amounts of recently conquered territory. The Crown neutralized them through economic and political incentives – tax exemptions, titles, grants, and the legitimation of their new landholdings and offices. This quid pro quo was great for the nobility's pocketbooks, but it also meant they had almost no bargaining power with the Crown over laws and policies.[3] Ferdinand and Isabella were also able to successfully petition Rome to support their preferred candidates for high ecclesiastical office, helping bring the Spanish religious establishment under their purview.[4]

Ferdinand and Isabella passed this institutional legacy down to their Habsburg grandson Charles V – who also became emperor of the Holy Roman Empire and inherited the crown of Spain in 1516 – and his son Philip II, who succeeded Charles in 1556. Charles V inherited the Spanish crown through his mother (Joanna the Mad), who was the daughter of Ferdinand and Isabella. He also inherited the Low Countries from his Habsburg father, Philip of Burgundy. Combined with the Spanish possessions in the New World and the Aragon possessions in Sicily, Sardinia, Naples, and northern Africa, the Habsburg kings were heirs to a global empire.

Charles V and Philip II desired above all to grow their empire. Hence they engaged Spain in numerous expensive and bloody conflicts between the large and growing European imperial powers. Spain fought nineteen wars in the sixteenth century against all of the major powers: eleven against France, eight against the Ottoman Empire, six against England, three against the Dutch, and three against Venice, among others (these numbers sum to more than nineteen due to alliances). Throughout the sixteenth century, Spain was not at war for all of eighteen years. Some of these conflicts were over religion; others were merely imperial expansion. Importantly, these wars were costly, and one of the key economic stories of the sixteenth century – in Spain as well as elsewhere in Europe – was the search for revenue to fund wars. As with England, the Dutch Republic, and other European nations, how the Spanish Crown funded these costly wars depended on the manner in which they propagated their rule and the access they had to funds beyond the control of the economic elite.

The framework proposed in this book sheds light on why and how Charles V and Philip II pursued the laws and policies that defined their reigns. Like other European rulers, Charles V and Philip II had numerous goals – gaining "glory" and wealth from the expansion and protection of territory, increasing specie production from the New World, and "battles against Islam," to name a few – and they faced budget constraints based largely on the funds they were allotted by the Cortes and the vast amount of gold and silver flowing in from the New World. The strength of their bargaining position against the Cortes was a result of the manner in which they propagated their rule. On top of being the legitimate heirs through heredity, the Habsburgs inherited the role of "Catholic monarchs." In the sixteenth century, the Spanish Crown co-opted the Spanish church, winning the right to appoint bishops. In return for these lucrative appointments, tax exemptions, and the occasional call to arms against enemies of the Church, the Church provided support to the king. For example, the see of Toledo – the second-wealthiest see in Christendom outside of Rome – granted the king 300,000 ducats for the fight against Protestant England and the rebuilding of the Spanish Armada.[5] The papacy also provided the Crown with funds from time to time. To support the Spanish fight against the Ottomans, the pope renewed the crusade subsidy (*cruzada*), which it gave to Ferdinand and Isabella in the fight against Granada, and it became a regular source of revenue.

The Crown's relationship with the Church and its role as a "protector of Christendom" goes a long way in explaining why Protestantism never took hold in Spain. Even prior to the Reformation, Ferdinand and Isabella sought to purge nonorthodox belief through the Inquisition. Charles V and Philip II continued this policy in the sixteenth century, and Philip II used the machinery of the Inquisition to stamp out any perceived Protestant sentiment seeping into Catalonia via France in the 1560s. In 1551–1552, the Inquisition published a list of prohibited Protestant books that was much more extensive than the lists produced elsewhere. Anyone suspected of even remotely deviating from Catholic orthodoxy could be branded a Lutheran and subject to torture and secret trial.[6]

The Church's support gave the Habsburgs an upper hand in their relations with the Cortes. At the beginning of Charles V's reign, the elite viewed him with suspicion as an outsider prince (Charles V grew up in Belgium and never set foot in Spain prior to his arrival as king). Nevertheless, the Cortes of Castile granted him 600,000 ducats without conditions merely for the promise that he would respect the laws of Castile and learn Spanish.[7] The Castilian economic elite's suspicion of their new king came to a boiling point in 1520, in an event known as the *comuneros* revolt. The urban lower nobility engineered this revolt against the monarchy and aristocracy, in a fashion similar to the English Civil War more than a century later. The *comuneros* had numerous grievances: they felt threatened by the growing concentration of power and wealth in the hands of the Habsburg king and a small group of nobles and clergy, they felt that Charles V's imperial ambitions threatened to subjugate Castile, and they sought more generally to curb royal and aristocratic power.[8] Unfortunately for the *comuneros*, the violent failure of their revolt exacerbated the very thing they revolted against. Since they no longer posed a threat to the king, he no longer needed to cede much to them in return for revenues. In the immediate aftermath of the revolt, a royal edict removed the power of the Cortes to withhold funds from the king or have any say in how he used his funds. After the failed revolt, the power of the monarchy was all the more concentrated and the Cortes remained "little more than a rubber stamp for the demands of the sovereign."[9] Charles V made it clear that the funds he requested were not conditional on his meeting the demands of the Cortes, telling them, "Yesterday I asked for your funds; today I want your advice."[10]

Unlike in England and the Dutch Republic, the weakened Spanish economic elite ended up having little input into the policies pursued by Charles V and Philip II. As the Holy Roman Emperor, Charles V led the opposition to the growing Protestant sentiment that spread throughout his German lands. Despite having little to do with Spanish economic or political interests, the fight against Protestants was one of Charles's top priorities. The Cortes of the Castile refused Charles money to fight in central Europe, but he was powerful and wealthy enough that this hardly affected his actions.[11] Charles also used Spanish resources in wars in the Low Countries that were ostensibly about containing Protestantism. The fight with Dutch Protestants began as early as 1521, when Charles V ordered the burning of all Lutheran books. It eventually led to the violent persecution of suspected heretics. Philip II also refused to tolerate the spread of Protestantism in the Low Countries, and he used the Inquisition to stamp out Calvinism beginning in 1565.[12] What began as religious suppression quickly spiraled into a revolt for political, economic, and religious freedom from Spanish rule (see Chapter 7). The fight against the Dutch was expensive for the Spanish Crown, and it was the primary source of sovereign default under Philip II. Philip's strained finances were readily apparent in the numerous delays in payments to Spanish troops garrisoned in the Low Countries. These troops mutinied forty-six times between 1572 and 1607, including the disastrous sack of Antwerp, where Spanish troops pillaged and virtually destroyed one of the wealthiest cities in Europe.[13]

The Spanish Crown also employed resources in conflicts with Muslims. In 1502, the Crown gave the Muslims of Castile the option to either convert to Christianity or leave, and it offered the same choice to the Muslims of Aragon in 1525. Converts (*moriscos*) were periodically harassed throughout the century and revolted in Granada in 1568–1570. The Ottomans presented an even more pressing threat against Spanish interests. For the first twenty years of Philip II's reign, the fight with the Ottomans for the Mediterranean dominated Spanish foreign policy.[14] Spain was in constant conflict with the Ottomans in the 1560s and 1570s, contesting control over North Africa and the Italian states. Spain received support from the papacy for these missions, including the *cruzada*. These wars culminated in the Battle of Leponto, where an alliance of Spain, Venice, and the papacy dealt a crushing naval blow to the Ottomans. This battle is widely viewed as the beginning of the end of Ottoman excursions into the Spanish-Italian sphere of influence in the Mediterranean. It also marked the peak of the Spanish fight against the Ottomans. After 1580, Spanish foreign policy focused much more intensely on northwest Europe.[15]

Of Philip II's forty-two years as king, Castile was at peace for all of six months. These wars were expensive – the military absorbed 60 percent of the Crown's expenditures[16] – and the story of Philip's reign was one of a search for revenue to fund these wars. Likewise, his father Charles V called the Cortes of Castile fifteen times, usually in search of funds. Although the Cortes complained about the Crown's demands, they generally gave him what he wanted without receiving much in return.[17] The Crown was successful in its negotiation with the Cortes for two related reasons: it had alternative means of propagation and alternative sources of revenue. One source of revenue was the Church, which provided funds outside the purview of the Cortes. More important, vast amounts of gold and silver flowed in from the Americas. At the peak of the treasure trade (1577–1607), treasure accounted for one-sixth to one-fourth of the Crown's total revenue, as ships coming in from America were required to pay the "royal fifth" – one fifth of the haul – into the Crown's coffers.[18] The treasure hauls also allowed the Crown to borrow large sums from Genoese and German bankers, with the treasure used as backing for the loans. These loans were not available on the open market; the Crown privately negotiated the terms with its lenders outside the purview of the Cortes. The preferred method of borrowing was through short-term loans called *asientos*, which did not require clearance from the Cortes.[19] An explosion of debt ensued. By 1600, interest payments alone were nearly three times the amount of treasure imports, and the level of outstanding debt was around five times yearly revenues.

Philip II spent more than he was taking in even with the treasure coming in from the Americas. This led him to take numerous illicit measures either to cut spending or increase revenue. His most famous illicit budget cuts entailed stopping payments to troops and failing to repay his other debts. He stopped all payments to his lenders four times, hurting his Genoese and German lenders. Bankers still lent to him in spite of his predilection for stopping payment, only because they were able to collude to cut off his access to funds when he acted poorly.[20] On the revenue side, the Crown was more than willing to confiscate private treasure when in a fiscal bind. The first confiscation occurred in 1523, when the Crown took 200,000 ducats to pay the army. The confiscations became policy over time whenever the Crown was under duress; in 1531–1534, 59 percent of the private treasure coming from America was confiscated and the entirety of the 1556 treasure fleet was confiscated.[21] The Crown also sold noble (*hidalgo*) status to those who could afford it. The rise in these grants narrowed the tax base – one of the primary reasons to attain *hidalgo* status was that nobles were tax exempt – but provided a quick source of revenue. Estimates from household censuses indicate that at least 12 percent of Spanish households had *hidalgo* status in 1542, and many more sales occurred in the following decades.[22]

How did Charles V and Philip II get away with these transgressions, which clearly harmed both the masses and the economic elite? The Cortes was not completely impotent; in fact, occasionally it was able to dictate policy when conditions were favorable. John Lynch (1991, p. 288) notes that, "given a grave issue, a popular cause, and a bankrupt government, the Cortes could find the will and the means to oppose the crown." But the fact remains that the Cortes's control over Spanish purse strings was weak. Control over funds was a primary reason that English and Dutch parliaments had so much bargaining power. In Spain, there were so many sources of revenue available to the Crown outside the purview of the Cortes of Castile – treasure from the Americas and loans from the Genoese and Germans being the two most important – that the Crown simply did not need to cede much to the economic elite.[23]

This institutional arrangement had disastrous consequences for the Spanish economic elite, and even more disastrous consequences for the wealthiest colonies in the Americas; the lingering effects of Spanish extractive institutions are still felt today in parts of Latin America.[24] Perhaps the best known short-run economic consequence of sixteenth-century Spanish policy was the rapid inflation brought on by the influx of precious metals from America. Inflationary pressures, which were much stronger in Spain than elsewhere in Europe, harmed Spanish exports. They even affected the Crown-protected wool industry.[25] The Crown also subjected the urban economic elite to an increasing tax burden.[26] The combination of additional revenue requested by the Crown and an ever-shrinking tax base meant the tax burden increasingly fell on the small urban middle class and the rural peasantry. This slowed down industrial development by directly depriving funds for investment. It also indirectly hindered industry by decreasing the size of the market for domestic goods – poor peasants do not a large market make – and by encouraging those with excess capital to invest it in land, which was tax exempt for those with titles.[27]

Another consequence of Spanish imperial policy was that most merchants who dealt in Spain were of Genoese, German, and Dutch origin. The Crown offered foreign merchants a share of the American treasure in return for access to credit. This gave foreign merchants incentive to involve themselves in Spanish trade while also giving them a privileged position in that trade.[28] But it gave them little incentive to establish their head offices in Spain. There was simply not enough commercial activity to warrant massive investments by financiers in anything but the treasure trade. So Madrid, Toledo, and Seville never became financial hubs like Amsterdam, despite all of the specie flowing into Spanish coffers. The historian Henry Kamen (2003, p. 298) argues this point succinctly: "[H]ad Spain really been the center of wealth, the great banking houses would have moved their head offices there. Instead they stayed where they were, in Antwerp, or Augsburg, or Genoa. Cities such as Lisbon, Seville, and Cartagena de Indias merited only commissioned agents."

The vast amount of American treasure also exacerbated the disincentive for the Crown to invest in industry. In the sixteenth century, Spain primarily exported raw materials, especially wool, and imported manufactured goods such as cloths and fabrics. They settled the balance of payments with ready cash from America rather than through industrial production.[29] The wars the Spanish fought against Protestants harmed these exporting industries. The Low Countries and England were the two most important export markets for Spanish wool, and trade with these countries slackened when the Spanish were at war in northwestern Europe. The negative effects of these policies were noticeable in Madrid, where a small political and aristocratic elite consumed primarily imported luxuries while the rest of the population was generally near subsistence and demanded only necessities.[30]

Other examples of Spanish economic mismanagement abound. In an attempt to lower prices, the Cortes of Castile moved in 1548 to forbid exports and encourage imports. They strengthened this law in 1552 with the enactment of a virtual prohibition of the export of goods made of wool, silk, and leather. This anti-trade policy had the effect that anyone familiar with basic economics would expect – industry suffered greatly – and the Cortes revoked the law in 1558.[31] But revocation was followed by a tax on exports, which grew further in 1564. The export tax was attractive to the Crown because it provided revenue that was outside the hands of the Cortes.[32] Unsurprisingly, these taxes further dampened Spanish economic production.

It is also hard to imagine that the expulsion of the Jews, Muslims, and Jewish and Muslim converts under the Inquisition and its aftermath had a trivial effect on the economy. Between 1609 and 1614, 275,000 *moriscos* were expelled from Spain, about a third of whom were from Castile. These *moriscos* primarily lived in towns and mostly took on undesirable menial jobs.[33] Although the economic effects of the expulsions were far from clear, they must have played a role in Spanish economic and social life. Yet another economically inhibitive religious policy was the conscious sealing off of Spanish intellectuals from the rest of the continent in the wake of the Reformation. In the 1530s, most Spanish humanist thinkers either fled Spain or were jailed by the Inquisition, and in the 1550s the Crown forbade Spanish students from attending foreign universities.[34]

Yet, as late as 1600, Spain was still an affluent country, with per capita GDP similar to England and trailing only the Low Countries and Italy in Europe (see Table 8.2).[35] But the Malthusian pressures that depressed wages and consumption throughout Western Europe, except in England and the Dutch Republic, were clearly present in Spain. At the time of Philip II's

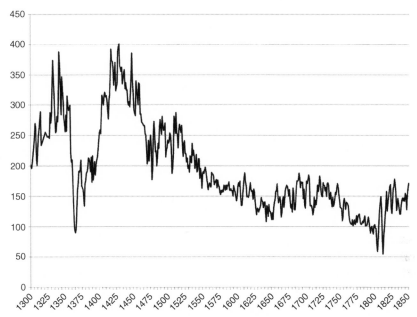

Figure 8.2 Real Wage Rates in Spain, 1300–1850 (1790s = 100)
Source: Alvarez-Nogal and de la Escosura (2013).

death in 1598, real wages were 41 percent lower than they were in the year that his father, Charles V, took the throne (1519), and per capita agriculture consumption was 24 percent lower (see Figures 8.2 and 8.3). Like most of the rest of Western Europe, Spanish real wages rose in the wake of the massive labor shortages following the Black Death in the late fourteenth century, and they fell slowly over the ensuing centuries, leveling off only in the seventeenth century.

It is puzzling that Spain did not follow a pattern similar to that of England and the Dutch Republic, especially given that Spanish per capita GDP was not far behind England's for much of the sixteenth century. Not only were England and the Dutch Republic able to avoid the Malthusian pressures that eventually crushed Spanish wages and consumption, but a massive divergence in real GDP emerged by the end of the seventeenth century between Spain and its northwest European rivals. The divergence was attributable to the fact that the features that foretell long-run economic growth were absent in sixteenth-century Spain. There was little incentive to invest Spain's newfound wealth in capital. A confluence of institutional and economic features diverted wealth elsewhere. Taxes discouraging exports and favoring landed wealth, wars with important trade partners, and the combination of rising

Figure 8.3 Real Per Capita Agricultural Consumption in Spain, 1300–1850 (1850s = 100)
Source: Alvarez-Nogal and de la Escosura (2013).

prices, stagnating wages, and increased taxes all combined to discourage investment in industry. The economic shortsightedness of such policies did not go unnoticed at the time. A group of reformers known as the *arbitristas* preached restraint on the importation of specie from the New World, the importance of manufacturing, increased political power for the economic elite, and many other reforms that would likely have halted Spain's long economic decline.[36] But this reform movement ultimately failed because the proposed measures, while good for the long-run health of the Spanish economy, did not benefit the short-run economic interests of the Crown and those that propagated its rule. Even the best philosophical arguments have difficulty making their way into policy if they do not benefit those at the bargaining table. The economic elite, who would have benefited the most from these reforms, were simply not strong enough propagators of rule in early modern Spain for these proposals to have a chance.

To reiterate, two distinct institutional features allowed the Spanish Crown to largely ignore the economic elite: its capacity to gain revenue outside the Cortes and its religious legitimacy. One could conjecture that the funds flowing in from the Americas and the Habsburgs' Italian and German bankers were the *sole* reason that the Spanish Crown was able to avoid negotiating with the Spanish economic elite. Yet, Charles V's and Philip II's actions speak loudly: they undertook *expensive* actions to gain the approval of the Church and maintain their status as the protectors of Christendom. The Inquisition was costly in terms of expenditure and loss of manpower and labor, but the Habsburgs continued to use it throughout the sixteenth century to persecute Jews and Muslims. Charles V fought the spread of the Reformation in the Holy Roman Empire with Spanish money, and Philip II continued this policy in the Low Countries. Philip II's successors, Philip III (r. 1598–1621) and Philip IV (r. 1621–1665), dragged Spain into the devastating Thirty Years War (1618–1648), which took place in Central Europe and began as a conflict between Catholic and Protestant belligerents. None of these policies were directly in Spanish interests – although they were in Habsburg interests – and they were all costly to Spain. But Spain's involvement in them makes sense in light of the Spanish Crown gaining legitimacy from the Church and in return fighting to protect the Church's interests.

In the long run, the Spanish economy declined in both absolute and relative terms.[37] By any metric of economic success, the Spanish economy struggled after the age of expansion in the sixteenth century. The average Spaniard was poorer in 1820 than in 1500, real wages did not reach their pre–Black Death levels even by the mid-nineteenth century, and consumption of agricultural goods plummeted. In relative terms, the Spanish economy also suffered. Spanish real per capita GDP was slightly higher than England's in 1570; by 1700 it was 60 percent of England's, and by 1750 it was less than 50 percent. Spanish per capita GDP was 78 percent of the Dutch in 1570 but fell to 46 percent of Dutch per capita GDP by 1650.[38] Cities also declined after the sixteenth century. The Spanish urbanization rate fell from 14.5 percent in 1591 to 13.5 percent by 1750; between 1594 and 1694, the cities of Valladolid, Toledo, and Segovia lost more than half their population.[39] The urban population only started to grow again in the late eighteenth century. This is the opposite of what occurred in England and the Netherlands, where urban populations exploded on the eve of industrialization. Even Spanish agricultural productivity declined in the seventeenth century, in sharp opposition to England, the Dutch Republic, and France, all of which achieved major productivity gains.[40]

The failure of Spain to develop an economy based on capital accumulation, secure property rights, and most of the other features generally associated with long-run economic success was among the great "lost opportunities" in European economic history. For a few generations, Spain seemed to be on the verge of breaking through and becoming an economic powerhouse of Europe. It should be clear by now that the fact that this did not happen was in part due to a deeply rooted institutional structure that did not favor economic growth. The strength of the Spanish Crown meant it rarely had to negotiate with the economic elite in order to gain revenue. This was the unfortunate irony of early modern Spain: the Crown's strength was precisely what facilitated Spanish long-run weakness.

Religious Legitimacy and Economic Stagnation in the Ottoman Empire

It is just as useful to think of the Ottoman sultan as "solving" a constrained optimization problem as it was English, Dutch, or Spanish rulers. The sultan chose the best laws and policies he could to propagate his rule, conditional on the constraints he faced from his propagating agents. However, the sultan's constraints were much different than those faced by Western European rulers, especially Protestant ones. The differences in these constraints were not random: they resulted from a long series of path-dependent processes, many of which this book highlights. This section spells out what those differences were, why they arose, and their economic consequences.

By the early sixteenth century, the Ottomans ruled over a vast and heterogeneous empire that included Arabs, Turks, Slavs, Muslims, Christians, and Jews. The differences in the ethnic and religious makeup of their many territories meant that what propagated rule effectively in some regions worked less well in others. Of course, religious legitimation by Islamic clerics was only effective where the population was largely Muslim. According to Barkan (1970), about 60 percent of Ottoman households outside of Istanbul were Muslim in the fifteenth century, although there was wide variation across the Empire. By the 1520s, the Ottomans controlled southeastern European cities with almost no Muslims, such as Athens, while other southeastern European cities were largely Muslim (see Table 8.3). Even in Anatolia (modern day Turkey), Christians made up a nontrivial portion of the population in many cities including Istanbul, which was only 58 percent Muslim. On the other hand, Muslims made up most of the population in the Arab provinces (see Table 8.4). It follows that religious authorities were good propagators of rule in some places – the Arab provinces and parts of Anatolia – but were much less effective in providing legitimacy in other areas.[41]

Over time, the Muslim population share grew in many of the previously Christian provinces, thereby increasing the efficacy of religious legitimacy. Even Athens, which had few Muslims in the beginning of the sixteenth

Table 8.3 *Religious Composition of Principal Ottoman Urban Populations, 1520–1535*

City	Muslim Share	Christian Share	Jewish Share
Turkey			
Konya	98.0%	2.0%	0.0%
Bursa	97.1%	1.1%	1.8%
Ankara	88.7%	10.2%	1.0%
Edirne	82.2%	12.9%	4.9%
Istanbul	58.3%	31.6%	10.1%
Tokat	53.9%	46.1%	0.0%
Sivas	25.8%	74.2%	0.0%
Greece			
Larissa	90.2%	9.8%	0.0%
Serres	61.4%	32.7%	5.9%
Nicopolis	37.7%	62.3%	0.0%
Trikkala	36.5%	41.6%	21.9%
Thessaloniki	25.3%	20.3%	54.4%
Athens	0.5%	99.5%	0.0%
Southeastern Europe (besides Greece)			
Monastir	75.7%	20.2%	4.0%
Skopje	74.8%	23.8%	1.4%
Sofia	66.4%	33.6%	0.0%

Sources: Barkan (1970), Westcott (2013).

Table 8.4 *Religious Composition of Certain Arab Provinces circa 1570–1590*

City	Modern Country	Muslim Share	Christian Share	Jewish Share
Basra	Iraq	100.0%	0.0%	0.0%
Aleppo	Syria	97.3%	2.6%	0.2%
Baghdad	Iraq	93.2%	5.9%	0.9%
Damascus	Syria	90.1%	7.8%	2.1%
Tripoli	Libya	76.4%	23.0%	0.6%

Sources: Barkan (1970), Westcott (2013).

century, was 29 percent Muslim by 1675. More generally, Southeastern Europe became increasingly Muslim over the course of the sixteenth and seventeenth centuries, especially in the larger cities (see Table 8.5). This increased the efficacy of religious legitimacy precisely in the places where it was least effective in the early Ottoman period.

Table 8.5 *Muslim Population Share in the Sixteenth–*
Seventeenth Centuries, Select Southeastern European Cities

City	Muslim Share, 16th century	Muslim Share, 17th century	Years of Observation
Athens	5%	29%	1540, 1675
Belgrade	29%	78%	1536, 1660
Ioannina	4%	49%	1564, 1670
Nicosia	15%	50%	1596, 1683
Prizren	40%	80%	1530, 1643
Sarajevo	27%	98%	1477, 1600
Seres	55%	70%	1500, 1659

Sources: Westcott (2013), Bearman et al. (2005).

In the fifteenth and sixteenth centuries, the Ottoman combination of military prowess and religious legitimacy allowed them to embark on expansionary conquests. The Ottomans gained military strength by bargaining with the Turcoman military elite, who supported the sultan's expansionist efforts in return for land in the newly conquered territories. As a result, the size of the Ottoman Empire expanded immensely in its first few centuries. After the initial years of expansion in the northwestern Anatolian peninsula (Turkey), the Ottomans conquered the Balkan Peninsula and the rest of the Anatolian peninsula by the mid-fifteenth century. The Ottomans expanded their empire in the sixteenth century, conquering modern-day Hungary, Romania, Moldova, Azerbaijan, Armenia, Iraq, Syria, Lebanon, Jordan, Israel, parts of the Arabian peninsula (including Mecca and Medina), and almost the entire north African coast (see Figure 8.1).

Like their Western European rivals, the Ottomans were constantly engaged in war in the sixteenth century. Wars required money, and to address their fiscal needs the Ottomans tapped the resources of their expanding provinces. Their fiscal apparatus was on par with that of the major European powers in the sixteenth century. Only France was able to collect significantly more revenue than the Ottomans did, although the powerful European states were able to extract much more per citizen than did the Ottomans (see Table 8.6). Indeed, the Ottomans had nearly three times the amount of revenue at their disposal than the English did in the 1550s, and more than twice the revenue of the Venetians, their most important rival in the struggle for dominance over the Eastern Mediterranean. Two-thirds to three-quarters of tax revenues came through the *timar*, a military lease contract whereby the provincial cavalry collected agricultural taxes directly from the peasantry as remuneration for their military services

Table 8.6 *State Revenues, 1550–1559, Annual Averages in Tons of Silver (Total) and Grams of Silver (Per Capita)*

	Total Tax Revenue	Per Capita Tax Revenue
France	151.6	10.9
Spain	107.1	19.1
Ottoman Empire	*106.1*	*5.6*
Venice	48.9	29.6
England	35.9	8.9
Poland-Lithuania	6.5	0.9

Sources: Karaman and Pamuk (2010).

to the state.[42] The *timar* system was similar to the tax collection system of feudal Europe, where local feudal lords controlled revenues in return for military service. The major benefit of the *timar* system to the Ottomans was that it allowed them to pay wages to their military despite facing currency shortages that made it impossible for peasants to pay taxes in currency. Religious jurists (*kadis*) delegated control over who could collect taxes, and all feudal incomes and privileges came only from the sultan.[43] In order to prevent these jurists and *timar* holders from becoming too powerful in a region, sultans rotated both at least every three years.[44]

Chapter 5 noted how important religious legitimacy was for the Ottomans, especially after the conquests of Constantinople (1453) and Mecca and Medina (1517). These military achievements bestowed religious legitimacy on the sultans even though they lacked a bloodline to the Prophet or Arab heritage. They bolstered their religious legitimacy by "acting Muslim" in setting laws and policies, a necessary task for any ruler claiming legitimacy from an Islamic religious establishment (see Chapter 3). The Ottomans further secured the support of the religious establishment by bringing them into the government, which gave the clerics a greater role in governance in return for their public approval of laws and policies. In the late fifteenth century, the Ottomans established the office of the Grand Mufti, a powerful position that oversaw the hierarchy of religious jurists.

Bringing the religious establishment into the state did decrease its capacity to legitimize. Perceived as under the thumb of the sultan, the religious hierarchy was not an independent source of legitimacy like the Islamic clerical class was in previous centuries. This was a calculated decision by the Ottomans, where two factors made the benefits of religious centralization within the state greater than the costs of weakened legitimizing capacity. First, the growing and heterogeneous empire required judicial decisions that favored Ottoman policy under a range of environments. By creating a hierarchy with the top positions gaining power, wealth, and prestige, the Ottomans helped incentivize jurists of all ranks to support their policies; any jurist who challenged Ottoman policy was unlikely to rise within the hierarchy. Second, and more important, the Ottomans pursued controversial policies – particularly with respect to territorial expansion – many of which flew in the face of Islam. As early as 1485, the Ottomans had their sights set on invading the Muslim Mamluk Empire, which controlled Egypt, parts of the Middle East, and the holy cities Mecca and Medina. By 1517, the Ottomans conquered the Mamluks. This war against another Muslim empire clearly needed the support of the Ottoman religious establishment, as invading and killing Muslims was much more difficult to justify within an Islamic context than invasions against states outside the world of Islam. The Ottomans soon thereafter (1532–1555) fought against another Islamic Empire on their eastern flank, the Persian Safavids. In short, these were not wars consistent with "acting like a good Muslim." It was more advantageous for the Ottomans to have a weakened religious establishment supporting its decisions than to have a strong but independent religious establishment who was unlikely to give the Ottomans support for their expansionist ambitions.

The symbiotic relationship between the sultan and religious establishment was most famously exemplified by the powerful Grand Mufti Ebu's-su'ud, who was the primary religious official under the important sultan Suleiman I (r. 1520–1566). Ebu's-su'ud was famous for harmonizing the desires of the sultan with Hanafi Islamic law, going as far as justifying the title of Caliph for Suleiman I even though the Ottomans lacked a blood connection to Muhammad and were not Arab. Ebu's-su'ud, like most other Grand Muftis, was also willing to cede to the state's needs with respect to administration: he systematized and legitimized laws of crime, property, trusts, taxation, and marriage in favor of the sultan's desires and in a manner consistent with Islamic law.[45]

The sultan's ability to manipulate the religious establishment, along with his support from the provincial military elite, had economic consequences. Unlike many Western European rulers, especially Protestant ones, the Ottomans *did not have to negotiate with the economic elite* in order to propagate their rule or attain tax revenues. This is not to say that the Ottomans never gave concessions to local landholders – they did, especially under the *timar* system. Nor is it to say that sultans never negotiated with non-Ottoman economic elite – they did, and as the Ottoman economy weakened in the eighteenth and nineteenth centuries, sultans broadened the commercial privileges of foreign merchants via capitulations. The point here is simply that the Ottoman economic elite – merchants, money changers, and manufacturers – had very little say in government policies.

This stands in stark contrast to Western European rulers, even Catholic rulers, who began to negotiate with the economic elite in parliaments as early as the twelfth century. European rulers at various times gave up some rights over property and people to the economic elite in parliaments in return for revenue and political propagation. This was especially true after the Reformation, when the Church lost its capacity to legitimize Protestant rulers. But there was no institution akin to a parliament in the Ottoman Empire. No organized groups of elites met regularly to constrain the sultan. This was in part because there were no independent cities with which to negotiate,[46] but there was also little need for the sultan to negotiate with the economic elite prior to the seventeenth century. The reason is simple: the sultan had no reason to relinquish rights to the economic elite because it could acquire revenue and legitimacy without them.

The constraints on Ottoman sultans were hardly set in stone. It is possible to see how these constraints changed over time by briefly focusing on institutional changes that occurred in the seventeenth century. The Ottoman propagating regime changed dramatically over the course of this century, as Ottoman expansion through conquest began to recede due to push back from Western Europe and the Safavid Empire. Meanwhile, the costs of warfare were increasing as the Ottomans realized the need to have a permanent standing army in order to compete with the growing European powers. Reduced access to conquest revenues and increased costs of warfare altered the Ottoman fiscal situation. By the mid-seventeenth century the Ottomans collected substantially less revenue than the major European powers did. Even though the population of the Ottoman Empire was about four times that of England and more than ten times that of the Dutch Republic, the Ottomans were able to extract less tax revenue from their citizens by the 1650s than these two nations (see Table 8.7).

For these reasons, the Ottomans decentralized both the tax collection system and local law and order in the seventeenth century. They turned to local power brokers, known as "notables" (*ayan*), to propagate their rule and collect taxes in regions that could not easily be controlled from Istanbul. The Ottomans employed notables for many purposes: collecting taxes, mobilizing troops, maintaining public order, and managing civil disputes (see Chapter 6). Notables possessed some form of local social, economic, or political power – they were *elites* – owing their position to their capacity to maintain law and order. The Ottomans initially decentralized

Table 8.7 *State Revenues in the Seventeenth Century, Annual Averages in Tons of Silver (Total) and Grams of Silver (Per Capita)*

	Total Tax Revenue		Per Capita Tax Revenue	
	1600–1609	1650–1659	1600–1609	1650–1659
Spain	430.8	412.7	62.6	57.3
France	294.2	1053.7	18.1	56.5
Ottoman Empire	*122.6*	*150.1*	*5.8*	*7.4*
Dutch Republic	116.8	213.9	76.2	114.0
Venice	67.6	68.0	37.5	42.5
England	65.7	196.1	15.2	38.7
Poland-Lithuania	15.2	39.9	1.6	5.0
Prussia	3.5	6.3	2.4	9.0

Sources: Karaman and Pamuk (2010).

their fiscal and legal capacity by granting notables the right to farm taxes for a year in return for an upfront cash payment. As fiscal demands grew, they extended the length of these contracts. Because there were no financial markets in which the state could borrow on a large scale, extending these contracts was a method that allowed the Ottomans to borrow large sums of money with future tax revenue as collateral. Beginning in 1695, the state sought large short-term payouts in return for lifetime tax farms under an institution known as the *malikane* system.

On the surface, the shift away from propagation by the religious and military elite to the notables seems similar to the post-Reformation changes that occurred in Europe, where parliaments played a larger role in financing and propagating kings. In both Protestant Europe and the Ottoman Empire, rulers ceded power in order to increase their access to revenue. However, there were two fundamental differences between the notables and Western European parliaments. For one, the notables did not collectively organize as a group, so they could not bargain with or constrain the sultan. Prior to the seventeenth century, the sultan did not need to bargain with local elites, since he was able to attain revenue and the support of the provincial military by giving them tax farms and the promise of future conquest. Individual, not group, ties were the basis for the relationship between the sultan and the military elite. The military elite did not bargain collectively for their tax farms – the sultan provided each member his own fiefdom. Unlike European rulers, who occasionally faced serious threats to their legitimacy, which forced them to bargain with the elites as a group, the Ottomans never faced a serious threat to their legitimacy after they conquered Constantinople in 1453.[47] Hence, the sultans never ceded privileges to the economic elite on the scale of their Western European counterparts. This meant that when the Ottoman fiscal situation deteriorated after their conquests ceased in the seventeenth century, there was no institutionalized collection of elites for the sultan to bargain with. So the sultans turned to the notables, who were the only people who could collect taxes without military force due to their social position.

Theoretically, the notables could have banded together to bargain with the sultan collectively. For instance, they could have consolidated their tax farms into larger farms, which would have unified their interests in opposition to the sultan. Eliana Balla and Noel Johnson (2009) note that seventeenth-century French tax farmers did so, thus acquiring the power to constrain the king. By combining their farms into a large partnership known as the Company of General Farms, French tax farmers could jointly withhold revenues from the king if he acted contrary to their wishes. Ottoman tax farmers, on the other hand, faced little incentive to act collectively in such a manner. For one, Islamic law disincentivized such partnerships. Islamic inheritance law mandates apportioning estates according to a preordained formula, and any heir could dissolve a partnership of which they inherited any part.[48] Hence, a partnership of tax farmers unknown to each other from diverse locations would have been a highly risky proposition, as any heir could have dissolved the partnership upon the death of a member.

Yet, even had Islamic law been more conducive to large partnerships, there was still less incentive for Ottoman notables to act collectively than there was for European tax farmers. The notables had power over their local population due to their family lineage – they were often descendants of Janissaries – so they were in a much better bargaining position vis-à-vis the sultan than individual European tax farmers were vis-à-vis their king. If the sultan transgressed the rights of notables or asked for exorbitant exactions, the notables could simply ignore the sultan while maintaining control over their locality. This was in fact a common occurrence. Notables frequently passed down their tax farms to their heirs instead of returning them to the state, causing the sultan to lose his ability to extract revenues from the farms. Some notables stopped sending revenues to the sultan altogether.[49] This greatly decreased the state's revenues – Ottoman tax revenues were much lower in the seventeenth and eighteenth centuries than in the previous two centuries – and it ultimately led to the failure of the *malikane* system, which the Ottomans phased out in the 1840s as part of a broader series of economic reforms.[50]

There was another important difference between the notables and members of Western European parliaments: notables were *seldom concerned with commercial activities*. Some were involved in commercial agriculture, but those notables mainly sold cash crops to Europe using Christian merchants. Still other notables were involved in trade, but this was relatively uncommon. Notables generally gained their position through the administrative ranks or through family or tribal ties – not through involvement in economic activities. Indeed, the decentralized nature of Ottoman tax farming arrangements and weak property rights over the farms created perverse incentives. Tax farming was far more lucrative than investing in agriculture, trade, or industry was. Since property rights over the tax farms were insecure – the sultan regularly confiscated tax farms in the eighteenth century – notables generally focused on extracting tax revenue at the expense of commerce. Even though more commercial activity would have meant greater future tax receipts, tax farmers had no assurance that the sultan would refrain from seizing the assets of the most successful farms.[51]

As a result, merchants, manufacturers, and money changers never gained a say in government that was close to resembling their power over local economic issues, and they certainly had much less ability to affect policy than their European counterparts.[52] The upshot was that policies favored the state and the notables at the expense of the economic elite. Policies restricting private capital accumulation and favoring state ownership of land and other property remained throughout most of the 600-year life of the empire. Property rights were highly irregular, and the sultan could revoke them in time of need. For instance, Mehmed II (r. 1444–1446 and 1451–1481) confiscated land held by both private owners and pious foundations (*waqf*) multiple times during his reign.[53] Mehmed "the Conqueror" was able to get away with such transgressions because he was one of the most legitimate rulers in Ottoman history due to his status as the "conqueror of Constantinople." But these confiscations were wildly unpopular with the many constituencies harmed by them; their magnitude alarmed even the religious establishment. This presented a problem for Mehmed II's son and successor, Bayezid II (r. 1481–1512), who did not have his father's legitimacy via personal accomplishment and needed these groups to propagate his rule. Bayezid II sought reconciliation with them and reversed many of his father's confiscations.[54] Centuries later, after the prospect of gaining additional revenues from territorial expansion became a fading memory, sultans turned back to transgressing property rights. For instance, in 1714, the sultan retracted tax farming contracts in many of the provinces, only to reinstate them three years later at 50 percent of their original bids. By the late eighteenth century, confiscations of tax farms were commonplace.[55]

This situation was fundamentally different from the one in Western Europe, and especially Protestant Europe, where the relatively weaker position of rulers required them to bargain with all of the economically powerful parties: the nobility, church, and the economic elite. Had Protestant rulers, and to a lesser extent Catholic rulers, ignored any of these three factions, they not only stood to lose tax revenue but also faced a greater threat of revolt. Yet, the irony noted in the Spanish case was even starker for the Ottomans: the sultan's strength was precisely what facilitated Ottoman long-run weakness. By relying on the notables, the Ottomans captured much of the available tax revenue while also limiting the possibility of revolt.[56] Sure, the sultan could have increased tax revenues even further by bringing the economic elite into the fold, but this would have come at the cost of ceding rights and bargaining power. Their cost-benefit calculation was different than the one faced by Protestant rulers. While this calculation incentivized Protestant rulers to make concessions to the economic elite in order to bolster their tax revenue and propagate rule, the lower benefits available to the Ottomans from doing so did not outweigh the significant costs of these concessions. In other words, the sultan's strength vis-à-vis other elites discouraged them from pursuing policies that would ultimately enrich the state.

These differences between the Ottoman Empire and Protestant nations affected the types of policies enacted in each region. Since the Ottomans did not negotiate with the economic elite, there was never much incentive to adapt commercial law codified in the Shari'a to reflect the changing needs of merchants and money changers. Doing so would have threatened the religious elite, who were the sole interpreters of religious law – and hence the sole interpreters of commercial law as codified in Islamic doctrine. Why should the sultan have undermined the clerical class – his primary source of legitimacy – for the benefit of the economic elite, a group with no seat at the bargaining table? There was simply little incentive for the Ottomans to modify commercial laws in response to changing economic circumstances, since they were able to acquire tax revenue without ceding much to the economic elite. This logic also helps explain why there was little demand from the economic elite for changes in commercial law, as noted in numerous works by Timur Kuran. If the sultan was unlikely to grant such changes in any case, why would one circumvent laws or appeal directly to the sultan, when doing so carried potential sanctions from both the religious and

political elite? Such a "double cost," as described in Chapter 2, disincentivized the economic elite from seeking changes to commercial laws.[57]

The Ottomans did, however, readily modify some laws. Since the Shari'a
was more of an ideal law and not always practicable, the *kanun* (the Law
of the Empire) supplemented the ideal with laws supporting the day-to-
day needs of the state, particularly in criminal and fiscal law. The *kanun*
and Shari'a were not always mutually consistent, and when they clashed,
the religious establishment generally found some way to cloak the sultan's desires in a veil consistent with Islamic principles. The first major
reform of the Ottoman legal code offers an example. Soon after Mehmed II
conquered Constantinople, he instituted his first legal code, which systematized tax collection across all aspects of society.[58] After his reign, the
Ottomans applied secular law in tax matters, allowing the sultan to skirt
Islamic dictates. Where tax law ran contrary to Islamic law, the sultan was
more than willing to augment the law in his favor.[59] Since the Ottomans
negotiated with individual military elite and eventually notables over tax
revenues, they had much to gain from flexibility with respect to tax law and
land tenure. There was much less to gain from flexibility in commercial law,
so the Ottomans largely allowed this to remain the purview of the religious
establishment.

Allowing religious authorities purview over commercial law affected
Ottoman commercial and financial policies as well as the type of economic
institutions and financial instruments employed by the Ottoman economic
elite. For instance, Chapter 4 noted that although merchants and lenders
were easily able to circumvent Islamic restrictions on taking interest, they
did so by incurring transaction costs that stifled the development of such
large-scale lending institutions as banks. As a result, lending remained
relatively small in scale and conducted primarily among known relations.
It was not until 1856 that the first successful bank opened, and even this
bank's financial backers were primarily British and French.

Timur Kuran spelled out in a series of articles and books numerous other
ways in which the Ottoman reliance on Islamic law in commercial transactions stifled economic growth. One of his important examples involves the
widespread use of *waqfs*, or pious trusts, in the provision of public goods.
The *waqf* functioned similarly to an English trust, but with a mission fixed in
perpetuity. *Waqfs* generally funded some immovable public good like a foun-
tain or school. This meant that if a *waqf* founder ordered that the *waqf* fund a
madrasa, then funds emanating from that *waqf* could only support *madrasa*
expenses. *Waqfs* had a religious dimension, too; the provision of a *waqf* was
viewed as a pious act, and *waqf* founders generally gained social prestige. An

unintended consequence of *waqf* law was that wealthy Muslims founded them as a means of evading inheritance laws. Since a *waqf* was a perpetual entity, one could found a *waqf* and pay a handsome sum to an heir to run it. The upshot is that the *waqf* gave wealthy Muslims a means for avoiding the splitting up of assets required by Islamic law. Kuran (2001, 2005b, 2011) argues that *waqfs* therefore absorbed capital that could have been invested in more productive pursuits, or at least in investments whose mission was not fixed.

Kuran (2005b, 2011) also argues that Islamic laws of inheritance were a primary reason that partnerships remained relatively simple throughout most of Islamic history. In both medieval Europe and the Ottoman Empire, partnerships constituted a key vehicle for combining capital and expertise. As such, they allowed for economies of scale and complementarities that would have otherwise been unavailable. Such economies of scale grew even greater as partnerships expanded to include many members. This type of growth occurred in Europe as basic partnerships (*commenda*) grew into family firms, joint-stock companies, and eventually corporations. A similar progression never occurred in the Ottoman Empire or the broader Islamic world. Indeed, Islamic partnerships remained small in scale and limited in time horizon. Kuran points to Islamic laws of inheritance and laws on partnerships as joint culprits. He notes that Islamic inheritance law split up inheritances among numerous heirs according to predetermined Qur'anic dictates, while partnerships immediately dissolved upon the death of any member. Although the heirs of a deceased partner could immediately reconstitute the dissolved partnership, the cooperation of all heirs was required. This clearly dampened the incentive to form partnerships with many members, or even to form long-lasting partnerships within a family, as was common in late medieval Italy. Whenever any member died, numerous heirs split their portion of the partnership, any of whom could prevent the partnership from continuing as it had. Hence, if any of the heirs were in a financial bind, the partnership was likely to dissolve. The dissolution could strike a major blow to partnership operations and the financial fortunes of all involved. It could force the original partners to dishonor already agreed-on contracts for lack of available funds, force the selling off of indivisible goods, or force the cancellation of operations critical to the partnership's viability, such as shipments or large purchases. The easiest way to avoid this fate was to simply avoid partnerships with many members, as each additional member increased the probability that the partnership would unexpectedly dissolve. It also discouraged partnerships engaged in long-term dealings, since the longer the horizon of the undertaking, the greater the likelihood that one of the partners would unexpectedly die.[60]

Ottoman jurists could have addressed the foregoing problem had they desired. But changes to inheritance or partnership laws would have required a reinterpretation of Islamic law, which was costly to the religious establishment because one of their key sources of influence – what made them elite – was their monopoly over the interpretation of *eternal* laws (see Chapter 2). Since such reinterpretation was costly, it would have taken a valuable reward to encourage it. But such rewards never arose, and the argument laid out earlier explains why. An equilibrium emerged where the sultan was happy to give the religious establishment purview over commercial law; the religious establishment in turn legitimized the sultan; and the economic elite remained relatively powerless. Had the sultan been in a more precarious position or relied on the economic elite for revenue, he might have modified commercial law to address their changing needs. However, the economic elite had no capacity to encourage legal changes more conducive to large, long-lasting partnerships. The two parties who interpreted and enforced the law had little interest in reinterpreting the law in such a manner.

A different process evolved in Europe, and particularly in England, where the corporate form emerged in part due to the prevalence of trusts, the closest Western equivalent to the *waqf*. The Statute of Uses (1535) encouraged English landowners to place their property into trusts that owners could use in nearly any desired manner – contrasting markedly with Islamic *waqf* law (see Chapter 7). The Statute of Wills (1540) made land devisable by will, allowing landowners to bequeath land to anyone they desired by writing a will. This too differed markedly from Islamic inheritance law, which prescribed preordained splits of inheritance. These two English laws encouraged the concentration of wealth and, over time, investment in large ventures. On the other hand, the strict and complex code of Islamic inheritance encouraged wealthy Ottoman subjects to invest their wealth in *waqf*s. *Waqf*s had the benefit of perpetual life while also allowing for asset concentration, but this came at the cost of inflexibility for trustees as economic conditions changed. The Ottomans could have avoided such problems with the types of wills and flexible trusts that emerged in post-Reformation England. Wills help prevent the fragmentation of inheritances, while flexible trusts allow heirs to invest assets efficiently. Neither of these were attributes of Islamic law, however. And since the sultan had little incentive to remove authority over commercial law from the religious establishment, partnerships remained relatively simple, exchange remained relatively personal, and the corporate form never emerged indigenously.

Unconstrained by the economic elite, the sultan had numerous tools at his disposal in times of fiscal crisis. One such tool used in the late sixteenth century, at the start of the first serious fiscal crises, was currency debasement. A major currency debasement took place in 1589, causing the Janissary corps to revolt; the sultan paid the corps in nominally fixed wages, so the debasement diminished the purchasing power of their wages. Many debasements followed, and in the 1640s, European coins replaced Ottoman coinage, which disappeared from circulation.[61] Indeed, Şevket Pamuk (2000) argues that debasements were the primary cause of increasing price levels throughout Ottoman history. The economic elite and laborers despised debasements, as they were ostensibly an additional tax on income and wealth.[62]

The Ottomans were not the only great power that debased their currency in the early modern period. Henry VIII instituted England's "Great Debasement" in 1542 in order to pay for the growing fiscal burden of war, and between 1542 and 1551, the value of English currency dropped dramatically. But there were two important points of contrast between the English and Ottoman debasements. First, Henry VIII debased the currency precisely *because* the power of Parliament had just increased with the Reformation. Debasement was one of the few fiscal policies the English Crown had at its disposal that did not require Parliament's consent. Second, the English Crown was far from immune to monetary pressures created by the debasement. Edward VI's government installed a set of reforms in 1551 to "rebase" the currency, ultimately culminating in the Elizabethan rebasement of 1560.[63]

Another feature of a well-functioning economy that was lacking in the Ottoman Empire was an impartial judicial system. Analyzing court registers from seventeenth-century Istanbul, Timur Kuran and Scott Lustig (2012) found that Islamic courts showed bias against non-Muslims and in favor of government officials. The pro-Muslim biases almost certainly stemmed from Islam's legal requirement of a higher level of evidence to prosecute Muslims than for prosecuting non-Muslims. As for the biases in favor of government officials, they were likely due to the fact that judicial appointments were made by the sultan; judges concerned about their careers sought to please litigants working directly for the sultan.[64]

Having access to courts that decide guilt based on the available evidence rather than political or social power is a fundamental determinant of the magnitude of commercial transactions in a society. A merchant is unlikely to enter into a contract with another party if he knows that his associate might renege on the contract without penalty. Hence, a partial judicial system reduces the number of mutually beneficial transactions that occur. Western Europeans solved this problem in the late medieval period with institutions such as the merchant guild and the community responsibility system, both of which incentivized rulers to provide impartial jurisprudence.[65] But these problems were not solved in the Ottoman Empire, at least until reforms were undertaken in the nineteenth century. Timur Kuran and I (Kuran and Rubin 2017) identified a further consequence of biased courts: privileged Ottoman subjects (men, Muslims, and elite) paid higher interest rates on loans than non-privileged subjects did. This is the opposite of what one expects in a modern context, where the privileged pay lower interest rates because their default risk is lower. In the Ottoman Empire, privileged borrowers were more likely to get away with reneging, so lenders imposed surcharges on them to make up for the risk associated with lending to them. We found that in the seventeenth and eighteenth centuries, men, Muslims, and elites paid about three to four percentage points higher interest on their loans, which was about one-sixth of the average interest paid for all loans. This feature of Ottoman lending markets likely exacerbated the divergence between the Ottoman and Western European economies. Since long-run economic development depends substantially on investment in capital, which itself depends in large part on the free flow of funds, the fact that the privileged paid higher interest rates indicates that those who were in the best position to invest paid the *highest* cost to do so. This must have had a dampening effect on capital accumulation in the early modern Ottoman Empire.

A final casualty of the manner in which the Ottomans propagated their rule was that Ottoman literacy remained low throughout the early modern period. As late as the nineteenth century, the Ottoman literacy rate was around 2–3 percent, while it surpassed 50 percent in England and the Netherlands by 1700, and reached at least 20 percent in the rest of Europe by 1800. Ottoman literacy rates remained strikingly low for two reasons: a low supply of books and a low demand for literacy. *Both* of these factors are attributable to the manner in which the Ottomans propagated their rule. The low supply of books resulted directly from the restrictions on presses printing in the Arabic script, which were in turn a consequence of Ottoman reliance on religious legitimation (see Chapter 5). The low demand for literacy was also a consequence of the many outcomes described in this book. As long as merchants remained engaged primarily in personal exchange, neither literacy nor numeracy were critical to conducting business. As long as the religious establishment had a monopoly on both education and the interpretation of legal and religious thought, they had incentive to restrict the number of potential challengers. And they had the capacity to do so by restricting access to madrasas, setting the curriculum for madrasas, and seeking favorable laws and policies from the sultan when necessary. Moreover, as the wages of Ottoman workers began to fall behind their Western European counterparts, the returns from literacy diverged in tandem. The vast interregional differences in literacy that emerged in the early modern period did not cause the relative Ottoman decline; rather, they were a consequence of the deeper features responsible for the divergence.

It Matters Who Propagates Rule

By now, the key point of the last two chapters should be clear: *it matters who propagates political rule*. In Spain and the Ottoman Empire, a mix of religious authorities, local power brokers, and military elite propagated rule, leaving rulers with little incentive to negotiate with the economic elite. In England and the Dutch Republic, the Reformation provided the death knell to the Church as an agent that could provide religious legitimacy, forcing (in England) the Crown to negotiate with the economic elite or (in the Dutch Republic) propelling the economic elite to a position of political power. The long-run effects of these institutional differences are clear. After the Reformation in England and the Dutch Republic, rulers and parliaments drafted laws and policies conducive to long-run economic success. These included stronger and clearer property rights, new institutions for the provision of public goods, poor relief, and investment in transportation networks. Spanish and Ottoman rulers did not undertake such reforms. Their policies gave their citizens less incentive to invest in productive pursuits, and the bases for sustained economic growth were largely missing.

These rule-propagating institutions did not arise out of thin air. Chapters 3 through 6 suggest that these institutions *evolved over centuries*, and institutional differences are traceable to the births of Islam and Christianity. This book thus provides a partial answer to two important and interrelated questions: "What does a society need to achieve economic prosperity?" and "How does a society maintain the fruits of prosperity in the long run?" The first question is a static one – at any point in time, it is possible to observe how rulers propagate their rule and analyze what this means for the types of laws and policies its government pursues. The second question is inherently historical and dynamic. Establishing the "right" institutions for sustained economic growth is an endogenous, historical process. There are many ways to get the "right" institutions, and there are many possible "right" institutional forms. For instance, the economic and political histories of England and the Low Countries are different in many ways, yet both eventually culminated in a setting conducive to growth. There is no one catch-all recipe for long-run economic success. But once the "correct" elements are in place, they tend to reinforce each other in a manner that further perpetuates economic growth, because it is in the interests of the key players for this outcome to arise. The opposite occurs when the "incorrect" elements are in place. In these settings, powerful individuals and groups perpetuate their own power and wealth at the expense of long-run economic growth, and stagnation results.

9

Conclusion

The degree to which the Middle East, and to a greater extent the Islamic world, fell behind Western Europe can be gathered by viewing a political map of the two regions in the early twentieth century. On the eve of World War I – the war that would serve as the final death knell to the long-suffering Ottoman Empire – much of the Islamic world was under the control of European powers (see Figure 9.1). France, Italy, and England split control over North Africa, and England controlled the southern Arabian Peninsula, with its important strategic position as gatekeeper of the Red Sea and Persian Gulf. Elsewhere in the Islamic world, England ruled over much of south Asia, and large swaths of central Asia were under Russian rule. The Ottoman Empire was crumbling, and tribal warfare pervaded the Arabian Peninsula.

The signs of Middle Eastern stagnation were apparent well before World War I. Even by the turn of the nineteenth century, Middle Eastern economic, technological, and military prowess had fallen visibly behind Western Europe. The Ottoman Empire was at best a peripheral economic power in the early nineteenth century and posed no serious military threat to Western Europe. An obvious symbol of its relative economic decline was the concessionary trade regime offered by the Ottoman government to the European powers at the expense of its own merchants. The economic disadvantages rooted in the capitulations were symptomatic of a much broader reversal of fortunes that were centuries in the making.

A central thesis of this book is that the environments under which Christianity and Islam were born spawned institutions that had important and unforeseen long-run consequences for the "rise of the West" and the stagnation of the Middle East. The thesis is hardly straightforward; the chain connecting the births of Islam and Christianity to economic outcomes

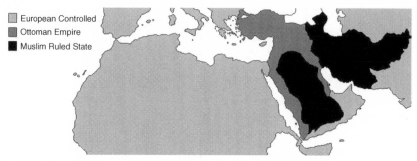

Figure 9.1 Middle East and North Africa on the Eve of World War I
Sources: Data from map available from UK National Archives, www.nationalarchives
.gov.uk/cabinetpapers/themes/maps-interactive/maps-in-time.htm

more than a millennium later has many links. A summary of the argument
follows, beginning with the first link.

The fundamental difference between Western Europe and the Middle
East explored in this book – and the *only* doctrinal difference between Islam
and Christianity that matters for the argument – is that Islamic doctrine is
more conducive to legitimizing rule than Christian doctrine is. The reason
for this doctrinal difference was the circumstances under which the religions were born. Christianity was born in the Roman Empire, which had
well-functioning legal and political institutions. Moreover, early Christians
were in no position to legitimize the Roman emperor. Islam, on the other
hand, formed initially alongside the expansion of a political state under
Muhammad. The corpus of Islamic law grew further under the empires of
the First Four Caliphs and the Umayyads – the largest empires the world
had ever seen at the time. A natural consequence of this coevolution – especially given the important religious role played by the early caliphs – was the
formation of Islamic doctrine supporting the legitimation of rule by Islam.

Subsequent Middle Eastern rulers thus had the capacity to derive legitimacy from a unifying ideology. The spread of a relatively uniform Islamic
legal framework helped foster this ideology, which could accommodate
divergent tribal interests. This had a number of beneficial consequences for
the economies of the Middle East, North Africa, and Iberian Peninsula. The
spread of Islamic political rule helped promote trade by providing greater
security for merchants, a common social and religious network, a common
currency, a common language, and common financial instruments.

Any convincing explanation for the decline of Middle Eastern economies relative to those of Western Europe must *also* explain why the
Middle East was so far ahead for so long. As we have seen, the same

feature can account for both the economic rise *and* decline of the Middle East: the strength of early Muslim rulers, due in large part to their ability to derive legitimacy from Islam, allowed Muslim-governed states to support trade in a manner unachievable by the more decentralized states of the pre-Islamic Middle East and post–Roman Europe. But this strength ultimately became a weakness. As trade expanded, new laws and policies were required for further expansion, none of which were imaginable in the context of the seventh-century economy. Yet, Middle Eastern rulers had little incentive to adopt such laws and policies. Doing so would have undermined the religious elite, who were the primary interpreters of commercial law and were largely responsible for the rulers' strength in the first place.

There was nothing predetermined about this outcome. Indeed, it was hardly unthinkable that Muslim rulers circa 1000 could have reformed Islamic law in a manner that would have benefited the economic elite. This book has provided two historical processes – one static and one dynamic – that can account for their failure to do so. The static process consists of the "game" a ruler plays to determine how to best propagate his rule. He considers the costs and benefits of different forms of propagation – both of which stem from institutions formed in the historical past – and chooses some combination of propagating agents that best help him stay in power. These choices have dynamic consequences over the long run, many of which are unforeseeable or occur so far in the future that they are of minimal concern to the ruler in the present. These consequences stem from the fact that propagating agents do not support the ruler for free – they expect some say in laws and policies in return. Their choices can have unintended, path-dependent consequences for future rulers.

Each link in the chain of these path-dependent processes makes sense in isolation, but rarely is it obvious how the end link connects to the first. This analysis is thus inherently historical. It identifies each link of a long chain, up to the ultimate outcome. Not only can this framework explain why Middle Eastern rulers had little incentive to make pro-commercial reforms circa 1000; it can *also* explain why the incentives fell over time. Moreover, it also makes sense of why Western European rulers were ultimately more incentivized to do so, especially after the Reformation. Importantly, nothing about this argument relies on old, easily dismissed arguments that Islam was antithetical to commerce or that it was inherently more conservative than Christianity. Indeed, *nothing* about this framework relies on any tenet of Islam and Christianity, except for Islamic doctrine being more conducive to legitimizing political rule.

The book first considers the static consequences of the relatively weaker capacity of Christian rulers to derive religious legitimacy. It meant that Western European and Middle Eastern rulers faced different incentives when deciding how to propagate their rule. Middle Eastern rulers derived greater benefits from religious legitimation, so they gave the religious elite an important seat at the bargaining table. In the short run, the rulers of the two regions pursued different laws and policies, especially with respect to commerce. After commerce began to revive in Western Europe in the late tenth century, merchants ran into constraints imposed by laws and policies unsuited for a commercial economy. European rulers ultimately gave the economic elite a seat at the bargaining table – at the expense of and occasionally in defiance of the Church – because the benefits of doing so outweighed the costs of less propagation from the Church. Muslim rulers faced a different set of costs and benefits from enacting laws and policies opposed by the religious elite. On the one hand, the benefits of ceding to the interests of the economic elite were actually *greater* in the Middle East for most of the medieval period than in Western Europe, as Middle Eastern economies were ahead of Western European ones. But the costs of upsetting the religious establishment were also far greater for Middle Eastern rulers, who relied more critically on clerics for legitimacy.

These static decisions made by Western European and Middle Eastern rulers had dynamic, unforeseen consequences. First, the decisions made by Western European rulers placed the Church in a no-win situation: either it would update its doctrine to reflect changing commercial needs (and risk losing its claim to hold "eternal" doctrine), or it would hold steady in the face of changing circumstances (and risk losing its moral authority). Either way, the Church's influence over its subjects, and especially the economic elite, weakened over time. Second, laws and policies favoring commerce had the unintended consequences of spurring on further economic and financial innovation. The widespread use of usurious financial instruments such as bills of exchange encouraged innovations in the structure of partnerships. In turn, these innovations ultimately led to the emergence of the banking system and the rise of impersonal exchange. These consequences arose hundreds of years after the Commercial Revolution sparked the initial changes in laws and policies, and they were unintentional and unforeseeable. Yet, it is difficult to imagine a world where the "rise of the West" would have occurred when and where it did without these initial changes. Meanwhile, in the Middle East, rulers rarely enacted laws that openly transgressed the wishes of religious authorities, and Islamic religious authorities never faced the no-win situation their Catholic counterparts did.

Thus, religious legitimation remained an important part of the propagating regime. As a result, what were once relatively small differences in the manner in which Middle Eastern and Western European rulers propagated their rule diverged immensely over time.

Another important path-dependent consequence of the differences in rule propagation involved different reactions to the spread of the printing press. From a static perspective, the responses of the Ottomans and Western Europeans are understandable given the costs and benefits of their choices. The printing press posed a threat to Islamic religious authorities: not only would it have threatened their control over information and the high barriers to producing Islamic thought; events in Western Europe showed just how quickly the press could undermine a vulnerable religious establishment. The sultan propagated his rule using a combination of religious legitimacy and military might; without the support of the religious establishment, his hold on power would have been much weaker. The Ottoman sultan therefore had an incentive to block the press. A very different sequence played out in Western Europe, where the press spread quickly after its invention in 1450. Had the Church wanted to stop its spread, it would have failed because its influence over secular rulers was relatively limited.

The dynamic, unforeseen consequences of printing were all the more important. The most monumental of these consequences was that the printing press helped facilitate the successful spread of the Reformation. Empirical tests indicate that the presence of a printing press prior to 1500 increased by 52.1 percentage points the probability that a city would become Protestant in 1530. The Reformers were successful where previous attempts at reforming the Church failed because they could spread their antipapal grievances quickly, before the Church could suppress them. Meanwhile, in the Ottoman Empire, even had there been anticlerical grievances like those expressed by the Protestant Reformers, any movement against the religious establishment was unlikely to spread quickly and was thus likely to be suppressed by the Ottoman sultan, who relied on clerics for legitimacy. In other words, the very thing that could have undermined the religious establishment – the printing press – did not spread in the Ottoman Empire *precisely because* religious legitimacy was so important.

The final link in the causal chain mapped out in this book is the connection between Protestantism and economic outcomes. A cursory reading of the argument might suggest that Protestantism is "better" for economic outcomes than Catholicism, which itself is better than Islam. Insofar as these readings make sense, they have *nothing* to do with the content of the religions. The connection between religion and economic outcomes involves the capacity of the religious elite to legitimize political rule. It was stronger in Islam than in Catholicism, and minimal in Protestantism. What was important about the Reformation, therefore, was not that it questioned the validity of certain church practices or even its religious nature. Instead, its importance lies in that it fundamentally altered the relationship between rulers and those who propagate their rule. This key point of the book has nothing to do with religion per se or, for that matter, culture in general. The argument is therefore in the spirit of Richard Tawney's (1926) classic rebuttal to Weber's "Protestant Ethic" hypothesis, which holds that the most important outcome of the Reformation was the secularization of law and political economy. Tawney's critique suggested that the Church had an ingrained anti-commercial philosophy, and capitalistic impulses spread only after the Reformation broke the Church's stranglehold over the marketplace. The argument proposed here is close in spirit to Tawney's argument, but with an important twist. Instead of focusing on how the Church affected the political and economic culture of the medieval period or on how this culture changed with the Reformation, I highlight the pathway through which religious propagation of political rule affected economic outcomes. In the process, I have answered why the religious elite had the power to affect decisions made by rulers in the first place and how this power manifested itself in policy.

The historical examples analyzed in Chapters 7 and 8 support this idea. By 1600, the manner in which rule was propagated in Protestant Northwestern Europe differed greatly from that in Catholic Europe, and even more so from that in the Middle East. In Protestant England and the Dutch Republic, the Reformation undermined the capacity of the Church to legitimize rule. As a response, rulers turned to parliaments comprised mostly of economic elites to propagate their rule and provide tax revenue. The economic elite thus obtained a seat at the bargaining table, which they used to enact laws and policies that benefited their interests. And the interests of the economic elite generally aligned more with laws and policies consistent with macroeconomic success. In England, the Crown and Parliament passed new laws providing clarity to property rights, relaxing usury laws, and improving poor relief. In the Dutch Republic, the economic elite negotiated for the provision of public goods such as vastly improved transport networks and land reclamation. Meanwhile, the Catholic Spanish Crown continued to derive legitimacy from the Church; the Pope crowned Ferdinand and Isabella the "Catholic Monarchs" for their role in the "fight against Islam." This source of legitimacy, combined with mountains of gold and silver flowing in from the Americas, allowed the Spanish Crown to essentially ignore their economic elite. The Spanish Crown therefore pursued policies that damaged economic interests at the expense of other key constituencies; examples include religious wars in the Holy Roman Empire, the Inquisition of Jews and Muslims, protection for the sheep-owners' guild, high taxes on the peasantry and urbanites, and export tariffs on key goods. In the Ottoman Empire, Islamic religious authorities had an even greater capacity to legitimize, and the sultan had little incentive to bring the economic elite to the bargaining table. This was especially true in the period of Ottoman expansion through the end of the sixteenth century, when the military elite also propagated the sultan. Ottoman merchants, manufacturers, and money changers never had a say in governance, and Ottoman policy reflected this. Property rights were relatively insecure, Islamic courts settled commercial issues, and the Ottomans frequently debased their currency.

In other words, differences in the capacity of Christian and Muslim religious authorities to legitimize rule, which arose due to circumstances surrounding the births of the two religions, had important long-run economic consequences. In the Middle East, this relationship was self-reinforcing. Middle Eastern rulers were strong, and *the very thing* that kept them strong – religious legitimation – discouraged them to negotiate with other potential propagating agents or to permit laws and policies capable of undermining the religious establishment. On the other hand, the relative weakness of Western European rulers encouraged them to engage in more costly negotiations with the economic elite. The unintended, path-dependent consequences of these negotiations further weakened the capacity of the Church to legitimize rule, especially after the Reformation. This further encouraged Western European rulers to negotiate with the economic elite. Consequently, they enacted laws and policies more beneficial to the economy.

Possible Misconceptions

Throughout the book, I attempt to discredit four misconceptions that a skeptical reader might attribute to its arguments. It is worthwhile to reconsider them in turn.

> Misconception #1: Increasing the political power of the economic elite is always good for long-run economic development.

An important part of the historical argument is that Protestant Northwestern Europe was primed for long-run economic success following the Reformation because the Church lost its propagating role to the economic elite in parliaments. A casual reader could easily take the argument to imply "economic elite = good, religious elite = bad." Far from it. The point is simply that, like the religious elite, the economic elite look after their own self-interest. It so happens that their self-interest more often encourages them to seek laws and policies that benefit the entire economy. But the incentives of the economic elite do not *always* align with laws and policies that portend economic success. Rent seeking, which is ubiquitous in every economy, offers an example. Powerful economic elite can often use their power to line their pockets through monopoly grants, government subsidies, and advantageous tax policy. Such privileges tend to create more losers than winners and end up redistributing wealth to those who already have it. Indeed, this was touched on in the overview of the eighteenth-century Dutch Republic (see Chapter 7). The Dutch rose to prominence in the seventeenth century with an economy based on trade, manufacturing, and highly productive agriculture. The economic elite played an important role in governing the Republic, and they were in large part responsible for laws and policies favoring interests in these sectors. But with economic success came special interests. After the 1670s, these interests dominated Dutch politics, pushing through industrial regulations favoring their own interests at the expense of newcomers, taxes that served a narrow slice of society disproportionately, and numerous other measures benefiting some at the expense of many.

Nothing in this book suggests, then, that giving more political power to the economic elite always improves the economy. What is true is that giving *zero* political power to the economic elite is definitely harmful to economic growth. Since other propagating agents are less likely to have interests conducive to economic success, giving those interests more say over a society's decisions will result in laws and policies less conducive to economic success. In the terms of economics, there is an "internal optimum" for the share of power held by the economic elite. The best fraction is not zero; neither is it one. Just as the economic elite's political powerlessness harmed the long-run economic fortunes of early modern Spain and the Ottoman Empire, an economy run *entirely* by corporations and wealthy power brokers could also be devastating for the vast majority of the population.

> Misconception #2: An argument that addresses why Middle Eastern economies fell behind Western European economies cannot account for the Middle East's lead over Europe during Islam's first few centuries.

This is perhaps the most frustrating misconception because I go through great pains to explain how the early expansion of the Islamic Middle East is compatible with its subsequent stagnation. It is also the misconception of readers who might ask why the book says little about the positives of Islam. Let me begin by noting that the book hardly shines a positive light on Christianity, either. This is hardly a serious criticism anyways. A good hypothesis is one that has an empirical basis, not one that skirts controversy or simply tells people what they want to hear.

This book states that in a premodern economic environment, Islam's unifying ideology provided a more favorable context for trade than the fractured regimes pervading the Middle East and Western Europe following the fall of the Roman Empire. Islam's conduciveness to legitimizing rule meant that Middle Eastern rulers were encouraged to enforce the growing corpus of Islamic law, which covered commerce and was well suited to the adjudication of premodern economic disputes. The question this book proceeds to answer is why the Middle East became "stuck" in this medieval equilibrium, which is why laws and policies barely evolved to meet the changing needs of merchants and other economic actors, needs that could not possibly have been foreseen during the first four Islamic centuries. But it would be a misreading to suggest that this is where the book's argument begins. Although many more pages are dedicated to the relative "reversal of fortunes" between the Middle East and Western Europe, the book focuses on an explanation that accounts *also* for the original ascent of the Middle East.

Misconception #3: Religion is harmful.

Writing on religion is tricky, and there is always the chance of offending. This is especially true when the primary hypothesis is that the "rise of the (Protestant) West" is in part attributable to the loss of political power for religious authorities. But nothing in the argument relies on the content of any Islamic or Christian dictates, save those that facilitate political legitimation. Moreover, the argument says absolutely nothing about the role of religion in daily life. Religion can be a powerful source of good, and it can be a powerful source of bad, especially when used to justify despicable acts. In my opinion, religion provides a net positive for the world – the benefits that it brings to individuals and communities well outweigh its costs. But my personal views are irrelevant to the argument, as is the fact that religion can be a source of both good and bad. All that matters is that religion can propagate rule.

The book does argue that religious propagation of rule is worse for long-run economic prosperity than propagation by the economic elite is. This is a falsifiable, positive statement – it is about how the world "is," not how it "should be." The argument makes no normative claims about whether economic prosperity is a good goal or not for a society. The aim of the book is to understand why the West became rich and the Middle East did not. It makes no claim at all regarding the morality of prosperity. That is the subject of an entirely different study.

It is made clear repeatedly that there is nothing *uniquely* bad about religious propagation. Indeed, propagation by military or police coercion is likely to have an equal, if not stronger, retarding impact on economic development. The reason is simple: propagating agents look after their own self-interest. This is as true of the religious elite as it is of the economic or military elite. And while the religious elite do have some interests aligned with economic success, such as keeping social order via poor relief, they have many other interests that are not, such as restrictions on taking interest. The military likewise has some interests consistent with economic success and other interests inconsistent with success. Increasing military resources may provide protection against foreign invasion or help quell social unrest. Alternatively, it can terrorize the population or keep an unpopular ruler in power. The key point is simply that the desired policies of the economic elite, based on their own self-interest, tend to align better than those of the religious elite with policies that promote economic success.

Misconception #4: The Middle East was destined to fall behind Western Europe because of the role that Islam plays in politics.

There is nothing deterministic about the argument presented in this book. History is not destiny, and it takes a major misreading to draw this implication. Instead, the framework points to what incentivized actors to make certain decisions at certain times, and to how these decisions affected the incentives of future decision-makers. There is nothing deterministic about this argument, and nothing implies that the economic paths of Western Europe and the Middle East *had* to diverge in the manner observed. Instead, it simply notes that actions of Middle Eastern and Western European rulers had unintended and unforeseen consequences for the incentives faced by future rulers, who themselves took actions that had unforeseen consequences for rulers even further in the future.

Each step in the described path-dependent chain made prosperity *more likely* to occur in Protestant Western Europe and not the Middle East. The case of the Ottomans blocking the printing press highlights the lack of determinism in these path-dependent processes. It is certainly possible that an inspired sultan could have fundamentally changed the course of economic history by permitting the press and encouraging its spread. Yet, for centuries no sultan had the right incentives. While it is by no means self-evident that long-run economic trends were reversible had the Ottomans permitted the printing press, it does provide a fascinating opportunity to conduct counterfactual history. The most direct consequence of Ottoman printing could have been the religious establishment facing opposition to its legitimizing power. The opposition could have come from the masses, the Janissary corps, or local power brokers like the notables, and it would have been relatively easy to spread an anticlerical message via the printing press. With a weakened religious establishment less capable of providing legitimacy, the Ottomans would have had incentive to bring *all* of the economically powerful parties to the negotiating table in order to propagate their rule and ensure sufficient tax collection. This probably would have included the military, notables, and economic elite. Had the Ottomans propagated their rule in this manner, then laws encouraging property rights, innovation, exploration, and economic expansion would have been more likely to arise. This counterfactual sequence of events obviously did not happen. But a lack of institutional change did not occur because of some ad hoc process or cultural conservatism. It resulted from processes deeply, though not inevitably, rooted in the historical past.

Implications for the Rise of the West

The arguments presented in this book have implications for our understanding of the "rise of the West." But there is one implication that readers should *not* take too far: very little has been said here about the specific mechanisms that led to industrialization. Indeed, the book's primary arguments attempt only to explain the larger institutional differences between Western (and northwestern) Europe and the Middle East up through the turn of the seventeenth century. The fascinating accounts of England's industrial rise put forth by renowned economic historians like Joel Mokyr and Robert Allen delve much deeper into the factors that permitted the onset of industrialization in the eighteenth century, and it is not my intention to confront these arguments.

This book has aimed to identify the preconditions of the economic revolution brought on by industrialization and to explain why, by 1600, northwestern Europe was a likely candidate for such a revolution. It places the roots of this revolution in the political changes that followed the Reformation. But I do not argue that the Reformation was an isolated, exogenous event that randomly hit certain "lucky" nations. Rather, the Reformation was the culmination of a long series of path-dependent events, each explainable by taking into account the previous step in the path and the resulting institutional environment. And while this book follows this path all the way back to the births of Christianity and Islam, most of the action occurs in the latter half of the medieval period (c. 1000–1517). It was then that the Commercial Revolution facilitated the undermining of the legitimizing relationship between church and state in Western Europe. It was also then that a deeply entrenched equilibrium arose in the Islamic world whereby religious authorities gained power at the political bargaining table due to their role as legitimizers of political authority. Finally, it was at the end of the medieval period that the printing press spread in Western Europe while the Ottomans suppressed it, for reasons entirely consistent with the manner in which rulers in both regions propagated their rule.

These were the preconditions that enabled the Reformation to take hold in certain parts of Western Europe, while a similar undermining of the religious establishment was unthinkable in the Middle East. This book therefore follows in the spirit of works by Robert Lopez, Douglass North, Avner Greif, Timur Kuran, Deirdre McCloskey, and Jan Luiten van Zanden, all of whom look for the roots of the modern economy in the medieval period. Where I depart from these scholars is in my focus on the manner in which rulers propagated their rule. The players at the bargaining table were different in Western Europe than in the Middle East, and they were ultimately different in Protestant and Catholic Europe.

The process through which this occurred was inherently historical. In other words, it was far from predetermined. Understanding the mechanisms through which it occurred is important, and not just for the sake of historical knowledge. The keys to modern wealth are still only available to a minority of the world's population, so knowing what actually did happen in England – and ultimately its followers in Europe, North America, and, much later, East Asia – provides an example of *one* path that did work.

Is this path replicable? In short, no. The nature of path-dependent processes is that one event builds on another, and random, uncontrollable events determine the exact trajectory. Would Henry VIII have brought the Reformation to England had Catherine of Aragon borne him a son or the pope granted him a divorce? We will never know. What we do know is that the unforeseen consequences of Henry VIII's decision were world-changing. Would the Dutch have had the world's leading economy in the late sixteenth and seventeenth centuries had the Spanish crushed the Dutch Revolt in its early stages (which almost happened multiple times)? Probably not: the Dutch "bargaining table" would have looked very different, with the economic elite having much less say in laws and policies.

Nevertheless, the English and Dutch cases are worth studying, even though they are not perfectly replicable. Not all of the steps along their paths were random. Many resulted from institutions whose importance is clear when contrasted with institutions of the Middle East. This is not to make the generic claim that "institutions matter," but the much more specific claim that it *matters who propagates rule.* How the English and Dutch – and, eventually, other European nations and the United States – got to the point where a "good enough" propagation regime was in place is of course critical to the story. Equally important is understanding the outcomes that followed once those regimes were in place. The latter pursuit has relevance for contemporary problems.

Implications for the Twenty-First Century and Beyond

Nearly half of the world's population lives on less than $2 a day, and around one-fifth live on less than $1 a day. Clearly the fruits of the modern economy have not spread far enough. One of the most depressing aspects of widespread poverty is that it is unnecessary. Unlike, say, five hundred years ago, humans have the technological capability to provide a comfortable lifestyle for the entirety of the world's population. Why, then, do so many people still live in abject poverty?

There are of course many answers to this question, and context clearly matters. The poverty of sub-Saharan Africa has different causes than the poverty of South or Central Asia. History, culture, and geography all play a role in separating the haves from the have-nots, and no one panacea exists for global poverty. But one thing common to most impoverished areas – as well as many wealthier but far from "developed" regions – is bad governance, especially with respect to economic issues.

This book provides a first-order reason why bad governance exists despite the presence of low-hanging economic fruits. Most of the time, it is a result of the manner in which rule is propagated. In the twenty-first century, bad governance is generally associated with propagation by a military or militia. They help keep otherwise unpopular rulers in power in return for a seat at the bargaining table. Generally this ends up meaning that their pockets are well-lined. Religious propagation is also sometimes associated with bad governance – Afghanistan and Saudi Arabia stand out as two nations whose leaders rely heavily on the support of religious authorities to the detriment of their people's economic well-being.

A skeptic might ask: Aren't some of the wealthiest countries (in per capita terms) Arab countries whose leaders rely on religious legitimacy? Indeed,

Qatar, Kuwait, and the United Arab Emirates all have higher per capita income than the average OECD country – but with one obvious caveat. *All* of the wealthy Middle Eastern countries derive most of their wealth from oil, with the exception of Turkey, which is middle income.

It is far from clear that the oil-producing nations of the Middle East are primed for long run economic success. As long as the oil is flowing, their governments can easily stay afloat, although they must distribute the oil wealth in a manner to forestall discontent. But what happens when the oil starts to run dry? Or what happens when alternative, cleaner fuels become more cost-effective – thereby driving down the demand, and therefore the price, of oil? Likewise, what happens if the price of oil drops due to excess supply?

This book provides a historical example of a case very similar to the one facing the oil-producing countries in the twenty-first century: sixteenth-century Spain. Consider the facts. The Spanish Crown received a huge wealth boost from the gold and silver flowing in from the Americas, and it received legitimacy from the Church. On that basis it could ignore the economic elite and pursue any type of policy it wanted. As a result, precious few laws and policies were enacted that protected property rights, encouraged capital accumulation, provided public goods, or supported domestic finance. Over time, the Spanish economy fell further and further behind its Western European counterparts in both relative and absolute terms. The average Spaniard was poorer in the early nineteenth century than in the sixteenth century.

The good news is that the oil-producing nations can avoid Spain's fate. The key will be to bring a wider swath of economic interests to the bargaining table – not just oil producers, but specialists in finance, trade, tourism, agriculture, manufacturing, and other services. This is all the more important for large oil-producing states, like Saudi Arabia, with populations large enough to make industrial diversification feasible. The United Arab Emirates has begun to diversify away from oil, but almost all "diversified" work is done by foreigners, who will leave if oil revenues dry up.

I am not optimistic that the large oil-producing nations will escape this fate. Their rulers are highly autocratic, and most restrict the freedom of their citizens. They are able to successfully rule in this manner – at least, for the time being – for the same reason that the sixteenth-century Spanish monarchs did so: they have independent sources of wealth as well as access to religious legitimacy. They can avoid long-run stagnation by seizing the short-term opportunity provided by oil to build economies capable of long-term success. Whether they do so remains to be seen, but history does not suggest reason for optimism.

Identifying the "problem" of the religious elite playing too much of a role in governance relative to the economic elite is one thing. It is very much another to change a society's institutions to the point where rulers have incentive to turn to the economic elite over the religious elite to propagate their rule. This book only diagnoses the problem; it does not offer a solution. It does, however, draw historical lessons that can help shape the solution.

Democracy is the most obvious contemporary solution for governance that considers the voice of the economic elite while also ensuring that their power is sufficiently constrained to keep their narrow interests from taking precedence over the rest of society. It is not much of a stretch to say that for at least the last century or two, "good" propagating arrangements were usually found in democracies, and "bad" propagating arrangements were found in non-democracies, where "good" and "bad" are used only to reflect their association with economic outcomes. Of course, not all democracies are well-functioning; India is a good example of a democracy with glaringly inefficient regulatory and legal systems. And economic improvement can certainly happen in non-democracies; China since its pro-market reforms of 1978 provides an important example.

But does this simply mean that poor, nondemocratic countries should have democracy imposed on them and everything will be flowery after that? Of course not. One cannot simply impose democracy on a country, regardless of context, and expect it to work. This is hardly an original point, although it was one the United States failed to heed in Iraq in the early 2000s. But why can't democracy simply be imposed on a society and be expected to work? What are the obstacles to transitioning to a successful democracy? This book offers some insight. Most importantly, democracy imposed by the outside can only work in a state that has institutions that are conducive to rule propagated by democratic elections. If potential rulers can rely on other sources of propagation, democracy can easily be undermined. In such a state, any enterprising outsider that enjoys the support of the religious establishment or the military can instigate the overthrow of democratically elected leaders. And even democratically elected leaders may find it hard to relinquish power if they have propagating agents at their disposal that can keep them in power.

This, more than anything else, is likely why democracy has had such a difficult time of it in the Middle East and North Africa. Of the 167 countries surveyed in the *Economist*'s 2014 Democracy Index, the most highly ranked countries in the region were Tunisia (70th) – ironically, the birth-place of the Arab Spring – and Turkey (98th). Most nations in the region fell under the category "authoritarian regime" (i.e., the least democratic type of regime): Morocco (116th), Algeria (117th), Libya (119th), Kuwait (120th), Jordan (121st), Qatar (136th), Egypt (138th), Oman (139th), Bahrain (147th), Yemen (149th), United Arab Emirates (152nd), Iran (158th), Saudi Arabia (161st), and Syria (163rd). In all of these nations, there appears to be only three possible types of propagating arrangements: brutal authoritarian rule propagated by force (e.g., Syria, Libya), oil-funded monarchies propagated by the religious establishment (e.g., Saudi Arabia, Qatar, Bahrain), or some combination of the two.

This is not surprising. Islam is highly conducive to propagating rule, and the cost of using Islam and Islamic religious authorities is much lower than using democratic elections. Indeed, it appears on the surface that the only mechanism that can support rule in the Islamic world without appeal to religion is brute force. For examples, one need look no further than the reigns of Saddam Hussein, Muammar Gaddafi, or Bashar al-Assad. One consequence of these propagating arrangements is that "imposing" democracy on an Islamic country may be a fool's errand, at least in the early twenty-first century.

This is hardly to say that Islam and democracy are incompatible with each other. The largest Muslim-majority country in the world – Indonesia – has, since 2004, held direct presidential elections. The only point made here is that political Islam is a more potent force than political Christianity. Accordingly, democracy works differently in Christian-majority countries than in Muslim-majority countries. Importantly, it is nearly impossible to imagine democracy working in the Middle East without a major role for religious authorities in the election and governing process.

It is even more difficult to see how a transition toward democracy – or any form of government that gives more political power to the economic elite – could arise *indigenously* in the Middle East unless the religious elite played an important role in governance. This is a point also made in Noah Feldman's penetrating book *The Fall and Rise of the Islamic State*. Feldman argues that the primary reason why religious legitimation was historically important in the Islamic world was that it checked the autocratic tendencies of rulers. When a series of unsuccessful nineteenth-century Ottoman reforms aimed at emulating Western forms of governance undermined the "traditional" Islamic state, the check provided by the religious establishment fell with it. This, according to Feldman, is why autocracy was the twentieth-century norm in the former Ottoman lands in North Africa and the Levant.

Feldman goes on to argue that one possible solution to bad Middle Eastern governance is democratically elected Islamic parties. These insights are consistent with the arguments of this book. Under ideal circumstances, Islamic parties could insulate themselves from religious extremism by co-opting the religious establishment while also feeling the need to bring the economic elite to the bargaining table in order to win future elections.

As of 2016, such a possibility has not come to pass and, not surprisingly, democracy has not flourished in the Middle East. One cause and consequence of this democracy deficit is that most Middle Eastern rulers are much weaker than they were historically. It may not seem so on the surface, as many of the late twentieth-century Middle Eastern leaders ruled with an iron fist. Yet, as the Arab Spring revealed, autocrats who rely primarily on military propagation are susceptible to revolt. And the rulers of the "oil states" are vulnerable to declines in the price of oil. One consequence of this relative weakness, and one of the themes laid out in Chapters 5 and 6, is that Middle Eastern rulers often restrict freedoms – particularly access to information on the Internet – to keep power out of the hands of potential rivals. Those chapters argued that efforts to monopolize information were successful in the early modern Middle East because it was in the interest of rulers and their propagating agents to inhibit the spread of information. If such anti-technology motivations were present in the fifteenth and sixteenth centuries, they are present even more visibly in the twenty-first century, where information technology allows for subversive ideas to spread in milliseconds.

Indeed, the Islamic world has been at the forefront of Internet censorship. While censorship certainly exists in non-Muslim authoritarian regimes (e.g., China, North Korea), it is especially in vogue for governments of Muslim-majority countries. By 2015, regimes in Iran, Syria, Afghanistan, Pakistan, Turkmenistan, Tajikistan, Libya, Bangladesh, and Sudan blocked YouTube. Facebook is highly censored in Iran, Saudi Arabia, Turkmenistan, Uzbekistan, and Syria. In Turkey, the Erdoğan regime attempted to ban Twitter and YouTube. The reason for these restrictions is similar in all cases: rulers simply cannot control social media, and threats to their power can spiral out of their control. The Arab Spring is the most potent example of what can happen when censorship weakens. What began with the self-immolation of Mohamed Bouazizi – a Tunisian street-vendor who was fed up with the government confiscating his goods – spread like wildfire throughout the Middle East and North Africa.

Although the Arab Spring was not successful everywhere it spread – the Bahrain government repressed it, it triggered a savage civil war in Syria, and it created a power vacuum in Egypt and Libya – its contagion was in no small part due to the power of social media to instantaneously spread information. Social media provides citizens the ability to coordinate protests and, more importantly, coordinate information about each other's preferences vis-à-vis their governments. The latter type of information frightens authoritarian governments the most. Throughout most of the history of the Islamic world, the power to coordinate opinion on all sorts of issues was normally the purview of religious authorities. This is what made them so powerful, and it was among the reasons why rulers were so eager to bring them to the bargaining table.

Can social media undermine religious authority in the twenty-first-century Islamic world in the same manner that the printing press undermined the Church in large parts of Western Europe in the sixteenth century? The obstacles are larger in the Middle East than they were in Western Europe. But twenty-first-century information technology is also much more potent than it was in the sixteenth century. The Reformation took decades to spread and even longer to fundamentally undermine propagating arrangements. If twenty-first-century information technology is going to have a similar effect in the Islamic world, it is reasonable to expect that it will transform society much more quickly. This, of course, is a big "if": numerous powerful groups, including religious authorities, have an interest in maintaining the status quo. Even if revolts undermine the status quo propagation regime, it is far from clear who will fill the power vacuum: the Egyptian and Iraqi experiences suggest that radicalized Islamic groups will play an important role in the power struggle. Nevertheless, a fundamental change in the manner in which rulers propagate their rule – spurred on by information technology – seems to be the primary hope in the Middle East for the emergence of institutions where the economic elite play some role in propagating rule. Whether or not this happens is one of the most important determinants of the twenty-first-century economic fortunes of the Middle East.

Concluding Thoughts

There is nothing about Islam per se that led to the economic stagnation of the Middle East except its conduciveness to legitimizing political rule. To be clear, this legitimate use of Islam by political rulers is very different from its misuse to "justify" the actions of violent jihadists in al Qaeda, the Taliban, or Islamic State. Islam is as open to misinterpretation and misuse as its Abrahamic brethren, Christianity and Judaism. Islam is no more culpable than religion itself for its cynical misuse. There will always be some type of ideology available to justify power grabs. In some parts of the world, it is Islam. In other parts it is some other religion or secular ideology.

Too many Westerners confuse correlation with causation when connecting Islam with terrorism or anti-Westernism. Those who think that Islam offers a uniquely violent ideology need only read the Old Testament to see the falsity of those claims. A simple thought experiment further illustrates this confusion. Imagine a world – say, an imaginary twenty-third century – in which the Middle East is the world's economic and military powerhouse: Middle Eastern governments are constantly interfering in European and American politics while Middle Eastern militaries are ubiquitous throughout the West. Poverty is common in the West, and autocratic rule is the norm. Is it really too difficult to imagine Western sentiment focusing on the "Middle Eastern devil," as some Middle Eastern sentiment is focused on the "American devil" in the twentieth and twenty-first centuries? Is it at all a stretch to think that anti–Middle Eastern sentiment would appeal to Christianity? I do not believe it is at all. After all, this imaginary world is not too different from the one faced by Europeans around the time of the Crusades, although with eleventh-century technology and less direct conflict between European and Middle Eastern states.

There is nothing about Islam per se that is anti-Western, antidemocratic, or anti–economic growth. Anti-Western sentiment in the Middle East results mainly from imperial policies, colonization, Western support of ruthless dictators, bloody one-sided conflicts, and Western extraction of resources – not Islam. Islam provides a nice and simple cover for such sentiment, but it is not its source. Instead, the sources of these sentiments lie in the factors that allowed the "West" to rise in the first place. The purpose of this book has been to shed some light on these factors. In the process, it hopefully has contributed to our understanding of which factors are actually important to economic stagnation and political instability, and which factors are merely symptoms of stagnation and instability.

There is room for cautious optimism for the future of the Middle East and the broader Islamic world, and this optimism links closely to economic activity. Where Muslims have had a taste for the much higher standards of living associated with the modern economy, rulers have found that sound economic management can be a powerful source of propagation, and their citizens place less importance on their religious credentials. Complete integration with the world economy will not be easy, and many powerful vested interests stand to lose their seat at the bargaining table. But integration still stands as the best hope to spring

the Middle East into a "virtuous cycle" whereby prosperity encourages changes in the manner in which rulers propagate their rule, which
encourages more prosperity and so on. This means integration well
beyond trading oil, arms, and a few other goods. It means political integration. It means a reduction of the role of the religious elite in politics,
but not at the expense of ceding to authoritarian rule. It probably means
democracy, or at least some hybrid form of it. Most importantly, it means
some political power for the economic elite. It is far from clear whether
Middle Eastern nations will take this path in the twenty-first century.
Too many unknowable future events could trigger a path in any direction, although it is likely that the price of oil will play a role in determining the shape of this path. History gives us reason to be both pessimistic
and optimistic. Time will tell which sentiment is correct.

Notes

1 Introduction

1 I use the term "Middle East" somewhat broadly throughout this book, comprising North Africa, the entire Arab world, Iran, Turkey, and Islamized Spain under Umayyad rule. Essentially, I use the term to represent the Islamic world west of South Asia. I apologize if this broad use of the term offends, but repeatedly using the term "Islamic world west of South Asia" would be an incredible nuisance, both for you and for me.

2 See Lewis (2002).

3 For more on the connection between urbanization and economic development, see de Vries (1984), Bairoch et al. (1988), and Bosker et al. (2013). Numerous works of economic history have employed city size as a proxy for premodern economic development; a few of these works include de Long and Shleifer (1993), Acemoglu, Johnson, and Robinson (2005), Dittmar (2011), and Cantoni (2015).

4 In 800, there are twenty-two cities, because four cities tie for nineteenth place on the list. I am extremely grateful to Maarten Bosker, Eltjo Buringh, and Jan Luiten van Zanden for sharing their data from their 2013 paper with me. These data were used to create the maps in Figures 1.1–1.4.

5 For more on these data, see Pamuk (2011).

6 Wages were comparable in Istanbul with parts of southern and central Europe. For more on European wage data, see Allen (2001). For more on Ottoman wage data, see Özmucur and Pamuk (2002).

7 For more on European and Asian wage data, see Allen et al. (2011). These wage data are broadly consistent with Angus Maddison's GDP data, updated in Bolt and van Zanden (2014). Allen et al. (2011) provide evidence, consistent with Maddison's evidence that real incomes of Chinese workers were well behind those of workers in northwest Europe in the eighteenth century.

8 Examples of these views are found in Weber (1922), Cromer (1908), von Grunebaum (1966), and Lewis (1982, 2002). For an overview of this literature, see Kuran (1997, pp. 49–53). For a classic criticism of this approach, see Said (1978).

9 This certainly does not mean that all economic arguments that depend on cultural explanations are wrong. Greif (1994a), Guiso, Sapienza, and Zingales (2006, 2009), and Tabellini (2010) are among a small set of good economic works that take culture

seriously. Alston et al. (2016) provide an insightful example from Brazil in the late twentieth and early twenty-first centuries of how culture is endogenous to beliefs and institutions. Alesina and Giuliano (2015) provide a nice review of this literature.

10 Numerous scholars have challenged Weber's thesis since it was first proposed. The most damning criticism is that the "capitalist spirit" predated the Reformation – the Italian city-states of the late medieval period were highly capitalist, yet they did not spark modern economic growth. On this point, see in particular Sombart (1967 [1913]) and Tawney (1926 [1954]). For a more general overview of the literature from the last century on Weber's hypothesis, see Iannaccone (1998), Delacroix and Nielsen (2001), and Iyer (2016).

11 This book adds to works such as those of Robert Allen (2009), who argues that relatively high wages in London encouraged more investment in capital-saving technologies than in the rest of the world, and these technologies were at the heart of the Industrial Revolution. Allen's hypothesis is convincing on many fronts, although it is less strong on the reasons for high wages in London in the first place. An institutional story consistent with the one presented in this book may help set the stage where Allen's story begins.

12 van Zanden (2009, pp. 59–60) has a nice discussion of some alternative arguments for the presence of relatively weak family ties in medieval Europe.

13 Also see Greif, Iyigun, and Sasson (2012) and Greif and Iyigun (2013) for how differences in family structures encouraged different institutional responses for risk-sharing in England and China, and see Greif and Tabellini (2015) for how these differences affected inter- and intragroup cooperation in Europe and China.

14 This is not to say that Kuran ignores the supply side or that I ignore the demand side. Both sides enter into both of our arguments. I simply place more weight on the supply side, and Kuran places more weight on the demand side.

15 This theory gives a historical twist to endogenous growth theory – formulated by Paul Romer (1986) and Robert Lucas (1988) and extended by Oded Galor (2011) – which places human capital at the center of perpetual economic growth. Galor is the leader in the "unified growth theory" field, which argues in favor of the importance of prehistorical forces such as geography and endowments. Galor suggests that these forces affected demographic transitions, the evolution of technology, and the acquisition of human capital in ways that explain modern day development. Unlike the geography hypotheses explored in this section, unified growth theory can account for reversals of fortune, although it has a very hard time accounting for the *timing* of the reversals of fortune.

16 Besley and Persson (2009, 2010) and Acemoglu (2005) extend this argument, noting that investments in fiscal capacity arise endogenously because of common interests in the provision of public goods. Gennaioli and Voth (2015) take this argument one step further, noting that once fiscal and state capacity becomes important for war-making, a divergence arises between internally cohesive states and those without cohesion, with the latter set of states dropping out of existence. Bates (2001) takes a slightly different interpretation of the "war made the state" argument, suggesting that since European states invested in war, they could ultimately use their increased capacity to coerce for economically beneficial activities, such as the protection of property rights and the termination of feuds. Other important works in this literature, especially those of Dincecco (2009, 2011), stress the role that representative

institutions played in generating fiscal capacity through increased taxation and lower sovereign credit risk. Also see Karaman and Pamuk (2013), who argue that the connection between representative institutions, war, and fiscal capacity is dependent on the economic structure of the regime. They suggest that the interests of representative assemblies align with the ruler with respect to war in urban settings, where the ruler and elites jointly govern, but not in rural settings, where local control over coercive power dominates.

17 These insights have spurred a large literature. For instance, Irigoin and Grafe (2013) argue that fiscal capacity is a function of coercive power and it follows an inverted-U shape; initial investments in coercion pay off well, but eventually diminishing returns kick in. If coercion is too great, the legitimacy of the ruler may be undermined. Dincecco, Fenske, and Onorato (2016) argue that the type of conflict matters for long-run fiscal capacity, as they find no correlation between historical warfare and per capita GDP in sub-Saharan Africa. Johnson and Koyama (2014) and Anderson, Johnson, and Koyama (2016) argue in a series of papers for an important – although nonobvious – effect of increased legal and fiscal capacity: it reduced persecution (of witches, minority religions, and so forth) in Europe in the early modern period.

18 One hypothesis in this literature that deserves special attention, because it focuses on the Western Europe-Middle East comparison, is Blaydes and Chaney (2013). They argue that European feudalism arose because of the weak fiscal capacity of rulers following the fall of the Roman Empire, and in this system economic elites were able to negotiate with rulers through parliaments. They also argue that such negotiating organizations never emerged in the Middle East because rulers relied on slave armies to extend their power and collect taxes and therefore did not need to negotiate with the elite. Both Blaydes and Chaney and I argue that the lack of constraint by the elite on Middle Eastern rulers relative to their European counterparts was a crucial piece of the long-run economic divergence between Western Europe and the Middle East, but we differ on the reasons why the elite did not constrain Middle Eastern rulers. For example, it is not completely clear within the Blaydes and Chaney framework why the Ottoman military elites in the provinces, who maintained relations with the central government under the *timar* system, could not have come together in a manner similar to European parliaments to constrain the sultan. My explanation is that European kings needed to negotiate with the elite to a greater degree than Ottoman sultans did because their position was weaker due to their weaker legitimacy. At the same time, my explanation does not address exactly why parliaments arose in Western Europe in the first place in the manner that they did, except to say that rulers were in a weaker position vis-à-vis the elite because of weaker legitimacy. Blaydes and Chaney shed light on this point, noting that parliaments arose after a long tradition of feudal relations slowly evolved into semi-organized bodies throughout Western Europe.

19 For more on this argument, also see Hoffman (2011, 2012). For a comprehensive account of the role that military might had on world economic history, see Findlay and O'Rourke (2007).

20 Numerous reasons have been given for the relative fractionalization of Europe, including the presence of outside threats (Alesina and Spolaore 2005; Ko, Koyama,

and Sng 2016), trade patterns (Friedman 1977; Alesina and Spolaore 1997), and geography (Diamond 1997). Others have noted that the presence of numerous independent city states helped foster the rise of a merchant class (Pirenne 1925; Jones 1981; Stasavage [2014] takes an alternative view, arguing that independent cities initially had higher growth rates but ultimately failed, possibly due to the stifling of trade by guilds), and that fractionalization encouraged technological discovery (Lagerlöf 2014).

21 In fairness to Jones and Mokyr, they are hesitant to make a causal claim connecting conservatism to bad outcomes. Goldstone (2000) presents an alternative take on Mokyr's argument, suggesting that the key technological advances – along with the acceptance of Newtonian science and the Glorious Revolution settlement – were "accidents" of history and are not explainable causally. While the present book acknowledges the importance of individual events and in no way suggests that history is deterministic, it argues that institutional environments make certain outcomes, including the important ones Goldstone studies, *more likely* to arise in certain places at certain times.

22 Cross-country regressions do suggest a possible connection between religion, especially Islam, and economic development. See Grier (1997), Barro and McCleary (2003), and Guiso, Sapienza, and Zingales (2003). For a different view, see Noland (2005). Yet, it is far from clear that these works are picking up anything more than a correlation – causation is a very different story. There are certainly aspects of religious belief that affect economic performance, however. In particular, religion may incentivize (or disincentivize) one to attain education (see, e.g., Berman 2000, Becker and Wößmann 2008, 2009; Botticini and Eckstein 2012; Chaudhary and Rubin 2011, 2016; Meyersson 2013). Such incentives have clearly played an important role in long-run economic outcomes, although they cannot account on their own for the "reversal of fortunes," the long-run rise of Europe, *and* intra-European differences. They are important contributing influences nonetheless.

23 Gregory Clark lists eighty reviews of his book on his website, a very large number for an academic book.

24 Some of Clark's comparisons rest on data from the revisionist literature spearheaded by Pomeranz (2000), who argues that China and Europe were economic equals as late as the eighteenth century. Allen et al. (2011) provide evidence that this was not the case, especially in the comparison between northwestern Europe and China.

25 Blaming Sykes-Picot is a common trope in the popular press, who reinvigorated the thesis when Islamic State declared the goal of creating a new map in the Middle East. For a sample of articles on this topic, see Osman (2013), Sazak (2014), Ignatius (2014), and Howorth (2014). Danforth (2013) presents this argument with a twist, suggesting that the "divide-and-rule" policies of the British and French are responsible for persistent violence. Academic contributions to the debate generally focus on the trade capitulations the Ottoman government gave to the European powers. For instance, see Ahmad (2000).

26 Of course, geography may affect the types of institutions a society has. For example, Michalopoulos, Naghavi, and Prarolo (2015) argue that numerous features of the Islamic economic system stem from the agricultural endowments and pre-Islamic trade routes of the Muslim world. Rodrik, Subramanian, and Trebbi (2004) test the role of geography versus the role of institutions and economic openness and find

that institutions can account for most of the difference in worldwide economic outcomes. Kenneth Pomeranz (2000) also makes an argument in *The Great Divergence* that places importance on geography. Pomeranz is primarily concerned with the divergence between Europe and China. He makes the "revisionist" argument that Europe and China were on relatively equal economic footing in the eighteenth century, and that fortuitous circumstances allowed Europe to pull ahead (e.g., access to coal, discovery of the New World). There is convincing evidence suggesting that the timing of the divergence is not as Pomeranz suggests (see Allen et al. 2011), and Pomeranz's theory has difficulty explaining intra-European differences.

2 The Propagation of Rule

1 An example that has received significant attention from economists is the degree to which the law protects corporate investors from expropriation by corporate insiders. Such protections are important because they encourage investment. La Porta et al. (1997, 1998) show that these protections are more prevalent in countries with a legal tradition based in common law than in civil law–based countries, and consequently financial development is much greater in common law countries. The legal origins literature has provided many nice insights (see, most prominently, La Porta et al. 1999, Glaeser and Shleifer 2002, Djankov et al. 2002, 2003, Glaeser et al. 2004, and La Porta et al. 2008). That literature seeks the specific effects of the transplantation of different strains of common and civil law. This is not the point of the present chapter, which seeks to understand how the *content* of specific laws emerges and persists.

2 See van Bavel et al. (2015).

3 Wintrobe (1998) provides a comprehensive overview of the constraints facing dictators and how these constraints affect the manner in which the dictator rules.

4 This definition of elite is similar to the one proposed in Wallis and North (2014).

5 My definition is similar to the definition of legitimacy proposed by Seymour Martin Lipset (1959, p. 86), who defined legitimacy as "the capacity of a political system to engender and maintain the belief that existing political institutions are the most appropriate or proper ones for the society." The definition proposed in this book is also similar to those suggested by Greif (2010) and Greif and Tadelis (2010), who define legitimacy of a political authority as "the extent to which people feel morally obliged to follow the authority." A more expansive definition would include beliefs about the beliefs of others. That is, people may view a rule-maker as legitimate if they believe that others believe the rule-maker has the right to make the rules. Since this aspect of legitimacy is not the focus of this book, I do not include it here.

6 This motivation of course does not fit all types of rulers. For example, Ronald Wintrobe (1998) analyzes "tinpot" rulers, like many dictators of sub-Saharan Africa, who aim to minimize the cost of staying in power so they can pocket excess rents produced by society. Yet, most goals that one might ascribe to a ruler – even growing wealthy – are not possible if the ruler is not in power. Similar points are made in Gill (1998, ch. 3; 2008, ch. 2).

7 This idea is similar to Wintrobe's (1998) insights on dictators, who maintain their rule by investing in repression and loyalty.

8 For an extended discussion on the concept of legitimizing agents, see Coşgel, Miceli, and Rubin (2012a, 2012b) and Greif and Rubin (2015).

9 For a nice rational choice analysis of how and why religious authorities legitimize political rule, see Gill (1998, especially ch. 1, 3; 2008, ch. 2).

10 These examples and many more are in Masud et al. (1996).

11 Chaney is quoting Robert Irwin's 1986 book *The Middle East in the Middle Ages* (p. 50).

12 For more on the economic effects of the "Pax Mongolia", see Needham (1954) and Findlay and O'Rourke (2007). For more on the use of violence to promote economic good in general, see Bates (2001).

13 Avner Greif (2006b, p. 30) also proposes a definition of institutions favored in this book: "[institutions are] ... a system of rules, beliefs, norms, and organizations, that together generate a regularity of (social) behavior ... Each component of this system is social in being a man-made, nonphysical factor that is exogenous to each individual whose behavior it influences." Other important works discussing the nature and consequences of institutions include Greif (1993), North (1981), North, Wallis, and Weingast (2009), Williamson (1985, 2000), Ostrom (1990, 2005), Aoki (2001), Acemoglu, Johnson, and Robinson (2001, 2002, 2005), Acemoglu and Robinson (2006, 2012), David (1994), and Helpman (2004, ch. 7).

14 This idea is consistent with Greif's (2006b) insight that institutions can only persist when they are *self-enforcing*. Greif considers an institution to be self-enforcing if everyone who is affected by the institution has incentive to act in the manner the institution supports.

15 The intuition laid out in this section largely comes from Rubin (2011). It also incorporates insights from Coşgel, Miceli, and Rubin (2012a, 2012b).

16 For more, see Gill (1998, ch. 3; 2008). Also see Coşgel and Miceli (2009), who argue that the trade-off between legitimacy concerns and the amount of religious goods provided by the religious establishment affects the relationship between church and state.

17 For more on this point, see Stark and Bainbridge (1985, ch. 22).

18 Another straightforward example of how institutionalized rules establish costs for propagating rule is how rulers recruited military elite in medieval Europe and the Middle East. Blaydes and Chaney (2013) argue that feudal institutions were the basis for military recruitment in medieval Europe, meaning that rulers had to concede numerous rights to feudal lords in return for military service. In the Middle East, Muslim sultans relied on slave armies for military service, meaning that local elites had relatively little bargaining power with the sultan, and thus their support was less expensive than their European counterparts.

19 Greif (2006b) calls such an institution self-reinforcing. His important insights provide the subtext for the ones elaborated in this chapter, but I attempt to confine as much jargon as possible to the footnotes.

20 For much more on this argument, see Kuran (1995).

21 Gill (1998, 53) makes a similar point: "[P]riests who consistently make poor political endorsements will discover that their followers will question not only their political judgment, but the spiritual guidance they offer as well." For more on this point, see Rodinson (1973), Noonan (1993, 2005), Ekelund et al. (1996), and Hallaq (2001).

22 Paul David (1985, p. 332) eloquently defined a path-dependent sequence of events as those in which "important influences upon the eventual outcome [are] exerted by temporally remote events, including happenings dominated by chance elements rather than systematic forces." His example of the QWERTY keyboard layout as a path dependent process is a classic example, even if it is with its detractors.

3 Historical Origins of Rule Propagation

1 See Hallaq (2005, ch. 1).

2 This insight has a long tradition nicely overviewed in Ensminger (1997). Also see Udovitch (1970), Rodinson (1973), and Lewis (1993). Jha (2013) carries this argument one step further, noting how trade fostered interethnic and interreligious cooperation in South Asia, which fostered the creation of institutions that bolstered interethnic trust in the twentieth century.

3 See Lopez (1971).

4 See Michalopoulos, Naghavi, and Prarolo (2015).

5 For an in-depth account on this point, see Watson (1983). For a brief overview of trade in Islamic history, see Rubin (2012).

6 Quoted in Lewis (1995, p. 149). For more on the intersection of the religious and the legal in early Islam, see Lewis (1974, 1995, 2002), Hassan (1981), and Hallaq (2005). Razi (1990) argues that this intersection is in part responsible for the outsized importance of Islam in legitimating political rule in the present day. Platteau (2011) argues that Islamic political authorities were easily able to bring the religious establishment under their aegis from an early time, and only used Islam to legitimize their rule when there was a vacuum of centralized power. This argument is consistent with the one proposed in this book, although this book places a greater emphasis on the constraints that religious authorities were able to place on the actions of political authorities.

7 These insights, along with the associated Qur'anic verses, are from the website www .free-minds.org. All Qur'an quotes are from www.quran.com.

8 These passages are from www.sahih-bukhari.com.

9 For more on these points, see Goodenough (1931, pp. 37, 54), Jones (1964, p. 96), Gager (1975, pp. 94, 96) and Goody (1983, pp. 92–93). Stark (1996) argues that the poor were underrepresented, in proportion to the Roman population, in early Christianity. Even if this is true, most Christians were from the poorer to middling classes.

10 For an extensive overview of the early separation of church and state in Christianity, see Mann (1986, ch. 10), Tierney (1988), and Feldman (1997).

11 Quoted in Johnson (1976, p. 70).

12 For more on this point, see Hyma (1938, p. 14) and Feldman (1997, pp. 25–27). Gelasius I is quoted in Tierney (1988, p. 13).

13 It is possible that Constantine's acceptance of Christianity was a political expedient aimed at gaining Christian support in the midst of civil wars fought with Maximinus II and Licinius over who would rule the empire. But Constantine's embrace of Christianity cannot have been solely to legitimize his regime. Although the Christian population was growing rapidly in the late third and early fourth

centuries, Christians still only made up around 10% of the Roman population around the time of the Edict of Milan. For more on Constantine's conversion to Christianity, see Jones (1949, ch. 6; 1964), Downey (1969, p. 21), and Stark (1996, ch. 1).

14 These numbers are from Stark (1996, p. 7). For more on this momentous period in Christian history, see Goodenough (1931, p. 53), Jones (1964, p. 96), Coleman-Norton (1966, pp. 85–86), Downey (1969, p. 34), Johnson (1976, p. 79), Goody (1983, p. 93), and Cameron (1993, pp. 71–72).

15 See Coşgel, Miceli, and Ahmed (2009).

16 See Crone and Hinds (1986, p. 1).

17 See Crone and Hinds (1986).

18 For more on this point, see Crone and Hinds (1986, chs. 4, 5).

19 For much more on the evolution of proto-kadis, see Hallaq (2005, ch. 2).

20 Hallaq (2005) notes that the Sunna was not complete in this period and there were actually multiple Sunna, including those of the first caliphs. Recognition of the Sunna of the Prophet as a source of law came later.

21 For much more on the early history of Sunna and hadith, see Hallaq (2005, ch. 5).

22 For more on the growth of the legal class in the first few Islamic centuries, see Masud et al. (1996), Berkey (2003), Hallaq (2005), and Coşgel, Miceli, and Ahmed (2009).

23 Quoted in Hallaq (2005, p. 184).

24 See Hallaq (2005, ch. 8).

25 See Hallaq (2005, ch. 8).

26 See Hallaq (2005, ch. 8).

27 See Hallaq (2005, p. 191).

28 For more on fatwas legitimizing actions by rulers or keeping their actions consistent with Islam, see Masud et al. (1996) and Fierro (1996).

29 For more, see Watt (1988, p. 28).

30 For more on the formation of the schools, see Hallaq (2005, ch. 7).

31 For more, see Schacht (1964, ch. 10), Coulson (1969), Weiss (1978), and Hallaq (2001, ch. 4).

32 Haim Gerber (1999, chs. 4–7) studied rulings by the important seventeenth-century Palestinian mufti Khayr al-Din al-Ramli in which numerous disagreements that remained unresolved in the classical and postclassical periods arose, necessitating an act of *ijtihad*. Wael Hallaq (1984, 2001) also notes numerous historical examples of *ijtihad*, suggesting that the "gate" never closed in theory or in practice. However, even if the "gate of *ijtihad*" were open, Hallaq's studies suggest that jurists indeed practiced *ijtihad* less frequently after the tenth century.

33 Chaney (2016) provides a complementary theory to the one proposed here. He argues that the rise and decline of Muslim science resulted from the incentives faced by the religious establishment. When the majority of the populations conquered by Islamic polities had converted to Islam, Chaney argues that studies in logic, philosophy, and science threatened to undermine the position of the religious elite.

34 See Tierney and Painter (1992, ch. 4).

35 Quoted in Tierney and Painter (1992, p. 73).

36 For more, see Tierney and Painter (1992, ch. 4).

37 See Berman (1983, ch. 1) and Tierney and Painter (1992, ch. 5).

38 For more on the economic consequences of these conditions, see Lopez (1971, chs. 1–2). For more of the effect of these conditions on the contractual forms found on manors, see North and Thomas (1971).

39 For more, see Goodenough (1931, p. 69) and Feldman (1997, p. 30).

40 See Tierney and Painter (1992, chs. 6, 7).

41 See Lopez (1971, chs. 2–3).

42 For more, see Greif, Milgrom, and Weingast (1994) and Greif (1994b). Putnam (1993), Guiso, Sapienza, and Zingales (2016), and Jacob (2010) contend that a key feature of medieval political institutions – the independence of certain cities in Northern Italy and the Holy Roman Empire – led to greater social capital and hence better subsequent economic outcomes.

43 For more on this point, see Lopez (1971), Jones (1997), and Greif (2006b).

44 For more, see North and Thomas (1971), Milgrom, North, and Weingast (1990), Greif, Milgrom, and Weingast (1994), Hunt and Murray (1999), and Greif (2004, 2006b).

45 See Berman (1983, p. 91).

46 Tierney (1988, pp. 33–95) gives an excellent overview of the Investiture Controversy, replete with translations of many of the important documents of the period.

47 For more on this period, see Berman (1983, ch. 2) and Tierney (1988, ch. 3).

48 On these last points, see Hyma (1938, pp. 30–32) and Feldman (1997, pp. 30–35).

49 See Berman (1983, ch. 7).

50 See Berman (1983) for an in-depth overview of the emergence of various types of law in this period.

51 See Berman (1983).

52 For an English translation and interpretation of this document, see Tierney (1988, ch. 3).

53 Quote from Berman (1983, p. 97).

54 See Tierney (1988, pp. 116–126).

55 See Tierney (1988, pp. 127–138).

56 See Tierney (1988, pp. 139–149).

57 Quoted in Tierney (1988, p. 171).

58 See van Zanden, Buringh, and Bosker (2012).

4 Bans on Taking Interest

1 Cash *waqf*s were also an important source of capital in the late Ottoman period. However, they had important differences from banks described later in this chapter.

2 Kuran (2005a) argues that "Islamic economics" as a whole is largely a guise for a modern economic system cloaked in Islamic doctrine.

3 Quoted in Kindleberger (1980). For more on this flavor of argument, see Labib (1969), Rodinson (1973), Udovitch (1975), Le Goff (1979), Jones (1988), and Pamuk (2004b). For arguments in favor of an impact of interest restrictions on economic and political outcomes, see de Roover (1948), Noonan (1957), Kuran (1986), Ekelund et al. (1996), Reed and Bekar (2003), Munro (2003, 2008), Rubin (2010, 2011), and Koyama (2010).

4 For more on interest restrictions in a premodern context, see Brenner (1983), Glaeser and Scheinkman (1998), and Rubin (2009).

5 See Rahman (1964) and Schacht (1995).

6 For more on *hiyal*, see Khan (1929), Schacht (1964, 2006), Coulson (1969), Grice-Hutchinson (1978), and Ray (1997).

7 Jahiz, an Arab writer living in Basra in the ninth century CE, documented a specific account of a double sale. He cited two Persian Gulf merchants who bought back for cash the same articles they had just sold on fixed term. Jahiz's account reveals that such transactions were commonplace for Muslims in this period. For more on this account, see Çağatay (1970, p. 57) and Rodinson (1973, pp. 38–40).

8 See Rodinson (1973, p. 39).

9 The scholars Abu Yusuf (d. 798) and Shaybani (d. 805) wrote two famous treatises.

10 In a detailed study of the early twelfth-century Cairo Geniza, Shelomo D. Goitein (1967, p. 170) observes that although credit and commerce flourished in Egypt, "even a cursory examination of the Geniza material reveals that lending money for interest was not only shunned religiously, but was also of limited significance economically … therefore, the economic role of financial investment today was then fulfilled by various forms of partnerships." Also see Udovitch (1979), Goitein (1967), and Gerber (1999, pp. 129, 141).

11 See Imber (1997, p. 146).

12 For more on *istiğlal*, see Gerber (1988, ch. 7).

13 On *waqf*s, see Imber (1997). On cash *waqf*s, see Çizakça (1995).

14 For more on the lack of banking, see Udovitch (1979) and Kuran (2004b, p. 73; 2011). Partnerships most frequently took the form of *mudaraba* (sleeping partnership) or *'inan*, in which both partners invested some capital. For an extended analysis of partnerships in the medieval Islamic world, see Udovitch (1970). For more, also see Goitein (1967) and Labib (1969).

15 This excludes cases involving *waqf*s.

16 For more, see Mandaville (1979), Çizakça (2000, ch. 3), and Kuran (2005c, pp. 606–8).

17 See Çizakça (2004, p. 10).

18 For more on the resolution to this controversy, see Mandaville (1979, pp. 297–8) and Imber (1997, pp. 144–5).

19 See Mandaville (1979, p. 292). Çizakça (2000, pp. 51–2) shows that the amount of capital injected into the economy by the cash *waqf*s was nearly ten times the amount withdrawn by the state through the tax farm of the silk press. On the other hand, Gerber (1988, pp. 132–40) provides data showing that the *waqf*'s role in providing credit in Bursa was relatively minor, and only 11% of all entries concerning credit were provided by *waqf*s in Jennings's (1973, p. 176) study of Kayseri sicils.

20 The approval of cash *waqf*s varied between schools of Sunni Islam. The Hanafi position (which was taken by the Ottomans) was relatively lenient, allowing them subject to custom. The Shafi'i, Maliki, and Hanbali schools also allowed the cash *waqf*, but only under certain conditions, with the Maliki school being the least rigid. For more, see Mandaville (1979, p. 293) and Çizakça (2000, pp. 27–40).

21 A few of the early Church fathers spoke out against interest, but modern scholars generally agree that these scattered early references to the evils of interest do not imply that taking interest was forbidden in the first three Christian centuries (Dow

1922; Divine 1959; Frierson 1969). The lack of anti-interest doctrine in this period is not attributable simply to the absence of a centralized Church. Numerous local synods met before the fourth century and would have been the primary forums to espouse anti-interest sentiments, as they were in the fourth century, but interest was not a topic that was widely discussed, if it was discussed at all (Hefele [1894] 1973).

22 See Hefele ([1894] 1973) and Maloney (1973). Elvira and Carthage explicitly extended the prohibition to laymen. Canons ten and thirteen of the Synod of Carthage of 345–348 stated, "As the taking of any kind of usury is condemned in laymen, much more is it condemned in clergymen" (Hefele [1894] 1973, vol. 2, pp. 186, 468).

23 Rubin (2009) provides a theory of interest restrictions that is consistent with this early history of the Church, arguing that once the Church gained wealth under Constantine in the early fourth century, it suddenly faced a problem whereby its commitment to provide aid to everyone in need encouraged risky behavior associated with taking loans at high interest. One way to mitigate this problem while remaining consistent with Old Testament doctrine was to ban interest. For other views on the emergence of interest restrictions in premodern economies, see Posner (1980), Brenner (1983), Glaeser and Scheinkman (1998), and Reed and Bekar (2003).

24 See Lopez (1971, p. 72).

25 See Le Goff (1979) and Munro (2003, 2008).

26 For more on these papal decrees, see Noonan (1957, pp. 19–22, 80–1; 1966, p. 63) and Munro (2003, 2008).

27 See Munro (2003), Lane (1966, ch. 6), and Mueller (1997, ch. 10–14).

28 See Pirenne (1937, pp. 133–4) and de Roover (1948, p. 104).

29 See Pirenne (1937, pp. 133–4), de Roover (1942, pp. 57–8; 1948, pp. 104–6, 161), Gilchrist (1969, p. 114), and Grice-Hutchinson (1978, ch. 1).

30 See Noonan (1957, ch. 7), Gelpi and Julien-Labruyère (2000, p. 32), and Munro (2003, 2008).

31 See Homer and Sylla (1991, ch. 5–6, p. 138).

32 Quote from Noonan (1957, p. 161, ch. 7). Also see Munro (2008).

33 See Noonan (1957, ch. 5, 12), Divine (1959), and Gilchrist (1969).

34 See Gilchrist (1969, p. 115) and Gelpi and Julien-Labruyère (2000, pp. 42–3).

35 By the sixteenth century, the interest ban was more or less a dead letter, although it was still the official position of the Church. The Protestant Reformation sped up the Church's relaxation of interest doctrine, but it is clear that the forces underlying the relaxation of the ban were in motion well before the Reformation. For more on the early Protestant views on interest, see Noonan (1957, ch. 18), Gelpi and Julien-Labruyère (2000, ch. 4–5), and Kerridge (2002). The ban was officially lifted in a series of decisions between 1822 and 1836 in which the Holy Office publicly declared moderate interest legal to everyone. In 1917, the Church offered the *Codex iuris canonici*, which replaced all earlier collections of canon law and allowed a legal title to interest.

36 Quoted in Hunt and Murray (1999, p. 65).

37 See Hunt and Murray (1999, p. 64) and Kohn (1999).

38 See Einzig (1970, p. 67).

39 See Hunt and Murray (1999). The operations of the Florentine Covoni family, who between 1336 and 1340 registered 443 exchange transactions, exemplifies the use

of bills of exchange as a financial instrument: 70 were trade-related and 373 were financial (Mueller 1997, p. 317–18). Bills of exchange evolved further in the late sixteenth and seventeenth centuries when they became negotiable and endorsable (the first use of endorsement occurred in the 1570s). As endorsable instruments, bills were similar to convertible money (Kohn 1999).

40   Merchants eventually adopted bills quoted in fictitious units of stable value in order to escape changes in exchange rates resulting from currency debasement and speculation, but their adoption of this measure instead of discounting suggests that currency exchange maintained its important role in the exchange transaction (Einzig 1970). Another way that bills simulated interest-bearing loans was through non-repayment by the payer. In this case, it was tacitly understood by all parties that a dishonored bill would be protested in court (for appearances) and returned to its place of issue, after which the taker was obligated to pay the deliverer back at the current rate of rechange, which acted as an interest payment (Einzig 1970).

41   If lenders could use differences in exchange rates to make an arbitrage-like profit, why did markets not eventually clear and exchange rates equalize? Raymond de Roover (1944) suggests that differences in exchange rates reflected a built-in interest payment, and hence such differences *had* to exist for an equilibrium to hold. If no differences in exchange rates existed, then there would not have been incentive for the capital-wealthy to lend. Meanwhile, some merchants were willing to pay a premium to have access to this capital. For instance, sellers of bills in London were often merchants who needed access to cash to pay for cloth, which they expected to sell in the Low Countries. One way of gaining access to this credit was by selling a bill in London and honored in Antwerp or Amsterdam. See de Roover (1944).

42   The *sakk* and *ruqʿa* acted like checks, and merchants employed them primarily in short-distance trade for relatively small sums (Goitein 1967, pp. 240–1; Udovitch 1975).

43   See Lieber (1968) and Udovitch (1979). Though it is certain that the *suftaja* predates the European bill of exchange, there is considerable debate concerning the Middle Eastern origins of the European bill. Early twentieth-century scholars such as Usher (1914) believed Western bills to be of Italian origin, while later "Orientalist" scholars such as Schacht (1964) and Lieber (1968) believe that European bills owe a great deal to the Islamic world. Ashtor (1973) reconciles the two viewpoints, noting that while Europeans were aware of *suftaja* and even dealt in them, the difference in the economic setting in which they emerged, which (as emphasized in this chapter) permitted an exchange transaction to be included in the European but not the Islamic bill, suggests that the European bill was a fundamentally different and unique credit instrument.

44   In a study of early *safatij*, Eliahu Ashtor (1973, p. 562) notes that "studying the texts referring to the *suftadjas* drawn up in Iraq and Egypt at the time of the Abbasid caliphs, we note that the sums sent to another city or another country had to be collected in the *same type of money* in which the loan was made" (italics added). The lack of a currency exchange associated with the *suftaja* extends well beyond the Abbasid period and is a salient feature of transactions registered in the Geniza in the twelfth and thirteenth centuries. Also see Udovitch (1975, 1979).

45   See Lieber (1968, p. 233), Ashtor (1973, pp. 556–7), Ray (1997, p. 71), and Pamuk (2004b).

46 Quoted in Goitein (1967, p. 243). Similarly, a characteristic "blank" *suftaja* read: "Give ____ all that he may demand, obtain a receipt from him, and debit the sum to me" (see Mez 1937, p. 476).

47 See Goitein (1967, p. 243).

48 The Hanafi permitted *safatij*.

49 An alternative hypothesis for the absence of an exchange transaction associated with the *suftaja* is that there were fewer opportunities to trade currencies, perhaps stemming from less fragmentation in the Middle East relative to Europe, and thus less scope to use currency exchange. Historical evidence indicating that numerous types of currencies, such as different types of dinars and dirhams, were available in the Middle East contradicts such a theory, however. Ashtor (1973, p. 560) notes that a "rich variety of money, that is to say the ease with which foreign monies could be obtained in the big cities, was a typical phenomenon of the monetary life of the Muslim countries at the time of the Abbasid caliphs and at that of the Crusades, distinguishing them signally, in this respect, from the countries of Western Europe." Moreover, the fact that differences in exchange rates in Europe were essential to bills being profitable does not mean that such differences could not have emerged in the Middle East, if they indeed did not exist. Once financiers used European bills of exchange as instruments of finance, differences in exchange rates emerged *endogenously* as interest payments. It thus follows that had Middle Eastern lenders been able to include an exchange transaction with the *suftaja*, differences in exchange rates in different Middle Eastern cities may have followed.

50 A lender could buy a *suftaja* in place A, have an agent turn in the *suftaja* in place B for the same currency, have the agent exchange the currency for a different currency in place B, buy another *suftaja* in place B with the new currency, turn in that *suftaja* in place A in the new currency, and finally exchange the currency in place A for the original currency.

51 Two schools of Sunni Islam (Maliki and Shafi'i) explicitly forbade *safatij*, though the Malikites permitted their use in cases of extreme danger to the traveling merchant. The Hanbali school permitted them as long as no fee was charged. They were disapproved of, though permitted, by the Hanafi school (Dien 1995). The Hanafites, however, insisted that the *suftaja* was only permissible when there was no agreement to pay elsewhere and where the sums paid and repaid were equal (Ashtor 1973).

52 The enforceability of fines for late repayment suggests another possible mechanism that lenders could have secured a profit via *safatij*. The lender and borrower could have had a tacit agreement that the agent in the distant land would be late in repayment with the fee paid serving as interest. Indeed, Western Europeans employed this type of agreement. It is unlikely that Muslim lenders used this tactic for a variety of reasons, all of which are consistent with the theory presented in this chapter. First and foremost, this would have been a clear violation of Islamic law. While Muslim lenders used numerous *hiyal* that were consistent with the letter but not the spirit of the law, any implicit understanding between parties would have made the contract voidable under Islamic law. Thus, the essential difference between the two regions is that a dishonored bill would have been enforceable in Western European courts *regardless* of the intent of the parties. Indeed, the Church considered such an arrangement usurious (*in fraudem usurarum*, see Munro [2003]) but had little power to impose secular sanctions after its power waned in the late thirteenth

century, whereas such a bill would not have been enforced in Islamic courts if it were obvious that the intent was to circumvent interest restrictions. Moreover, even if such a practice became widespread, it is unclear how it would have facilitated impersonal lending. The set of potential sanctions that could enforce this type of contract were personal or social.

53 See Einzig (1970).

54 See de Roover (1946b, 1963). The Medici house operated in a similar manner to its rival controlled by Francesco Datini. The Medici enterprise differed from the "super-company" organizations of the fourteenth century (such as the Peruzzi, Bardi, and Acciaiuoli companies), which were centralized under one partnership that controlled foreign branches.

55 See de Roover (1963, p. 87).

56 See de Roover (1946a, 1963).

57 See Goitein (1967, pp. 244–5) and Udovitch (1975).

58 Theoretically, Middle Eastern lenders could have extended their networks in order to increase their confidence in the partner on the other end of the transaction, who would have been a part of the same "business." This would have encouraged the writing of larger *safatij* at greater fees. Yet, in this case the incidence of personal exchange is even greater, as both the borrower and his agent are part of an even closer network. It is also possible that Middle Eastern lenders could have learned the potential benefits of adding exchange to the *suftaja* through contact with Christian minorities. Indeed, the Pact of Umar permitted Christian minorities (*dhimmis*) in Islamic lands to utilize Christian courts in transactions involving non-Muslims. Yet, it is unlikely that European bills of exchange could have been commonly employed as financial instruments in Muslim lands for two reasons: (1) bills of exchange were enforceable only by merchant law in Europe, which was not available in Islamic law; and (2) the viability of bills of exchange as financial instruments depended on the existence of a critical mass of (in this case, Christian) borrowers and lenders in more than one region. In fact, Christian minorities generally abided by Islamic law until the eighteenth century, by which time much more advanced financial instruments were available to European lenders. For more on these points, see Kuran (2004a, 2011).

59 See Mokyr (1990). For more on the importance of historical events and path dependence on the evolution of institutions, see David (1994), Kuran (2005a, 2011), and Greif (2006b, chs. 5, 7).

5 Restrictions on the Printing Press

1 I am only concerned here with the invention of the movable-type printing press in Europe. The Chinese knew of printing since the eleventh century, but it was not introduced to Europe until the 1450s.

2 See McCusker (2005) and Chilosi and Volckart (2010).

3 The actual number spans the period 500–1450, but it is almost certain that the number of manuscripts produced from 450 to 1450 was smaller than in the half-century following the invention of the press.

4 See Febvre and Martin (1958, p. 218).

5   See Spitz (1985) and Buringh and van Zanden (2009).
6   See Buringh and van Zanden (2009).
7   See Febvre and Martin (1958).
8   See Dittmar (2011).
9   See Eisenstein (1979).
10 See Febvre and Martin (1958, p. 249).
11 See Febvre and Martin (1958) and Eisenstein (1979).
12 See Swetz (1987).
13 Quoted in Swetz (1987, p. 25).
14 See Kertcher and Margalit (2006).
15 For more, see Febvre and Martin (1958), Eisenstein (1979), Love (1993), Johns (1998), and Kertcher and Margalit (2006).
16 Much of the next two sections are in Coşgel, Miceli, and Rubin (2012a). I thank Metin and Tom for their work and their permission to let me use the ideas we formulated together in this chapter. And I especially thank Metin for letting me use the Turkish works he translated.
17 Mystakidis (1911, p. 324) mentioned the presence of such an edict in the first volume of *Türk Tarih Encümeni Dergisi*, but the validity of this claim was challenged by Efdaleddin Tekiner (1916) in the same publication five years later on the grounds that Ottoman archives do not house edicts issued prior to 1553 and thus Mystakidis could not possibly have seen it. Despite this correction and the fact that no such edicts have since been uncovered, the secondary literature has for the most part accepted the presence of the edict as a matter of established fact. See, for example, Pedersen (1984, p. 133), Finkel (2005, p. 366) and Savage-Smith (2003, p. 656). I thank Metin Coşgel for the insights and translations on Mystakidis and Tekiner.
18 English translation from Göçek (1987, p. 112).
19 See Finkel (2005, p. 366).
20 For more see Coşgel, Miceli, and Rubin (2012a) and Frazee (1983).
21 See Pedersen (1984, p. 135).
22 See Finkel (2005, p. 366).
23 See Atiyeh (1995, p. 285).
24 See Göçek (1987, p. 110).
25 For more, see Pedersen (1984), Robinson (1993, p. 233), Sardar (1993), and Atiyeh (1995, p. 283).
26 On the Ottoman Empire, see Quataert (2000, p. 167). On Europe, see Baten and van Zanden (2008).
27 See Özmucur and Pamuk (2002).
28 See Sardar (1993, pp. 47–51).
29 See Sardar (1993, pp. 47–51).
30 See İnalcık (1973, p. 99) and Dale (2010).
31 See Hourani (1991, ch. 13), Imber (1997), and Dale (2010).
32 This process is described in Hourani (1991, p. 199) and Robinson (1993, p. 235).
33 See Sardar (1993, p. 50).
34 See Sardar (1993, pp. 45–6).
35 See Robinson (1993, p. 237).
36 Quoted in Robinson (1993, p. 237).
37 See Sardar (1993, pp. 52–3).

38 Chaney (2016) puts forth a similar argument. He argues that the fall of Muslim science was due to the fact that Islamic religious authorities faced little competition in the realm of ideas and hoped to keep it that way.

39 See Göçek (1987, p. 109).

40 See Buringh and van Zanden (2009).

41 See Tierney (1988).

42 See Schachner (1962).

43 See Schachner (1962, p. 50).

44 See Christ et al. (1984, pp. 297–310) and Febvre and Martin (1958, pp. 22–5).

45 See Haskins (1957, pp. 38–53), Schachner (1962), and Christ et al. (1984, pp. 237–8).

46 To be clear, the Ottoman suppression of printing in the Arabic script was *not* the result of idiosyncratic decisions made by a few sultans in the fifteenth and sixteenth centuries. If this were the case, it is likely that the long hand of history would have caught up with the Ottomans and pushed toward the adoption of printing. Instead, as this chapter suggests, the Ottoman blocking of printing was a calculated decision resulting from very deeply entrenched, institutionally imposed incentives faced by the sultan. The Ottoman non-adoption of the press was a *self-enforcing equilibrium* outcome, not a choice made by a few foolish sultans.

6 Printing and the Reformation

1 Spenkuch (2016) provides possible support for Weber's hypothesis. He finds that Protestantism induces people to work longer hours – leading to higher earnings – and that human capital or institutional differences cannot account for these results. This leaves many possible causal channels open, including the one proposed by Weber.

2 Becker and Wößmann (2008, 2009) propose that the causal pathway connecting Protestantism to long-run economic success is education. They argue that Luther encouraged reading the Bible, which in turn gave Protestants an early start on acquiring literacy. Arruñada (2010) argues that Protestants did not have a unique work ethic, but instead had a "social ethic" that favored market transactions. Young (2009) overviews a number of possible, non-mutually exclusive reasons that Protestant regions had better long-run outcomes than Catholic regions. Guiso et al. (2003) gives a contrary view. They find a positive correlation between Christian religions and attitudes conducive to economic growth.

3 As calculated in Allen (2001).

4 Allen (2001) gives data for 1900–1913, but Bairoch et al. (1988) does not provide population data for this period. Allen (2001) also does not have data for each city in each period. Where Allen's data are missing, I exclude these cities from the analysis. Population data from Bairoch et al. (1988) are from the beginning of the period in question. Bairoch and colleagues do not report population data for 1550 or 1650, so I derive these data by taking the geometric mean of the two surrounding points.

5 On the Reformation, see Weber (1905 [2002]), Tawney (1926), Becker and Wößmann (2008, 2009), and Arruñada (2010). On the printing press, see Eisenstein (1979), Baten and Van Zanden (2008), Buringh and van Zanden (2009), and Dittmar

(2011). On the New World, see Pomeranz (2000) and Acemoglu, Johnson, and Robinson (2005). On the Renaissance, see Mokyr (2002) and McCloskey (2010). On the Ottomans, see Iyigun (2008, 2015).

6 Rubin (2014a) suggests that centralized institutions like the medieval Church are particularly vulnerable to rapid revolt because they have numerous means of suppressing dissent. This means that the publicly stated preferences of people often differ from their privately held preferences (as in Kuran [1995]). Makowsky and Rubin (2013) further this argument, suggesting that information technology further increases the likelihood of revolt in economies with centralized institutions, as previously suppressed anti-authority preferences are more likely to rise to the surface.

7 Much of this section is from Rubin (2014b).

8 See Cameron (1991).

9 See Blickle (1984). Ekelund, Hébert, and Tollison (2002) suggest, in a similar manner, that civil authorities sought an alternative provider of legal services and a less costly path to salvation through the Reformation, as the Church (a monopolist) was overcharging. Their analysis highlights yet another necessary precondition of the Reformation, complementing the one proposed in this chapter.

10 See Scribner (1989).

11 See Holborn (1942) and Edwards (1994).

12 For more on the debate between papism and conciliarism, and especially the role played by Gerson, see Dolan (1965, ch. 4).

13 See Weber (1912).

14 See Wilhelm (1910).

15 A city is considered to have been part of the Holy Roman Empire if it were de facto subject to the Emperor and the empire's institutions throughout the sixteenth century. This includes cities in present-day Germany, Austria, Czech Republic, Belgium, Luxembourg, eastern France, and western Poland. This excludes Switzerland, which de facto broke away from the Empire in 1499; the Netherlands, which revolted and broke away from the Holy Roman Empire in the 1570s; and northern Italy (e.g., the Duchies of Savoy and Milan), which was not de facto subject to the Emperor. All results are robust to different definitions of the Holy Roman Empire.

16 Becker and Wößmann (2008, 2009) and Cantoni (2012) find that proximity to Wittenberg was a key factor determining whether towns in the Holy Roman Empire adopted the Reformation.

17 Pfaff and Corcoran (2012) argue that there are numerous other supply-and-demand features that contributed to cities adopting the Reformation. Curuk and Smulders (2016) suggest that princes may have demanded the Reformation to remove the power of the Church, and this demand was highest in regions that did not realize their economic potential. Their study suffers from a limited sample size, and it is unclear that their mechanism could have possibly worked in the free imperial cities, but their intuition is consistent with the arguments made in this book. For an overview of recent works on the economic, sociological, and political causes and consequences of the Reformation, see Becker, Pfaff, and Rubin (2016).

18 The variables controlled for are: whether the city housed a university by 1450, whether the city housed a bishop or archbishop by 1517, whether the city was a member of the Hanseatic League, whether the city was an independent, Free

Imperial city in 1517, whether a city belonged to a lay magnate (i.e., it was neither free nor subject to an ecclesiastical lord), a dummy for the presence of printing, whether the city was on water (ocean, sea, large lake, or river connected to another city), the city's urban potential (i.e., the sum of the populations of all other cities weighted by their distance from the city in question), the city's distance to Wittenberg, and the latitude, longitude, and interaction between the two. For more on these data, see Rubin (2014b).

19 Formally, Rubin (2014b) analyzes both a probit and a two-stage probit to control for endogeneity. The first-stage dependent variable is whether a city had a printing press by 1500, and the instrument used is the city's distance to Mainz, the birthplace of printing. This variable correlates with the spread of printing but should not have had an independent effect on the spread of the Reformation. More details are available in Rubin (2014b).

20 For the relevant recent citations in the fiscal capacity literature, see Chapter 1. In many historical and present-day societies, the economic elite held the government's purse strings and provided council to rulers, helping them solve information problems and problems associated with succession. For more, see Congleton (2011, chs. 2–5).

21 For much more on the incentive for rulers to maximize revenue through predation – and attempts at constraining this type of action by other players in society – see Brennan and Buchanan (1980), Levi (1988), North and Weingast (1989), Tilly (1990), and Irigoin and Grafe (2013).

22 Congleton (2011, ch. 5) has a nice discussion of how differing "king and council" arrangements affect policy outcomes in different situations. Congleton's analysis is consistent with the one offered in this book, although the emphasis here is more on why differing arrangements arose in the first place. Also see van Zanden, Buringh, and Bosker (2012).

23 See van Zanden, Buringh, and Bosker (2012, p. 838).

24 Monarchs also called parliaments to legitimize themselves early in their reign, establish laws affecting local commerce, and hear complaints from petitioners.

25 Not all parts of Bavaria were Catholic, but this was the least-Reformed German region. The figure does not look very different with Bavaria classified as Protestant. Also, I drop Russia from this figure, since it was primarily Orthodox.

26 van Zanden, Buringh, and Bosker (2012) argue that there was a "little divergence" in parliamentary development between northwestern Europe and southern Europe between 1500 and 1800, but they do not attribute this divergence to the Reformation. Their empirical observation is consistent with the argument proposed in this book; indeed, the present argument helps explain why this "little divergence" arose when and where it did.

27 See van Zanden, Buringh, and Bosker (2012).

28 Another important distinction between Christianity and Islam is that the former has more centralized institutions than the latter. This argument is highly complementary to the one proposed in this chapter, as explained in note 6. I do not discuss this argument in detail because doing so would necessitate at least two more chapters that would detract from the central focus of the book.

29 See İnalcık (1973, chs. 18–19).

30 Much of this section is from Coşgel, Miceli, and Rubin (2012a). I again thank Metin and Tom for their work and their permission to let me use these ideas we formulated together.

31 On wages, see Özmucur and Pamuk (2002). On literacy, see Quataert (2000, p. 167).

32 Calculated by Metin Coşgel from the information presented in Baysal (1968, pp. 40–2).

33 See Zilfi (1988, pp. 47–8).

34 See İnalcık (1973) and Hourani (1991, ch. 15).

35 See Hourani (1981), Özkaya (1994), and Karaman and Pamuk (2010).

36 Gill (1998, ch. 3) similarly notes, in the Latin American context, that one of the primary times in which states attack religious authority is when alternative sources of legitimacy arise. Gill focuses on the effects of alternative ideologies, such as nationalism or communism.

37 Quoted in Kurzman and Browers (2004, p. 5).

38 See Opwis (2004, pp. 30–3).

39 See Opwis (2004, p. 30). Opwis also notes that these events weakened the hold of religious authorities over the legal sphere as well.

40 See Kuran (2011) for an extensive analysis of the causes and consequences of the Ottoman capitulations.

41 Quoted in Kurzman and Browers (2004, p. 4). For more, also see Opwis (2004).

42 See Browers (2004).

43 See Opwis (2004, pp. 33–7).

44 Eickelman (1998) also points to mass education and communication as the impetus for an "Islamic Reformation," but he places the timing in the latter half of the twentieth century.

45 See Opwis (2004, p. 35).

46 See Opwis (2004, p. 38) and Browers (2004, p. 56).

47 Quoted in Kurzman and Browers (2004, p. 6).

7 Success: England and the Dutch Republic

1 See, for instance, North and Thomas (1973).

2 For an excellent overview of the Malthusian model and its usefulness in economic history, see Clark (2007).

3 See van Zanden, Buringh, and Bosker (2012).

4 See Graves (1985, p. 39).

5 See Congleton (2011, ch. 12) for more consequences of this arrangement.

6 Quoted in Hunt (2008, p. 43).

7 24 Henry VIII c.12.

8 26 Henry VIII c.1.

9 On the last point, see Graves (1985).

10 27 Henry VIII c.10 and 32 Henry VIII c.1.

11 See Ives (1967).

12 See Ives (1967).

13 See Holdsworth (1912), Bordwell (1926), Ives (1967), and North, Wallis, and Weingast (2009, ch. 3).

14 Mary was declared a bastard in the First Succession Act of 1533 (25 Henry VIII c.22), and Elizabeth was declared a bastard in the Second Succession Act of 1536 (28 Henry VIII c. 7).

15 35 Henry VIII c.1.

16 1 Mary st.2 c.1 and 1 Eliz. I c.3.

17 Burgess (1992) overviews the Tudor's and Stuart's use of the "divine right of kings" doctrine and the limitations of this doctrine.

18 For more on this history of usury legislation, see Munro (2012). The reinstitution of usury laws brought back a statute passed under Henry VIII in 1545 that was struck down in 1552.

19 See North and Weingast (1989).

20 See Brenner (1993) for a fantastically detailed exposition of the "new merchant" and Parliamentary alliances that were the key to the Royalist opposition in the Civil War.

21 There is a large literature citing the seventeenth-century political conflicts between Parliament and the Crown as a key determinant of long-run economic success in England. Most famously, Douglass North and Barry Weingast (1989) suggest that the ultimate upshot of the conflicts, especially the Glorious Revolution settlement, was that the Crown could credibly commit to upholding the property rights of the economic elite, as Parliament showed they could remove a monarch. The constitutional structure resulting from the Settlement allowed action in times of crisis, but also gave wealth-holders in Parliament a greater say in the daily happenings of government. North and Weingast's theory is not without its detractors, and the present book does not engage in this debate. See in particular Clark (1996), who argues that rates of return were stable well before the Glorious Revolution and did not spike around the Revolution, as would be expected if North and Weingast are correct. For other criticisms of North and Weingast's theory, see Carruthers (1990), Wells and Wills (2000), Quinn (2001), and Sussman and Yafeh (2006). Pincus and Robinson (2014) argue that North and Weingast were correct to focus on institutional changes heralded by the Glorious Revolution, but that party politics were at the root of the changes, not credible commitment. Cox (2012) argues that North and Weingast were correct to focus on institutional changes, but their focus on property rights was misplaced. Cox suggests that the important changes were constitutional in nature, giving Parliament greater ability to grant tax revenues and issue debt.

22 For much more on the commercial policies of the Interregnum government, see Brenner (1993, ch. 12).

23 See de Vries and van der Woude (1997) and de Vries (2000) for numbers attesting to Dutch growth during the Golden Age.

24 See Israel (1995, ch. 6), de Vries and van der Woude (1997), van Zanden (2002a, 2002b), and van Bavel (2003). van Zanden (2002a, 2002b) attempts to pin the rise of the Dutch economy to an earlier period than de Vries and van der Woude. van Zanden (2002b) goes so far as to say that Dutch economic growth over the sixteenth–eighteenth centuries was "unspectacular." I have no interest in entering into this argument; the only point made here is that the Dutch had a "head start" on much of the rest of Europe, a relatively uncontroversial point within this literature.

25 See Allen (2001) and van Zanden (2002a).

26 See van Zanden (2002b), van Bavel (2003), and van Zanden, Zuijderduijn, and de Moor (2012).

27 See North (1981, p. 152).

28 See Israel (1995, p. 106).

29 See de Vries and van der Woude (1997, ch. 5) and van Zanden, Zuijderduijn, and de Moor (2012). van Zanden (2002a) argues that the Dutch did indeed have a feudal past, and he cites a recent literature in support of this assertion. Regardless, it is clear that the feudal nobility were weaker relative to the urban classes in the Low Countries than they were elsewhere in Europe.

30 See van Zanden, Zuijderduijn, and de Moor (2012) for more on the accessibility of credit in late medieval Holland.

31 See Israel (1995, ch. 6).

32 See Parker (1977, p. 32), van Gelderen (1992, pp. 22–3), and van Zanden, Zuijderduijn, and de Moor (2012).

33 See Israel (1995, ch. 13).

34 See van Zanden and Prak (2006).

35 See Parker (1977, p. 179) and de Vries and van der Woude (1997, ch. 4).

36 van Gelderen (1992) gives an excellent overview of the political thought underlying the Dutch Revolt.

37 See Israel (1995, p. 79).

38 See Parker (1977, pp. 36–7).

39 See Parker (1977, ch. 2), van Gelderen (1992), and de Vries and van der Woude (1997, ch. 9).

40 See Parker (1977, p. 155). van Gelderen (1992, ch. 4) notes that by the mid-1570s, the Dutch made efforts to deny that the Revolt was religiously motivated, instead arguing that it was a fight for liberty.

41 See Fritschy (2003).

42 See de Vries and van der Woude (1997, ch. 4), Fritschy (2003), and van Zanden and Prak (2006).

43 See Israel (1995, ch. 14).

44 See Gelderblom and Jonker (2004).

45 See Gelderblom and Jonker (2005).

46 See de Vries and van der Woude (1997, chs. 2, 5, 9).

47 See Israel (1995, ch. 15).

48 See de Vries and van der Woude (1997, chs. 11, 12).

49 See Israel (1995, ch. 6).

50 See de Vries and van der Woude (1997, chs. 3, 11, 13).

51 See Israel (1995, ch. 14), de Vries and van der Woude (1997, chs. 3, 8), and van Bavel (2003).

52 See Israel (1995, ch. 12).

53 See de Vries and van der Woude (1997, chs. 5, 8). Priest (2006) gives an excellent overview of laws regarding the alienability of land in English history.

54 See de Vries and van der Woude (1997, ch. 4).

55 Cameron and Neal (2003) give a nice overview of the order in which the European countries industrialized.

56 See de Vries and van der Woude (1997, chs. 8, 11, 14).

57 See de Vries (2000).

8 Stagnation: Spain and the Ottoman Empire

1 See Kamen (2003).
2 The exact number of people expelled has long been the subject of debate. For example, Elliott (1961) claims that Hamilton (1938) vastly underestimated the number of expulsions and thus underestimated their economic impact. It is not my purpose to enter into this debate, only to note that the expulsions affected the Spanish Crown's basis for legitimacy.
3 See Simpson (1956) and Lynch (1991, ch. 1).
4 See Lynch (1991, ch. 1). The police forces (*hermandades*) also brought the nobility to heel, as they were able to force contributions from both the nobility and the Church.
5 See Lynch (1991, p. 154).
6 See Dunn (1979, ch. 1), Kamen (1988, ch. 5), and Lynch (1991, ch. 8). Kamen in particular argues that the Spanish history of squashing nonorthodox thought gave the Reformation little it could build on in Spain. Another possibility, which I do not wish to push too far, is that publishing never became a big business in Spain prior to the Reformation (Kamen 1988, p. 69). This is consistent with the argument made in Chapter 6, which notes the importance of printing to the propaganda efforts of the Reformers.
7 See Lynch (1991, ch. 2).
8 See Lynch (1991, ch. 2).
9 Quote from Drelichman (2005a). For more on the effect of the *comuneros* revolt, see Drelichman (2005a), Lynch (1991, ch. 2), and Simpson (1956). Kamen (1988) argues that the "rubber stamp" view of the Cortes is untenable, but he points to the late sixteenth and seventeenth centuries as evidence. This may be true in the period Kamen is considering, but it is not the object of discussion here.
10 Quote from Lynch (1991, p. 64).
11 See Kamen (2003, ch. 2).
12 See Lynch (1991, ch. 9).
13 See Parker (1973) and Lynch (1991, ch. 9). Parker (1973) gives an overview of the repeated mutinies of the Spanish army in the late sixteenth century, all of which occurred due to lack of payment.
14 See Dunn (1979, ch. 1) and Lynch (1991, ch. 7).
15 See Lynch (1991, ch. 7).
16 See Drelichman and Voth (2011).
17 See Lynch (1991, ch. 2).
18 See Drelichman (2005a). Drelichman (2005b) argues that the import of precious metals from America created a "Dutch disease" that undermined Spanish long-run economic growth. Irigoin and Grafe (2008) and Grafe and Irigoin (2012) note that the Crown was able to extract significant revenue despite having almost no fiscal apparatus by outsourcing fiscal functions to private individuals.
19 See Drelichman (2005a) and Drelichman and Voth (2011).
20 See Drelichman and Voth (2011).
21 See Drelichman (2005a).
22 See Drelichman (2005a).

23 See Irigoin and Grafe (2008, 2013) and Grafe and Irigoin (2012). The fiscal apparatus was weak and decentralized. The central government had almost no control over which taxes their tax farmers levied.

24 For more on the long-run effects of such extractive institutions, see Acemoglu, Johnson, and Robinson (2005) and Acemoglu and Robinson (2012).

25 Spanish policies regarding the wool industry were yet another cause of Spanish economic decline. The Mesta (sheep-owners' guild) was favored by the Crown, and the Crown therefore refrained from enclosing common lands and providing security of property rights for non-Mesta agriculturalists. See Hamilton (1938), Elliott (1961), North (1981), and Lynch (1991, ch. 4). Kamen (1978) argues that there is simply no plausible evidence to suggest that the Crown's favoring of the Mesta inhibited agriculture. I do not wish to enter into this argument here. I simply note that the arguments made in this book are consistent with the Crown's favoring of the Mesta at the expense of economic development, to the extent that this was historically the case.

26 Even where local finance and law and order were not under the control of the Crown, it was in the hands of the growing aristocracy and the Church, neither of whom were interested in commercial endeavors. See Kamen (1988, ch. 1).

27 See Lynch (1991, ch. 4).

28 See Lynch (1991, ch. 4) and Kamen (2003, chs. 2, 7).

29 See Lynch (1991, ch. 4).

30 See Lynch (1991, ch. 4).

31 See Elliott (1961) and Lynch (1991, pp. 172–3).

32 See Lynch (1991, pp. 198–9).

33 See Elliott (1961).

34 See Elliott (1961) and Lynch (1991, ch. 2).

35 Also see Álvarez-Nogal and de la Escosura (2007).

36 For more on the *arbitristas*, see Baeck (1988).

37 There is a long history of academic treatises trying to explain the "decline of Spain." For some of the relevant literature, see Hamilton (1938), Elliott (1961), and Kamen (1978). Kamen views the decline of Spain as a myth, arguing that Spain never really "rose" in the first place.

38 See Álvarez-Nogal and de la Escosura (2007). They show there was significant variation within Spain, but the general pattern over time appears robust.

39 See Hamilton (1938) and Álvarez-Nogal and de la Escosura (2007, 2013).

40 See Álvarez-Nogal and de la Escosura (2007, 2013).

41 For more on the varying sources of legitimacy employed by the Ottomans, see Coşgel, Miceli, and Rubin (2012a, 2012b).

42 For more, see İnalcık (1973, ch. 13), Hourani (1991, ch. 13), Pamuk (2004b), Coşgel and Miceli (2005), and Karaman and Pamuk (2010).

43 See İnalcık (1973).

44 See Karaman (2009).

45 For more on Ebu's-su'ud – his career, life, and place within the Ottoman hierarchy – see Imber (1997).

46 See van Zanden, Buringh, and Bosker (2012).

47 The Ottomans did face a threat in the early fifteenth century when Tamerlane overthrew them. Sultan Mehmed I (r. 1413–1421) won back the throne by ceding to

the demands of the elite. However, this was prior to their expansion outside of the Anatolian and Balkan peninsulas. See Karaman (2009).

48 See Kuran (2005b, 2011).

49 See Pamuk (2004a) and Balla and Johnson (2009).

50 See Pamuk (2004a) and Karaman and Pamuk (2010).

51 See Pamuk (2004b).

52 See Pamuk (2004a, 2004b).

53 See Karaman and Pamuk (2010).

54 See Karaman and Pamuk (2010).

55 See Balla and Johnson (2009).

56 See Karaman (2009) for an analysis of the Ottoman tradeoffs between tax collection and stifling revolt.

57 The Ottomans did occasionally modify commercial law. For instance, in the nineteenth century, after external pressures made it obvious that economic stagnation was harming the Ottomans' position vis-à-vis Europe, they imposed a series of economic reforms. Moreover, the Qur'an is hardly wholly antithetical to commerce; scores of verses sanctify private property and encourage enrichment. The point is simply that the costs of modifying commercial law frequently, but not always, outweighed its benefits.

58 See İnalcık (1973, ch. 10) and Karaman (2009).

59 For example, one of Ebu's-su'ud's great accomplishments was that he harmonized secular administration with religious law by allowing rulers wide discretion in setting tax rates. See Imber (1997).

60 See Kuran (2011).

61 See Pamuk (2000).

62 See Özmucur and Pamuk (2002).

63 For overviews of the Great Debasement, see Challis (1967) and Munro (2011). For more on the inflationary effect of the Great Debasement, see Brenner (1961).

64 Metin Coşgel and Bogac Ergene (2014) find similar patterns in their analysis of courts in eighteenth-century Kastamonu, an Ottoman town in north-central Turkey. They show that members from elite families did much better than those from poorer families, although they suggest that it is possible that this was not the result of judicial bias, but resulted from the fact that members of the elite would only risk going to court if they were confident they would win.

65 On the merchant guild, see Greif, Milgrom, and Weingast (1994) and Greif (2006b). On the community responsibility system, see Greif (2002, 2004, 2006b).

References

Acemoglu, Daron (2005), 'Politics and Economics in Weak and Strong States', *Journal of Monetary Economics*, 52, 1199–226.

Acemoglu, Daron, Johnson, Simon, and Robinson, James A. (2001), 'The Colonial Origins of Comparative Development: An Empirical Investigation', *American Economic Review*, 91 (5), 1369–401.

(2002), 'Reversal of Fortune: Geography and Institutions in the Making of the Modern World Income Distribution', *Quarterly Journal of Economics*, 118, 1231–94.

(2005), 'The Rise of Europe: Atlantic Trade, Institutional Change, and Economic Growth', *American Economic Review*, 95 (3), 546–79.

Acemoglu, Daron and Robinson, James A. (2006), 'Economic Backwardness in Political Perspective', *American Political Science Review*, 100, 115–31.

(2012), *Why Nations Fail: The Origins of Power, Prosperity, and Poverty* (New York: Crown).

Ahmad, Feroz (2000), 'Ottoman Perceptions of the Capitulations 1800–1914', *Journal of Islamic Studies*, 11 (1), 1–20.

Alesina, Alberto and Giuliano, Paola (2015), 'Culture and Institutions', *Journal of Economic Literature*, 53 (4), 898–944.

Alesina, Alberto and Spolaore, Enrico (1997), 'On the Number and Size of Nations', *Quarterly Journal of Economics*, 112 (4), 1027–56.

(2005), 'War, Peace, and the Size of Countries', *Journal of Public Economics*, 89 (7), 1333–54.

Allen, Robert C. (2001), 'The Great Divergence in European Wages and Prices from the Middle Ages to the First World War', *Explorations in Economic History*, 38, 411–47.

(2009), *The British Industrial Revolution in Global Perspective* (Cambridge: Cambridge University Press).

Allen, Robert C., et al. (2011), 'Wages, Prices, and Living Standards in China, 1738–1925: In Comparison with Europe, Japan, and India', *Economic History Review*, 64 (S1), 8–38.

Alston, Lee J., et al. (2016), *Beliefs, Leadership and Critical Transitions: Brazil, 1964–2012* (Princeton: Princeton University Press).

Álvarez-Nogal, Carlos and de la Escosura, Leandro Prados (2007), 'The Decline of Spain (1500–1850): Conjectural Estimates', *European Review of Economic History*, 11, 319–66.

(2013), 'The Rise and Fall of Spain (1270–1850)', *Economic History Review*, 66 (1), 1–37.

Anderson, Robert Warren, Johnson, Noel D., and Koyama, Mark (2016), 'Jewish Persecutions and Weather Shocks: 1100–1800', *Economic Journal*, Forthcoming.

Aoki, Masahiko (2001), *Toward a Comparative Institutional Analysis* (Cambridge, MA: MIT Press).

Arruñada, Benito (2010), 'Protestants and Catholics: Similar Work Ethic, Different Social Ethic', *Economic Journal*, 120 (547), 890–918.

Ashtor, Eliahu (1973), 'Banking Instruments between the Muslim East and the Christian West', *Journal of European Economic History*, 1, 553–73.

Atiyeh, George Nicholas (1995), *The Book in the Islamic World: The Written Word and Communication in the Middle East* (Albany: State University of New York Press).

Baeck, Louis (1988), 'Spanish Economic Thought: The School of Salamanca and the Arbitristas', *History of Political Economy*, 20 (3), 381–408.

Bairoch, Paul, Batou, Jean, and Chèvre, Pierre (1988), *La Population des Villes Européennes, 800–1850* (Geneva: Droz).

Balla, Eliana and Johnson, Noel D. (2009), 'Fiscal Crisis and Institutional Change in the Ottoman Empire and France', *Journal of Economic History*, 69 (3), 809–45.

Barkan, Ömer Lütfi (1970), 'Research on the Ottoman Fiscal Surveys', in M.A. Cook (ed.), *Studies in the Economic History of the Middle East* (London: Oxford University Press), 163–71.

Barro, Robert and McCleary, Rachel M. (2003), 'Religion and Economic Growth Across Countries', *American Sociological Review*, 68 (5), 760–81.

Baten, Joerg and Zanden, Jan Luiten van (2008), 'Book Production and the Onset of Modern Economic Growth', *Journal of Economic Growth*, 13 (3), 217–35.

Bates, Robert H. (2001), *Prosperity and Violence: The Political Economy of Development* (New York: Norton).

Baysal, Jale (1968), *Müteferrikadan Birinci Mesrutiyete kadar Osmanlı Türklerinin bastıkları Kitaplar* (Istanbul).

Bearman, P., et al. (2005), 'Brill Encyclopaedia of Islam', Second edn. (Leiden: Brill).

Becker, Sascha O., Pfaff, Steven, and Rubin, Jared (2016), 'Causes and Consequences of the Protestant Reformation', *Explorations in Economic History*, Forthcoming.

Becker, Sascha O. and Wößmann, Ludger (2008), 'Luther and the Girls: Religious Denomination and the Female Education Gap in 19th Century Prussia', *Scandinavian Journal of Economics*, 110 (4), 777–805.

(2009), 'Was Weber Wrong? A Human Capital Theory of Protestant Economic History', *Quarterly Journal of Economics*, 124 (2), 531–96.

Berkey, Jonathan P. (2003), *The Formation of Islam: Religion and Society in the Near East, 600–1800* (Cambridge: Cambridge University Press).

Berman, Eli (2000), 'Sect, Subsidy, and Sacrifice: An Economist's View of Ultra-Orthodox Jews', *Quarterly Journal of Economics*, 115 (3), 905–53.

Berman, Harold J. (1983), *Law and Revolution: The Formation of the Western Legal Tradition* (Cambridge, MA: Harvard University Press).

Besley, Timothy and Persson, Torsten (2009), 'The Origins of State Capacity: Property Rights, Taxation and Politics', *American Economic Review*, 99 (4), 1218–44.

(2010), 'State Capacity, Conflict and Development', *Econometrica*, 78, 1–34.

Blaydes, Lisa and Chaney, Eric (2013), 'The Feudal Revolution and Europe's Rise: Political Divergence of the Christian West and the Muslim World before 1500 CE', *American Political Science Review*, 107 (1), 16–34.

Blickle, Peter (1984), 'Social Protest and Reformation Theology', in Kaspar von Greyerz (ed.), *Religion, Politics and Social Protest: Three Studies on Early Modern Germany* (London: George Allen & Unwin).

Bogart, Dan (2011), 'Did the Glorious Revolution Contribute to the Transport Revolution? Evidence from Investment in Roads and Rivers', *Economic History Review*, 64 (4), 1073–112.

Bogart, Dan and Richardson, Gary (2009), 'Making Property Productive: Reorganizing Rights to Real and Equitable Estates in Britain, 1660–1830', *European Review of Economic History*, 13, 3–30.

  (2011), 'Property Rights and Parliament in Industrializing Britain', *Journal of Law and Economics*, 54 (2), 241–74.

Bolt, Jutta and van Zanden, Jan Luiten (2014), 'The Maddison Project: Collaborative Research on Historical National Accounts', *Economic History Review*, 67 (3), 627–51.

Bordwell, Percy (1926), 'The Repeal of the Statute of Uses', *Harvard Law Review*, 39 (4), 466–84.

Bosker, Maarten, Buringh, Eltjo, and van Zanden, Jan Luiten (2013), 'From Baghdad to London: Unraveling Urban Development in Europe, the Middle East, and North Africa, 800–1800', *Review of Economics & Statistics*, 95 (4), 1418–37.

Botticini, Maristella and Eckstein, Zvi (2012), *The Chosen Few: How Education Shaped Jewish History, 70–1492* (Princeton: Princeton University Press).

Brennan, Geoffrey and Buchanan, James M. (1980), *The Power to Tax: Analytical Foundations of a Fiscal Constitution* (Cambridge: Cambridge University Press).

Brenner, Reuven (1983), *History – The Human Gamble* (Chicago: University of Chicago Press).

Brenner, Robert (1993), *Merchants and Revolution: Commercial Change, Political Conflict, and London's Overseas Traders, 1550–1653* (Princeton: Princeton University Press).

Brenner, Y.S. (1961), 'The Inflation of Prices in Early Sixteenth Century England', *Economic History Review*, 14 (2), 225–39.

The British Library (2011), 'Incunabula Short Title Catalog (ISTC)', <www.bl.uk/catalogues/istc/>, accessed September 9, 2016.

Browers, Michaelle (2004), 'Islam and Political *Sinn*: The Hermeneutics of Contemporary Islamic Reformists', in Michaelle Browers and Charles Kurzman (eds.), *An Islamic Reformation?* (Lanham: Lexington).

Burgess, Glenn (1992), 'The Divine Right of Kings Reconsidered', *English Historical Review*, 107 (425), 837–61.

Buringh, Eltjo and van Zanden, Jan Luiten (2009), 'Charting the "Rise of the West": Manuscripts and Printed Books in Europe, A Long-Term Perspective from the Sixth through Eighteenth Centuries', *Journal of Economic History*, 69 (2), 409–45.

Çağatay, Neşet (1970), 'Ribā and Interest Concept and Banking in the Ottoman Empire', *Studia Islamica*, 32, 53–68.

Cameron, Averil (1993), *The Later Roman Empire: AD 284–430* (London: Fontana Press).

Cameron, Euan (1991), *The European Reformation* (Oxford: Oxford University Press).

Cameron, Rondo and Neal, Larry (2003), *A Concise Economic History of the World: From Paleolithic Times to the Present* (Oxford: Oxford University Press).

Cantoni, Davide (2012), 'Adopting a New Religion: The Case of Protestantism in 16th Century Germany', *Economic Journal*, 122 (560), 502–31.

(2015), 'The Economic Effects of the Protestant Reformation: Testing the Weber Hypothesis in the German Lands', *Journal of the European Economic Association*, 13 (4), 561–98.

Carruthers, Bruce G. (1990), 'Politics, Popery, and Property: A Comment on North and Weingast', *Journal of Economic History*, 50 (3), 693–98.

Challis, C.E. (1967), 'The Debasement of the Coinage, 1542–1551', *Economic History Review*, 20 (3), 441–55.

Chaney, Eric (2013), 'Revolt on the Nile: Economic Shocks, Religion, and Political Power', *Econometrica*, 81 (5), 2033–53.

(2016), 'Religion and the Rise and Fall of Muslim Science', Harvard University Press Working Paper.

Chaudhary, Latika and Rubin, Jared (2011), 'Reading, Writing, and Religion: Institutions and Human Capital Formation', *Journal of Comparative Economics*, 39 (1), 17–33.

(2016), 'Religious Identity and the Provision of Public Goods: Evidence from the Indian Princely States', *Journal of Comparative Economics*, 44 (3), 461–83.

Chilosi, David and Volckart, Oliver (2010), 'Books or Bullion? Printing, Mining and Financial Integration in Central Europe from the 1460s', LSE Working Paper 144/10.

Christ, Karl, Kern, Anton, and Otto, Theophil M. (1984), *The Handbook of Medieval Library History* (Metuchen, NJ: Scarecrow Press).

CIA (2014), 'The World Factbook' (Washington, DC).

Cipolla, Carlo M. (1967), *Money, Prices, and Civilization in the Mediterranean World: Fifth to Seventeenth Century* (New York: Gordian Press).

Çizakça, Murat (1995), 'Cash *Waqf*s of Bursa, 1555–1823', *Journal of the Economic and Social History of the Orient*, 38, 313–54.

(2000), *A History of Philanthropic Foundations: The Islamic World from the Seventh Century to the Present* (Istanbul: Bogazici University Press).

(2004), 'Ottoman Cash *Waqf*s Revisited: The Case of Bursa, 1555–1823', *Foundation for Science, Technology and Civilization* (June), 2–20.

Clair, Colin (1976), *A History of European Printing* (New York: Academic Press).

Clark, Gregory (1996), 'The Political Foundations of Modern Economic Growth: England, 1540–1800', *Journal of Interdisciplinary History*, 26 (4), 563–88.

(2007), *A Farewell to Alms: A Brief Economic History of the World* (Princeton: Princeton University Press).

Coleman-Norton, P.R. (1966), *Roman State & Christian Church: A Collection of Legal Documents to A.D. 535* (London: S.P.C.K.).

Congleton, Roger D. (2011), *Perfecting Parliament: Constitutional Reform, Liberalism, and the Rise of Western Democracy* (Cambridge: Cambridge University Press).

Coşgel, Metin M. and Ergene, Boğaç A. (2014), 'The Selection Bias in Court Records: Settlement and Trial in Eighteenth-Century Ottoman Kastamonu', *Economic History Review*, 67 (2), 517–34.

Coşgel, Metin M. and Miceli, Thomas J. (2005), 'Risk, Transaction Costs, and Government Finance: The Distribution of Tax Revenue in the Ottoman Empire', *Journal of Economic History*, 65 (3), 806–21.

(2009), 'State and Religion', *Journal of Comparative Economics*, 37, 402–16.

Coşgel, Metin M., Miceli, Thomas J., and Ahmed, Rasha (2009), 'Law, State Power, and Taxation in Islamic History', *Journal of Economic Behavior and Organization*, 71 (3), 704–17.

Coşgel, Metin M., Miceli, Thomas J., and Rubin, Jared (2012a), 'The Political Economy of Mass Printing: Legitimacy, Revolt, and Technology Change in the Ottoman Empire', *Journal of Comparative Economics*, 40 (3), 357–71.

(2012b), 'Political Legitimacy and Technology Adoption', *Journal of Institutional and Theoretical Economics*, 168 (3), 339–61.

Coulson, Noel J. (1969), *Conflicts and Tensions in Islamic Jurisprudence* (Chicago: University of Chicago Press).

Cox, Gary W. (2012), 'Was the Glorious Revolution a Constitutional Watershed?', *Journal of Economic History*, 72 (3), 567–600.

Cromer, Evelyn B. (1908), *Modern Egypt*, vol. 2 (London: Macmillan).

Crone, Patricia and Hinds, Martin (1986), *God's Caliph: Religious Authority in the First Centuries of Islam* (Cambridge: Cambridge University Press).

Curuk, Malik and Smulders, Sjak (2016), 'Malthus Meets Luther: The Economics Behind the German Reformation', CESifo Working Paper Series No. 6010.

Dale, Stephen F. (2010), *The Muslim Empires of the Ottomans, Safavids, and Mughals* (Cambridge: Cambridge University Press).

Danforth, Nick (2013), 'Stop Blaming Colonial Borders for the Middle East's Problems', *The Atlantic*, <www.theatlantic.com/international/archive/2013/09/stop-blaming-colonial-borders-for-the-middle-easts-problems/279561>.

David, Paul A. (1985), 'Clio and the Economics of QWERTY', *American Economic Review*, 75 (2), 332–37.

(1994), 'Why Are Institutions the 'Carriers of History'?: Path Dependence and the Evolution of Conventions, Organizations, and Institutions', *Structural Change and Economic Dynamics*, 5, 205–20.

de Long, J. Bradford and Shleifer, Andrei (1993), 'Princes and Merchants: European City Growth before the Industrial Revolution', *Journal of Law and Economics*, 36 (2), 671–702.

de Roover, Raymond (1942), 'Money, Banking, and Credit in Medieval Bruges', *Journal of Economic History*, 2 (Supplement), 52–65.

(1944), 'What Is Dry Exchange? A Contribution to the Study of English Mercantilism', *Journal of Political Economy*, 52, 250–66.

(1946a), 'The Medici Bank Financial and Commercial Operations', *Journal of Economic History*, 6, 153–72.

(1946b), 'The Medici Bank Organization and Management', *Journal of Economic History*, 6, 24–52.

(1948), *Money, Banking, and Credit in Mediæval Bruges* (Cambridge, MA: Mediaeval Academy of America).

(1963), *The Rise and Decline of the Medici Bank: 1397–1494* (New York: W.W. Norton.).

de Vries, Jan (1984), *European Urbanization 1500–1800* (Cambridge, MA: Harvard University Press).

(2000), 'Dutch Economic Growth in Comparative-Historical Perspective, 1500–2000', *De Economist*, 148 (4), 443–67.

de Vries, Jan and van der Woude, Ad (1997), *The First Modern Economy: Success, Failure, and Perseverance of the Dutch Economy, 1500–1815* (Cambridge: Cambridge University Press).

Delacroix, Jacques and Nielsen, Francois (2001), 'The Beloved Myth: Protestantism and the Rise of Industrial Capitalism in Nineteenth-Century Europe', *Social Forces*, 80 (2), 509–53.

Diamond, Jared (1997), *Guns, Germs, and Steel: The Fates of Human Societies* (New York: Norton).

Dickens, Arthur Geoffrey (1968), *Reformation and Society in Sixteenth Century Europe* (New York: Harcourt, Brace, & World).

(1974), *The German Nation and Martin Luther* (New York: Harper).

Dien, M.Y. Izzi (1995), 'Suftadja', in C.E. Bosworth et al. (eds.), *The Encyclopaedia of Islam: New Edition* (Leiden: Brill).

Dincecco, Mark (2009), 'Fiscal Centralization, Limited Government, and Public Revenues in Europe', *Journal of Economic History*, 69 (1), 48–103.

(2011), *Political Transformations and Public Finances: Europe, 1650–1913* (Cambridge: Cambridge University Press).

Dincecco, Mark, Fenske, James, and Onorato, Massimiliano Gaetano (2016), 'Is Africa Different? Historical Conflict and State Development', CSAE Working Paper 2014–35.

Dittmar, Jeremiah (2011), 'Information Technology and Economic Change: The Impact of the Printing Press', *Quarterly Journal of Economics*, 126 (3), 1133–72.

Divine, Thomas F. (1959), *Interest: An Historical and Analytical Study in Economics and Modern Ethics* (Milwaukee: Marquette University Press.).

Djankov, Simon, et al. (2002), 'The Regulation of Entry', *Quarterly Journal of Economics*, 117 (1), 1–37.

(2003), 'Courts', *Quarterly Journal of Economics*, 118 (2), 453–517.

Dolan, John P. (1965), *History of the Reformation: A Conciliatory Assessment of Opposite Views* (New York: Desclee).

Dow, John (1922), 'Usury (Christian)', in James Hastings (ed.), *Encyclopædia of Religion and Ethics*, vol. 12 (New York: Charles Scribner's Sons).

Downey, Glanville (1969), *The Late Roman Empire* (New York: Holt, Rinehart and Winston).

Drelichman, Mauricio (2005a), 'All That Glitters: Precious Metals, Rent Seeking and the Decline of Spain', *European Review of Economic History*, 9 (3), 313–36.

(2005b), 'The Curse of Moctezuma: American Silver and the Dutch Disease', *Explorations in Economic History*, 42 (3), 349–80.

Drelichman, Mauricio and Voth, Hans-Joachim (2011), 'Lending to the Borrower from Hell: Debt and Default in the Age of Philip II', *Economic Journal*, 121, 1205–27.

Dunn, Richard S. (1979), *The Age of Religious Wars, 1559–1715* (New York: Norton).

Edwards, Mark U. (1994), *Printing, Propaganda, and Martin Luther* (Berkeley: University of California Press).

Eickelman, Dale F. (1998), 'Inside the Islamic Reformation', *Wilson Quarterly*, 22 (1), 80–89.

Einzig, Paul (1970), *The History of Foreign Exchange*, 2nd edn. (London: Macmillan).

Eisenstein, Elizabeth L. (1979), *The Printing Press as an Agent of Change: Communications and Cultural Transformations in Early Modern Europe* (Cambridge: Cambridge University Press).

Ekelund, Robert B., Hébert, Robert F., and Tollison, Robert D. (2002), 'An Economic Analysis of the Protestant Reformation', *Journal of Political Economy*, 110 (3), 646–71.

Ekelund, Robert B., et al. (1996), *Sacred Trust: The Medieval Church as an Economic Firm* (Oxford: Oxford University Press).

Elliott, John H. (1961), 'The Decline of Spain', *Past & Present*, 20, 52–75.

Engerman, Stanley L. and Sokoloff, Kenneth L. (1997), 'Factor Endowments, Institutions, and Differential Paths of Growth among New World Economies: A View from Economic Historians of the United States', in Stephen Haber (ed.), *How Latin America Fell Behind: Essays on the Economic Histories of Brazil and Mexico, 1800–1914* (Stanford: Stanford University Press).

(2002), 'Factor Endowments, Inequality, and Paths of Development among New World Economies', NBER Working Paper 9259.

Ensminger, Jean (1997), 'Transaction Costs and Islam: Explaining Conversion in Africa', *Journal of Institutional and Theoretical Economics*, 153 (1), 4–29.

Febvre, Lucien and Martin, Henri-Jean (1958), *The Coming of the Book: The Impact of Printing, 1450–1800* (London: Verso).

Feldman, Noah (2008), *The Fall and Rise of the Islamic State* (Princeton: Princeton University Press).

Feldman, Stephen M. (1997), *Please Don't Wish Me a Merry Christmas: A Critical History of the Separation of Church and State* (New York: New York University Press).

Fierro, Maribel (1996), 'Caliphal Legitimacy and Expiation in al-Andalus', in Muhammad K. Masud, Brinkley Messick, and David S. Powers (eds.), *Islamic Legal Interpretation: Muftis and their Fatwas* (Cambridge, MA: Harvard University Press).

Findlay, Ronald and O'Rourke, Kevin H. (2007), *Power and Plenty: Trade, War, and the World Economy in the Second Millennium* (Princeton: Princeton University Press).

Finkel, Caroline (2005), *Osman's Dream: The Story of the Ottoman Empire, 1300–1923* (London: Perseus).

Frazee, Charles A. (1983), *Catholics and Sultans: The Church and the Ottoman Empire 1453–1923* (Cambridge: Cambridge University Press).

Friedman, David (1977), 'A Theory of the Size and Shape of Nations', *Journal of Political Economy*, 85 (1), 59–77.

Frierson, James G. (1969), 'Changing Concepts on Usury: Ancient Times through the Time of John Calvin', *American Business Law Journal*, 7, 115–25.

Fritschy, Wantje (2003), 'A 'Financial Revolution' Reconsidered: Public Finance in Holland during the Dutch Revolt, 1568–1648', *Economic History Review*, 56 (1), 57–89.

Gager, John G. (1975), *Kingdom and Community: The Social World of Early Christianity* (Englewood Cliffs: Prentice-Hall).

Galor, Oded (2011), *Unified Growth Theory* (Princeton: Princeton University Press).

Gelderblom, Oscar and Jonker, Joost (2004), 'Completing a Financial Revolution: The Finance of the Dutch East India Trade and the Rise of the Amsterdam Capital Market, 1595–1612', *Journal of Economic History*, 64 (3), 641–72.

(2005), 'Amsterdam as the Cradle of Modern Futures Trading and Options Trading, 1550–1650', in W.N. Goetzmann and K.G. Rouwenhorst (eds.), *The Origins of Value. The Financial Innovations that Created Modern Capital Markets* (Oxford: Oxford University Press).

Gelpi, Rosa-Maria and Julien-Labruyère, François (2000), *The History of Consumer Credit: Doctrines and Practices* (New York: St. Martin's).

Gennaioli, Nicola and Voth, Hans-Joachim (2015), 'State Capacity and Military Conflict', *Review of Economic Studies*, 83, 1–47.

Gerber, Haim (1988), *Economy and Society in an Ottoman City: Bursa, 1600–1700* (Jerusalem: The Hebrew University).

 (1999), *Islamic Law and Culture 1600–1840* (Leiden: Brill).

Gilchrist, John (1969), *The Church and Economic Activity in the Middle Ages* (London: Macmillan).

Gill, Anthony (1998), *Rendering Unto Caesar: The Catholic Church and the State in Latin America* (Chicago: University of Chicago Press).

 (2008), *The Political Origins of Religious Liberty* (Cambridge: Cambridge University Press).

Glaeser, Edward L. and Scheinkman, Jose (1998), 'Neither a Borrower nor a Lender Be: An Economic Analysis of Interest Restrictions and Usury Laws', *Journal of Law and Economics*, 41 (1), 1–36.

Glaeser, Edward L. and Shleifer, Andrei (2002), 'Legal Origins', *Quarterly Journal of Economics*, 117 (4), 1193–229.

Glaeser, Edward L., et al. (2004), 'Do Institutions Cause Growth?', *Journal of Economic Growth*, 9 (3), 271–303.

Göçek, Fatma Muge (1987), *East Encounters West: France and the Ottoman Empire in the Eighteenth Century* (Oxford: Oxford University Press).

Goitein, Shelomo D. (1967), *A Mediterranean Society: The Jewish Communities of the Arab World as Portrayed in the Documents of the Cairo Geniza*, vol. 1 (Berkeley: University of California Press).

Goldstone, Jack A. (2000), 'The Rise of the West – or Not? A Revision to Socio-economic History', *Sociological Theory*, 18 (2), 175–94.

Goodenough, Erwin R. (1931), *The Church in the Roman Empire* (New York: Henry Holt and Company).

Goody, Jack (1983), *The Development of the Family and Marriage in Europe* (Cambridge: Cambridge University Press).

Grafe, Regina and Irigoin, Alejandra (2012), 'A Stakeholder Empire: The Political Economy of Spanish Imperial Rule in America', *Economic History Review*, 65 (2), 609–51.

Graves, Michael A.R. (1985), *The Tudor Parliaments: Crown, Lords, and Commons, 1485–1603* (New York: Longman).

Greif, Avner (1993), 'Contract Enforceability and Economic Institutions in Early Trade: The Maghribi Traders' Coalition', *American Economic Review*, 83 (3), 525–48.

 (1994a), 'Cultural Beliefs and the Organization of Society: A Historical and Theoretical Reflection on Collectivist and Individualist Societies', *Journal of Political Economy*, 102 (5), 912–50.

 (1994b), 'On the Political Foundations of the Late Medieval Commercial Revolution: Genoa during the Twelfth and Thirteenth Centuries', *Journal of Economic History*, 54 (2), 271–87.

 (2002), 'The Islamic Equilibrium: Legitimacy and Political, Social, and Economic Outcomes', Mimeo.

(2004), 'Impersonal Exchange without Impartial Law: The Community Responsibility System', *Chicago Journal of International Law*, 5 (1), 109–38.

(2006a), 'Family Structure, Institutions, and Growth: The Origins and Implications of Western Corporations', *American Economic Review*, 96 (2), 308–12.

(2006b), *Institutions and the Path to the Modern Economy* (Cambridge: Cambridge University Press).

(2010), 'A Theory of Moral Authority: Moral Choices under Moral Networks Externalities', Mimeo.

Greif, Avner and Iyigun, Murat (2013), 'Social Organizations, Risk-Sharing Institutions and Industrialization', *American Economic Review*, 103 (3), 534–38.

Greif, Avner, Iyigun, Murat, and Sasson, Diego (2012), 'Social Institutions and Economic Growth: Why England and not China Became the First Modern Economy', Mimeo.

Greif, Avner, Milgrom, Paul, and Weingast, Barry R. (1994), 'Coordination, Commitment, and Enforcement: The Case of the Merchant Guild', *Journal of Political Economy*, 102 (4), 745–76.

Greif, Avner and Rubin, Jared (2015), 'Endogenous Political Legitimacy: The English Reformation and the Institutional Foundations of Limited Government', Mimeo.

Greif, Avner and Tabellini, Guido (2015), 'The Clan and the Corporation: Sustaining Cooperation in China and Europe', Stanford University working paper.

Greif, Avner and Tadelis, Steven (2010), 'A Theory of Moral Persistence: Crypto-Morality and Political Legitimacy', *Journal of Comparative Economics*, 38, 229–44.

Grice-Hutchinson, Marjorie (1978), *Early Economic Thought in Spain, 1177–1740* (London: George Allen & Unwin).

Grier, Robin (1997), 'The Effect of Religion on Economic Development: A Cross National Study of 63 Former Colonies', *Kyklos*, 50 (1), 47–62.

Guiso, Luigi, Sapienza, Paola, and Zingales, Luigi (2003), 'People's Opium? Religion and Economic Attitudes', *Journal of Monetary Economics*, 50 (1), 225–82.

(2006), 'Does Culture Affect Economic Outcomes?', *Journal of Economic Perspectives*, 20 (2), 23–48.

(2009), 'Cultural Biases in Economic Exchange?', *Quarterly Journal of Economics*, 124 (3), 1095–131.

(2016), 'Long-Term Persistence', *Journal of the European Economic Association*, Forthcoming.

Hallaq, Wael B. (1984), 'Was the Gate of Ijtihad Closed?', *International Journal of Middle East Studies*, 16 (1), 3–41.

(2001), *Authority, Continuity, and Change in Islamic Law* (Cambridge: Cambridge University Press).

(2005), *The Origins and Evolution of Islamic Law* (Cambridge: Cambridge University Press).

Hamilton, Earl J. (1938), 'Revisions in Economic History: VIII. – The Decline of Spain', *Economic History Review*, 8 (2), 168–79.

Haskins, Charles Homer (1957), *The Rise of Universities* (Ithaca: Great Seal Books).

Hassan, Farooq (1981), *The Concept of State and Law in Islam* (Washington, DC: University Press of America).

Hefele, Charles Joseph ([1894] 1973), *A History of the Christian Councils* (New York: AMS Press).

Helmholz, Richard H. (1986), 'Usury and the Medieval English Church Courts', *Speculum*, 61 (2), 364–80.

Helpman, Elhanan (2004), *The Mystery of Economic Growth* (Cambridge, MA: Harvard University Press).

Hoffman, Philip T. (2011), 'Prices, the Military Revolution, and Western Europe's Comparative Advantage in Violence', *Economic History Review*, 64 (S1), 39–59.

(2012), 'Why Was It Europeans Who Conquered the World?,' *Journal of Economic History*, 72 (3), 601–33.

(2015), *Why Did Europe Conquer the World?* (Princeton: Princeton University Press).

Holborn, Louise W. (1942), 'Printing and the Growth of a Protestant Movement in Germany from 1517 to 1524', *Church History*, 11 (2), 123–37.

Holdsworth, W.S. (1912), 'The Political Causes which Shaped the Statute of Uses', *Harvard Law Review*, 26 (2), 108–27.

Homer, Sidney and Sylla, Richard (1991), *A History of Interest Rates* (3rd edn.; New Brunswick: Rutgers University Press).

Hourani, Albert (1981), 'Ottoman Reform and the Politics of Notables', in Albert Hourani (ed.), *Emergence of the Modern Middle East* (Berkeley: University of California Press), 36–66.

(1991), *A History of the Arab Peoples* (Cambridge, MA: Harvard University Press).

Howorth, Jolyon (2014), 'Explainer: Why a Century-old Deal between Britain and France got ISIS Jihadis Excited', *The Conversation*, <http://theconversation.com/explainer-why-a-century-old-deal-between-britain-and-france-got-isis-jihadis-excited-28643>.

Hunt, Alice (2008), *The Drama of the Coronation: Medieval Ceremony in Early Modern England* (Cambridge: Cambridge University Press).

Hunt, Edwin S. and Murray, James M. (1999), *A History of Business in Medieval Europe, 1200–1550* (Cambridge: Cambridge University Press).

Hyma, Albert (1938), *Christianity and Politics: A History of the Principles and Struggles of Church and State* (Philadelphia: J.B. Lippincott).

Iannaccone, Laurence R. (1998), 'Introduction to the Economics of Religion', *Journal of Economic Literature*, 36 (3), 1465–95.

Ignatius, David (2014), 'Rethinking Woodrow Wilson's 14 Points', *The Washington Post*, <www.washingtonpost.com/opinions/david-ignatius-rethinking-woodrow-wilsons-14-points/2014/07/08/809c20b0-06c1-11e4-a0dd-f2b22a257353_story.html>.

Imber, Colin (1997), *Ebu's-su'ud: The Islamic Legal Tradition* (Stanford: Stanford University Press).

IMF (2012), 'World Economic Outlook Database'.

İnalcık, Halil (1973), *The Ottoman Empire* (New York: Praeger).

Irigoin, Alejandra and Grafe, Regina (2008), 'Bargaining for Absolutism: A Spanish Path to Nation-State and Empire Building', *Hispanic American Historical Review*, 88 (2), 173–209.

(2013), 'Bounded Leviathan: Fiscal Constraints and Financial Development in the Early Modern Hispanic World', in D'Maris Coffman, Adrian Leonard, and Larry Neal (eds.), *Questioning Credible Commitment: Perspectives on the Rise of Financial Capitalism* (Cambridge: Cambridge University Press).

Israel, Jonathan I. (1995), *The Dutch Republic: Its Rise, Greatness, and Fall 1477–1806* (Oxford: Oxford University Press).

Ives, E.W. (1967), 'The Genesis of the Statute of Uses', *English Historical Review*, 82 (325), 673–97.

Iyer, Sriya (2016), 'The New Economics of Religion', *Journal of Economic Literature*, 54 (2), 395–441.

Iyigun, Murat (2008), 'Luther and Suleyman', *Quarterly Journal of Economics*, 123 (4), 1465–94.

    (2010), 'Monotheism (From a Sociopolitical & Economic Perspective)', University of Colorado Working Paper.

    (2015), *War, Peace, and Prosperity in the Name of God: The Ottoman Role in Europe's Socioeconomic Evolution* (Chicago: University of Chicago Press).

Jacob, Marcus (2010), 'Long-Term Persistence: The Free and Imperial City Experience in Germany', SSRN Working Paper.

Jennings, Ronald C. (1973), 'Loans and Credit in Early 17th Century Ottoman Judicial Records: The Sharia Court of Anatolian Kayseri', *Journal of the Economic and Social History of the Orient*, 16 (2–3), 168–216.

Jha, Saumitra (2013), 'Trade, Institutions and Ethnic Tolerance: Evidence from South Asia', *American Political Science Review*, 107 (4), 806–32.

Johns, Adrian (1998), *The Nature of the Book: Print and Knowledge in the Making* (Chicago: University of Chicago Press).

Johnson, Noel D. and Koyama, Mark (2014), 'Taxes, Lawyers, and the Decline of Witch Trials in France', *Journal of Law and Economics*, 57 (1), 77–112.

Johnson, Paul (1976), *A History of Christianity* (New York: Simon & Schuster).

Johnson, Todd M. and Grim, Brian J. (2008), '*World Religion Database*', (Leiden and Boston: Brill).

Jones, A.H.M. (1949), *Constantine and the Conversion of Europe* (London: Macmillan).

    (1964), *The Later Roman Empire 284–602* (Norman: University of Oklahoma Press).

Jones, Eric L. (1981), *The European Miracle: Environments, Economics, and Geopolitics in the History of Europe and Asia* (Cambridge: Cambridge University Press).

    (1988), *Growth Recurring: Economic Change in World History* (Oxford: Clarendon Press).

Jones, Philip (1997), *The Italian City-State: From Commune to Signoria* (Oxford: Clarendon Press).

Kamen, Henry (1978), 'The Decline of Spain: A Historical Myth?', *Past & Present*, 81, 24–50.

    (1988), *Golden Age Spain* (New York: Palgrave Macmillan).

    (2003), *Empire: How Spain Became a World Power, 1492–1763* (New York: HarperCollins).

Karaman, Kıvanç (2009), 'Decentralized Coercion and Self-Restraint in Provincial Taxation: The Ottoman Empire, 15th–16th centuries', *Journal of Economic Behavior & Organization*, 71 (3), 690–703.

Karaman, Kıvanç and Pamuk, Şevket (2010), 'Ottoman State Finances in European Perspective, 1500–1914', *Journal of Economic History*, 70 (3), 593–629.

    (2013), 'Different Paths to the Modern State in Europe: The Interaction between Warfare, Economic Structure, and Political Regime', *American Political Science Review*, 107 (3), 603–26.

Kennedy, Paul M. (1987), *The Rise and Fall of the Great Powers: Economic Change and Military Conflict from 1500 to 2000* (New York: Random House).

Kerridge, Eric (2002), *Usury, Interest, and the Reformation* (Burlington: Ashgate).

Kertcher, Zack and Margalit, Ainat N. (2006), 'Challenges to Authority, Burdens of Legitimization: The Printing Press and the Internet', *Yale Journal of Law and Technology*, 8 (1), 1–31.

Khan, Mir S.A. (1929), 'The Mohammedan Laws against Usury and How They Are Evaded', *Journal of Comparative Legislation and International Law*, 11, 233–44.

Kim, Hyojoung and Pfaff, Steven (2012), 'Structure and Dynamics of Religious Insurgency: Students and the Spread of the Reformation', *American Sociological Review*, 77 (2), 188–215.

Kindleberger, Charles P. (1980), 'Review of The Dawn of Modern Banking by the Center for Medieval and Renaissance Studies', *Journal of Political Economy*, 88 (1), 217–19.

Ko, Chiu Yu, Koyama, Mark, and Sng, Tuan-Hwee (2016), 'Unified China; Divided Europe', *International Economic Review*, Forthcoming.

Kohn, Meir (1999), 'Bills of Exchange and the Money Market to 1600', SSRN working paper.

Koyama, Mark (2010), 'Evading the 'Taint of Usury': Complex Contracts and Segmented Capital Markets', *Explorations in Economic History*, 47 (4), 420–42.

Kuran, Timur (1986), 'The Economic System in Contemporary Islamic Thought: Interpretation and Assessment', *International Journal of Middle East Studies*, 18, 135–64.

    (1995), *Private Truths, Public Lies: The Social Consequences of Preference Falsification* (Cambridge, MA: Harvard University Press).

    (1997), 'Islam and Underdevelopment: An Old Puzzle Revisited', *Journal of Institutional and Theoretical Economics*, 153 (1), 41–71.

    (2001), 'The Provision of Public Goods under Islamic Law: Origins, Impact, and Limitations of the Waqf System', *Law and Society Review*, 35 (4), 841–97.

    (2004a), 'The Economic Ascent of the Middle East's Religious Minorities: The Role of Islamic Legal Pluralism', *Journal of Legal Studies*, 33, 475–515.

    (2004b), 'Why the Middle East is Economically Underdeveloped: Historical Mechanisms of Institutional Stagnation', *Journal of Economic Perspectives*, 18 (3), 71–90.

    (2005a), *Islam and Mammon: The Economic Predicaments of Islamism* (Princeton: Princeton University Press).

    (2005b), 'The Absence of the Corporation in Islamic Law: Origins and Persistence', *The American Journal of Comparative Law*, 53, 785–834.

    (2005c), 'The Logic of Financial Westernization in the Middle East', *Journal of Economic Behavior and Organization*, 56, 593–615.

    (2011), *The Long Divergence: How Islamic Law Held Back the Middle East* (Princeton: Princeton University Press).

    (ed.) (2013), *Social and Economic Life in Seventeenth-Century Istanbul: Glimpses from Court Records*, vols. 9–10 (Istanbul: İş Bankası Kültür Yayınları).

Kuran, Timur and Lustig, Scott (2012), 'Judicial Biases in Ottoman Istanbul: Islamic Justice and its Compatibility with Modern Economic Life', *Journal of Law and Economics*, 55 (3), 631–66.

Kuran, Timur and Rubin, Jared (in press), 'The Financial Power of the Powerless: Socio-Economic Status and Interest Rates under Partial Rule of Law', *Economic Journal*, Forthcoming.

Kurzman, Charles and Browers, Michaelle (2004), 'Introduction: Comparing Reformations', in Michaelle Browers and Charles Kurzman (eds.), *An Islamic Reformation?* (Lanham: Lexington).

La Porta, Rafael, Lopez-de-Silanes, Florencio, and Shleifer, Andrei (2008), 'The Economic Consequences of Legal Origins', *Journal of Economic Literature*, 46 (2), 285–332.

La Porta, Rafael, et al. (1997), 'Legal Determinants of External Finance', *Journal of Finance*, 52 (3), 1131–50.

—— (1998), 'Law and Finance', *Journal of Political Economy*, 106 (6), 1113–55.

—— (1999), 'The Quality of Government', *Journal of Law, Economics, & Organization*, 15 (1), 222–79.

Labib, Subhi Y. (1969), 'Capitalism in Medieval Islam', *Journal of Economic History*, 29, 79–96.

Lagerlöf, Nils-Peter (2014), 'Population, Technology and Fragmentation: The European Miracle Revisited', *Journal of Development Economics*, 108, 87–105.

Landes, David S. (1998), *The Wealth and Poverty of Nations: Why Some Are So Rich and Some So Poor* (New York: Norton).

Lane, Frederic C. (1966), *Venice and History: The Collected Papers of Frederic C. Lane* (Baltimore: Johns Hopkins Press).

le Goff, Jacques (1979), 'The Usurer and Purgatory', in Center for Medieval and Renaissance Studies (ed.), *The Dawn of Modern Banking* (New Haven: Yale University Press).

—— (1988), *Your Money or Your Life: Economy and Religion in the Middle Ages* (Cambridge, MA: MIT Press).

Levi, Margaret (1988), *Of Rule and Revenue* (Berkeley: University of California Press).

Lewis, Bernard (1974), *Islam: From the Prophet Muhammad to the Capture of Constantinople* (New York: Harper & Row).

—— (1982), *The Muslim Discovery of Europe* (New York: Norton).

—— (1993), *The Arabs in History* (Oxford: Oxford University Press).

—— (1995), *The Middle East* (New York: Scribner).

—— (2002), *What Went Wrong? The Clash between Islam and Modernity in the Middle East* (New York: HarperCollins).

Lieber, Alfred E. (1968), 'Eastern Business Practices and Medieval European Commerce', *Economic History Review*, 21, 230–43.

Lipset, Seymour Martin (1959), 'Some Social Requisites of Democracy: Economic Development and Political Legitimacy', *American Political Science Review*, 53 (1), 69–105.

Lopez, Robert S. (1971), *The Commercial Revolution of the Middle Ages, 950–1350* (Cambridge: Cambridge University Press).

Love, Harold (1993), *Scribal Publication in Seventeenth-Century England* (Oxford: Oxford University Press).

Lucas, Robert (1988), 'On the Mechanics of Economic Development', *Journal of Monetary Economics*, 22 (1), 3–42.

Lynch, John (1991), *Spain 1516–1598: From Nation State to World Empire* (Malden: Blackwell).

Makowsky, Michael and Rubin, Jared (2013), 'An Agent-Based Model of Centralized Institutions, Social Network Technology, and Revolution', *PLoS ONE*, 8 (11), e80380.

Maloney, Robert P. (1973), 'The Teaching of the Fathers on Usury: An Historical Study on the Development of Christian Thinking', *Vigiliae Christianae*, 27, 241–65.

Mandaville, Jon E. (1979), 'Usurious Piety: The Cash *Waqf* Controversy in the Ottoman Empire', *International Journal of Middle East Studies*, 10 (3), 289–308.

Mann, Michael (1986), *The Sources of Social Power: A History of Power from the Beginning to A.D. 1760* (Cambridge: Cambridge University Press).

Marshall, Monty G. and Cole, Benjamin R. (2014), *Global Report 2014: Conflict, Governance, and State Fragility* (Vienna, VA: Center for Systemic Peace).

Masud, Muhammad K., Messick, Brinkley, and Powers, David S. (1996), 'Muftis, Fatwas, and Islamic Legal Interpretation', in M.K. Masud, B. Messick, and D.S. Powers (eds.), *Islamic Legal Interpretation: Muftis and their Fatwas* (Cambridge, MA: Harvard University Press).

McCloskey, Deirdre (2010), *Bourgeois Dignity: Why Economics Can't Explain the Modern World* (Chicago: University of Chicago Press).

McCusker, John J. (2005), 'The Demise of Distance: The Business Press and the Origins of the Information Revolution in the Early Modern Atlantic World', *American Historical Review*, 110 (2), 295–321.

Meyersson, Erik (2013), 'Islamic Rule and the Emancipation of the Poor and Pious', *Econometrica*, 82 (1), 229–69.

Mez, Adam (1937), *Die Renaissance des Islam*, trans. S. Khuda Bukhsh and D.S. Margoliouth (London: Luzac & Co.).

Michalopoulos, Stelios, Naghavi, Alireza, and Prarolo, Giovanni (2015), 'Trade and Geography in the Spread of Islam', NBER working paper 18438.

Milgrom, Paul R., North, Douglass C., and Weingast, Barry R. (1990), 'The Role of Institutions in the Revival of Trade: The Law Merchant, Private Judges, and the Champagne Fairs', *Economics and Politics*, 2 (1), 1–23.

Mokyr, Joel (1990), *The Lever of Riches* (Oxford: Oxford University Press).

(2002), *The Gifts of Athena: Historical Origins of the Knowledge Economy* (Princeton: Princeton University Press).

(2009), *The Enlightened Economy: Britain and the Industrial Revolution 1700–1850* (New Haven: Yale University Press).

Mueller, Reinhold (1997), *The Venetian Money Market: Banks, Panics, and the Public Debt, 1200–1500* (Baltimore: Johns Hopkins University Press).

Munro, John (2003), 'The Medieval Origins of the Financial Revolution: Usury, Rentes, and Negotiablity', *The International History Review*, 25 (3), 505–62.

(2008), 'The Usury Doctrine and Urban Public Finances in Late-Medieval Flanders (1220–1550): Rentes (Annuities), Excise Taxes, and Income Transfers from the Poor to the Rich', in S. Cavaciocchi (ed.), *Fiscal Systems in the European Economy from the 13th to the 18th Centuries*, vol. 39 (Florence: University of Florence Press).

(2011), 'The Coinages and Monetary Policies of Henry VIII (r. 1509–47)', in James Estes (ed.), *The Collected Works of Erasmus: The Correspondence of Erasmus, Vol. 14: Letters 1926 to 2081, A.D. 1528* (Toronto: University of Toronto Press), 423–76.

(2012), 'Usury, Calvinism, and Credit in Protestant England: From the Sixteenth Century to the Industrial Revolution', in Francesco Ammannati (ed.), *Religion and Religious Institutions in the European Economy, 1000–1800* (Florence: Firenze University Press), 155–84.

Mystakidis, B.A. (1911), 'Hükümet-i Osmaniye Tarafından İlk Tesis Olunan Matbaa ve Bunun Sirayeti', *Türk Tarih Encümeni Dergisi*, 1.

Needham, Joseph (1954), *Science and Civilization in China*, vol. 1 (Cambridge: Cambridge University Press).

Noland, Marcus (2005), 'Religion and Economic Performance', *World Development*, 33 (8), 1215–32.

Noonan, John T. (1957), *The Scholastic Analysis of Usury* (Cambridge, MA: Harvard University Press).

(1966), 'Authority, Usury, and Contraception', *Cross Currents*, 16 (1), 55–79.

(1993), 'Development in Moral Doctrine', *Theological Studies*, 54, 662–77.

(2005), *A Church That Can and Cannot Change* (Notre Dame: University of Notre Dame Press).

North, Douglass C. (1981), *Structure and Change in Economic History* (New York: Norton).

(1990), *Institutions, Institutional Change and Economic Performance* (Cambridge: Cambridge University Press).

North, Douglass C. and Thomas, Robert P. (1971), 'The Rise and Fall of the Manorial System: A Theoretical Model', *Journal of Economic History*, 31 (4), 777–803.

(1973), *The Rise of the Western World: A New Economic History* (Cambridge: Cambridge University Press).

North, Douglass C., Wallis, John Joseph, and Weingast, Barry R. (2009), *Violence and Social Orders: A Conceptual Framework for Interpreting Recorded Human History* (Cambridge: Cambridge University Press).

North, Douglass C. and Weingast, Barry R. (1989), 'Constitutions and Commitment: The Evolution of Institutional Governing Public Choice in Seventeenth-Century England', *Journal of Economic History*, 49 (4), 803–32.

Opwis, Felicitas (2004), 'Changes in Modern Islamic Legal Theory: Reform or Reformation?', in Michaelle Browers and Charles Kurzman (eds.), *An Islamic Reformation?* (Lanham: Lexington).

Osman, O. (2013), 'Why Border Lines Drawn with a Ruler in WW1 Still Rock the Middle East', *BBC News*, <www.bbc.com/news/world-middle-east-25299553>.

Ostrom, Elinor (1990), *Governing the Commons: The Evolution of Institutions for Collective Action* (Cambridge: Cambridge University Press).

(2005), *Understanding Institutional Diversity* (Princeton: Princeton University Press).

Özkaya, Yücel (1994), *Osmanlı Imparatorlugu'nda Ayânlik* (Ankara: Türk Tarih Kurumu Basimevi).

Özmucur, Süleyman and Pamuk, Şevket (2002), 'Real Wages and Standards of Living in the Ottoman Empire, 1489–1914', *Journal of Economic History*, 62 (2), 293–321.

Pamuk, Şevket (2000), *A Monetary History of the Ottoman Empire* (Cambridge: Cambridge University Press).

(2004a), 'The Evolution of Financial Institutions in the Ottoman Empire, 1600–1914', *Financial History Review*, 11 (1), 7–32.

(2004b), 'Institutional Change and the Longevity of the Ottoman Empire, 1500–1800', *Journal of Interdisciplinary History*, 35, 225–47.

(2011), 'Real Wages and GDP Per Capita Estimates for the Middle East, 700 to 1800', mimeo.

Parker, Geoffrey (1973), 'Mutiny and Discontent in the Spanish Army of Flanders 1572–1607', *Past & Present*, 58, 38–52.

(1977), *The Dutch Revolt* (London: Penguin).

Pascali, Luigi (2016), 'Banks and Development: Jewish Communities in the Italian Renaissance and Current Economic Performance', *Review of Economics & Statistics*, 98 (1), 140–58.

Pedersen, Johannes (1984), *The Arabic Book*, trans. Geoffrey French (Princeton: Princeton University Press).

Pfaff, Steven and Corcoran, Katie E. (2012), 'Piety, Power, and the Purse: Religious Economies Theory and Urban Reform in the Holy Roman Empire', *Journal for the Scientific Study of Religion*, 51 (4), 757–76.

Pincus, Steven C.A. and Robinson, James (2014), 'What Really Happened During the Glorious Revolution?', in Sebastian Galiani and Itai Sened (eds.), *Institutions, Property Rights, and Economic Growth: The Legacy of Douglass North* (Cambridge: Cambridge University Press).

Pirenne, Henri (1925), *Medieval Cities: Their Origins and the Revival of Trade* (New York: Doubleday Anchor Books).

(1937), *Economic and Social History of Medieval Europe* (New York: Harcourt, Brace, and Company).

Platteau, Jean-Philippe (2011), 'Political Instrumentalization of Islam and the Risk of Obscurantist Deadlock', *World Development*, 39 (2), 243–60.

Pomeranz, Kenneth L. (2000), *The Great Divergence: China, Europe, and the Making of the Modern World Economy* (Princeton: Princeton University Press).

Posner, Richard A. (1980), 'A Theory of Primitive Society, with Special Reference to Law', *Journal of Law and Economics*, 23, 1–53.

Priest, Claire (2006), 'Creating an American Property Law: Alienability and its Limits in American History', *Harvard Law Review*, 120 (2), 385–458.

Putnam, Robert D. (1993), *Making Democracy Work: Civic Traditions in Modern Italy* (Princeton: Princeton University Press).

Quataert, Donald (2000), *The Ottoman Empire, 1700–1922* (Cambridge: Cambridge University Press).

Quinn, Stephen (2001), 'The Glorious Revolution's Effect on English Private Finance: A Microhistory, 1680–1705', *Journal of Economic History*, 61 (3), 593–615.

Rahman, Fazlur (1964), 'Ribā and Interest', *Islamic Studies*, 3, 1–43.

Ray, Nicholas D. (1997), 'The Medieval Islamic System of Credit and Banking: Legal and Historical Considerations', *Arab Law Quarterly*, 12, 43–90.

Razi, G. Hossein (1990), 'Legitimacy, Religion, and Nationalism in the Middle East', *American Political Science Review*, 84 (1), 69–91.

Reed, Clyde G. and Bekar, Cliff T. (2003), 'Religious Prohibitions Against Usury', *Explorations in Economic History*, 40, 347–68.

Robinson, Francis (1993), 'Technology and Religious Change: Islam and the Impact of Print', *Modern Asian Studies*, 27 (1), 229–51.

Rodinson, Maxime (1973), *Islam and Capitalism* (Austin: University of Texas Press).

Rodrik, Dani, Subramanian, Arvind, and Trebbi, Francesco (2004), 'Institutions Rule: The Primacy of Institutions Over Geography and Integration in Economic Development', *Journal of Economic Growth*, 9, 131–65.

Romer, Paul M. (1986), 'Increasing Returns and Long-Run Growth', *Journal of Political Economy*, 94 (5), 1002–37.

Rubin, Jared (2009), 'Social Insurance, Commitment, and the Origin of Law: An Economic Theory of the Emergence of Interest Bans', *Journal of Law and Economics*, 52 (4), 761–77.

——— (2010), 'Bills of Exchange, Interest Bans, and Impersonal Exchange in Islam and Christianity', *Explorations in Economic History*, 47 (2), 213–27.

——— (2011), 'Institutions, the Rise of Commerce, and the Persistence of Laws: Interest Restrictions in Islam & Christianity', *Economic Journal*, 557, 1310–39.

——— (2012), 'Trade and Commerce', in Gerhard Bowering et al. (eds.), *Encyclopedia of Islamic Political Thought* (Princeton: Princeton University Press).

——— (2014a), 'Centralized Institutions and Cascades', *Journal of Comparative Economics*, 42 (2), 340–57.

——— (2014b), 'Printing and Protestants: An Empirical Test of the Role of Printing in the Reformation', *Review of Economics & Statistics*, 96 (2), 270–86.

Sachs, Jeffrey D. (2001), 'Tropical Underdevelopment', NBER Working Paper 8119.

Said, Edward (1978), *Orientalism* (New York: Pantheon Books).

Sardar, Ziauddin (1993), 'Paper, Printing, and Compact Disks: The Making and Unmaking of Islamic Culture', *Media, Culture & Society*, 15, 43–59.

Savage-Smith, Emilie (2003), 'Islam', in R. Porter (ed.), *The Cambridge History of Science. Vol. 4. Eighteenth-Century Science* (Cambridge: Cambridge University Press).

Sazak, Selim Can (2014), 'Good Riddance to Sykes-Picot', *The National Interest*, <http://nationalinterest.org/commentary/good-riddance-sykes-picot-9868>.

Schachner, Nathan (1962), *The Mediaeval Universities* (New York: A.S. Barnes).

Schacht, Joseph (1964), *An Introduction to Islamic Law* (Oxford: Oxford University Press).

——— (1995), 'Ribā', in C.E. Bosworth et al. (eds.), *The Encyclopaedia of Islam: New Edition* (Leiden: Brill).

——— (2006), 'Hiyal', *Encyclopaedia of Islam Online Edition* (2nd edn.).

Scribner, R.W. (1989), 'Oral Culture and the Transmission of Reformation Ideas', in Helga Robinson-Hammerstein (ed.), *The Transmission of Ideas in the Lutheran Reformation* (Dublin: Irish Academic Press).

Simpson, Lesley Byrd (1956), 'The Cortes of Castile', *The Americas*, 12 (3), 223–33.

Sokoloff, Kenneth L. and Engerman, Stanley L. (2000), 'History Lessons: Institutions, Factor Endowments, and Paths of Development in the New World', *Journal of Economic Perspectives*, 14 (3), 217–32.

Sombart, Werner (1967 [1913]), *Luxury and Capitalism* (Ann Arbor: University of Michigan Press).

Spenkuch, Jörg L. (2016), 'Religion and Work: Micro Evidence from Contemporary Germany', Northwestern University working paper.

Spitz, Lewis S. (1985), *The Protestant Reformation, 1517–1559* (New York: Harper & Row).

Stark, Rodney (1996), *The Rise of Christianity* (Princeton: Princeton University Press).

Stark, Rodney and Bainbridge, William Sims (1985), *The Future of Religion: Secularization, Revival, and Cult Formation* (Berkeley and Los Angeles: University of California Press).

Stasavage, David (2014), 'Was Weber Right? The Role of Urban Autonomy in Europe's Rise', *American Political Science Review*, 108 (2), 337–54.

Sussman, Nathan and Yafeh, Yishay (2006), 'Institutional Reforms, Financial Development, and Sovereign Debt: Britain 1690–1790', *Journal of Economic History*, 66 (4), 906–35.

Swetz, Frank J. (1987), *Capitalism & Arithmetic: The New Math of the 15th Century* (La Salle: Open Court).

Tabellini, Guido (2010), 'Culture and Institutions: Economic Development in the Regions of Europe', *Journal of the European Economic Association*, 8 (4), 677–716.

Tawney, Richard H. (1926 [1954]), *Religion and the Rise of Capitalism* (New York: Mentor).

Tekiner, Efdaleddin (1916), 'Memâlik-i Osmaniye'de Tıbâatim Kıdemi', *Türk Tarih Encümeni Dergisi*, 7, 242–49.

Tierney, Brian (1988), *The Crisis of Church and State 1050–1300* (Toronto: University of Toronto Press).

Tierney, Brian and Painter, Sidney (1992), *Western Europe in the Middle Ages, 300–1475*, 5th edn. (New York: McGraw-Hill).

Tilly, Charles (1975), 'Reflections on the History of European State-Making', in Charles Tilly (ed.), *The Formation of States in Western Europe* (Princeton: Princeton University Press), 3–83.

(1990), *Coercion, Capital, and European States, AD 990–1990* (Oxford: Blackwell).

Turchin, Peter, Hall, Thomas D., and Adams, Jonathan M. (2006), 'East-West Orientation of Historical Empires and Modern States', *Journal of World-Systems Research*, 12 (2), 219–29.

Udovitch, Abraham L. (1970), *Partnership and Profit in Medieval Islam* (Princeton: Princeton University Press).

(1975), 'Reflections on the Institutions of Credits and Banking in the Medieval Islamic Near East', *Studia Islamica*, 41, 5–21.

(1979), 'Bankers without Banks: Commerce, Banking, and Society in the Islamic World of the Middle Ages', in Center for Medieval and Renaissance Studies (ed.), *The Dawn of Modern Banking* (New Haven: Yale University Press), 255–73.

United Nations Development Program (2014), 'Human Development Report'.

Usher, Abbott Payson (1914), 'The Origin of the Bill of Exchange', *Journal of Political Economy*, 22, 566–76.

van Bavel, Bas (2003), 'Early Proto-Industrialization in the Low Countries? The Importance and Nature of Market-Oriented Non-Agricultural Activities on the Countryside in Flanders and Holland, c. 1250–1570', *Revue belge de philology et d'histoire*, 81 (4), 1109–65.

van Bavel, Bas, Buringh, Eltjo, and Dijkman, Jessica (2015), 'Immovable Capital Goods in Medieval Muslim Lands: Why Water-Mills and Building Cranes Went Missing', Utrecht University Working Paper.

van Gelderen, Martin (1992), *The Political Thought of the Dutch Revolt, 1555–1590* (Cambridge: Cambridge University Press).

van Zanden, Jan Luiten (2002a), 'The 'Revolt of the Early Modernists' and the 'First Modern Economy': An Assessment', *Economic History Review*, 55 (4), 619–41.

(2002b), 'Taking the Measure of the Early Modern Economy: Historical National Accounts for Holland in 1510/14', *European Review of Economic History*, 6, 131–63.

(2009), *The Long Road to the Industrial Revolution: The European Economy in a Global Perspective, 1000–1800*, eds. Maarten Prak and Jan Luiten van Zanden (Global Economic History Series; Leiden: Brill).

van Zanden, Jan Luiten, Buringh, Eltjo, and Bosker, Maarten (2012), 'The Rise and Decline of European Parliaments, 1188–1789', *Economic History Review*, 65 (3), 835–61.

van Zanden, Jan Luiten and Prak, Maarten (2006), 'Towards an Economic Interpretation of Citizenship: The Dutch Republic between Medieval Communes and Modern Nation-States', *European Review of Economic History*, 10, 111–45.

van Zanden, Jan Luiten, Zuijderduijn, Jaco, and de Moor, Tine (2012), 'Small is Beautiful: The Efficiency of Credit Markets in Late Medieval Holland', *European Review of Economic History*, 16, 3–22.

von Grunebaum, Gustave E. (1966), *Medieval Islam: A Study in Cultural Orientation* (Chicago: University of Chicago Press).

Wallis, John Joseph and North, Douglass C. (2014), 'Leviathan Denied: Rules, Governments, and Social Dynamics', Mimeo.

Watson, Andrew W. (1983), *Agricultural Revolution in the Early Islamic World: The Diffusion of Crops and Farming Techniques 700–1100* (Cambridge: Cambridge University Press).

Watt, W. Montgomery (1988), *Islamic Fundamentalism and Modernity* (London: Routledge).

Weber, Max (1905 [2002]), *The Protestant Ethic and the 'Spirit' of Capitalism* (New York: Penguin).

(1922), *Economy and Society: An Outline of Interpretive Sociology* (Berkeley: University of California Press).

Weber, Nicholas (1912), 'Waldenses', *The Catholic Encyclopedia*, vol. 15 (New York: Robert Appleton Company).

Weiss, Bernard (1978), 'Interpretation in Islamic Law: The Theory of Ijtihad', *American Journal of Comparative Law*, 26 (2), 199–212.

Wells, John and Wills, Douglas (2000), 'Revolution, Restoration, and Debt Repudiation: The Jacobite Threat to England's Institutions and Economic Growth', *Journal of Economic History*, 60 (2), 418–41.

Westcott, Mark (2013), 'Muslims and Minorities: Religion and City Growth in the Ottoman Empire', Mimeo.

Wilhelm, Joseph (1910), 'Jan Hus', *The Catholic Encyclopedia*, vol. 7 (New York: Robert Appleton Company).

Williamson, Oliver E. (1985), *The Economic Institutions of Capitalism* (New York: Free Press).

(2000), 'The New Institutional Economics: Taking Stock, Looking Ahead', *Journal of Economic Literature*, 38 (3), 595–613.

Wintrobe, Ronald (1998), *The Political Economy of Dictatorship* (Cambridge: Cambridge University Press).

World Bank (2014), *World Development Indicators: GDP Per Capita (Current US$)* (Washington, DC: World Bank).

Young, Cristobal (2009), 'Religion and Economic Growth in Western Europe: 1500–2000', Stanford University working paper.

Zilfi, Madeline C. (1988), *The Politics of Piety: The Ottoman Ulema in the Postclassical Age (1600–1800)* (Minneapolis: Bibliotheca Islamica).

Index

AALIMS. *See* Association for Analytic
  Learning about Islam and Muslim Societies
Abbasid Caliphate, 33, 108; Europe and, 71,
  233n49; legitimacy and, 59–60; safatij and,
  94, 232n44, 233n49; size of, 4, 6, 7, 49, 50t;
  See also specific persons, topics
Abramitzky, Ran, xix–xx
Acemoglu, Daron, 18
Africa, 2, 8, 21, 65, 201, 213, 221n1
agriculture, 50, 63, 64, 159, 182f, 183, 243n25
al-Bukhari, Muhammad, 52
Alexander III (Pope), 84
Alexander the Great, 32, 49
Alfonso IX, 138
al-Jamali, Ali, 48
Allen, Robert, 211, 222n11, 236n4
al-Muntasir, 33
al-Qaeda, xiii
Anderson, Robert, 174
Aquinas, Thomas, 69
Arab Spring, 30, 216, 217
Arabic script, 105, 106, 109, 113, 142, 144,
  198, 236n46
ASREC. *See* Association for the Study of
  Religion, Economics, and Culture
Assad, Bashar al, 216
Association for Analytic Learning about Islam
  and Muslim Societies (AALIMS), xviii
Association for the Study of Religion,
  Economics, and Culture (ASREC), xviii
authoritarian rule, xiii, 216, 217, 218, 220. *See
  also specific rulers, topics*

Baghdad, 4, 7, 94, 108
Balla, Eliana, 39, 191

banking, 5, 81; bills of exchange, 2, 92–97, 204,
  231n38, 234n58; Europe and, 92, 96, 179,
  204 (*see also specific states, topics*); interest
  and, 75–132 (*see also* interest); Middle
  East and, 13, 75, 76, 81–82, 92–97, 230n10,
  230n14, 234n58 (*see also specific states,
  topics*); modern, 75, 81, 97; money and,
  75–132 (*see also* money); origins of, 5, 92,
  204; safatij and, 94, 96–97, 234n58
Bayezid II, 82, 105, 192
Becker, Sascha, 120
Becket, Thomas á, 68
Belgium, 152, 159–160, 162, 165, 166–167, 170
Berman, Harold J., 69
bills of exchange, 92–97, 204, 234n58
Black Death, 149, 151, 181
Blaydes, L., 223n18
Boniface VIII, 70
Bosker, Maarten, 137
Bouazizi, Mohamed, 217
Bourgeois Dignity (McCloskey), 20
Buringh, Eltjo, 100, 115, 137

Calvinism, 15, 159
capitalism, 16, 21, 119, 120
Carolingian Empire, 64, 83
Catholicism: anti-usury and, 91; canon
  law, 68–70; commerce and, 91, 189, 205;
  deposition, 69, 70; Dictatus Papae, 69;
  economic elites and, 189; economics and,
  205; England and, 155; fragmentation and,
  116; Holy Roman Empire (*see* Holy Roman
  Empire); Inquisition, 173; interest and,
  84–85, 90–91 (*see also* interest); Islam
  and, 121, 206; Lateran Councils, 84, 87;

265

Made in United States
Orlando, FL
19 May 2022

17929017R00178